RADICAL HISTORY

Issue 111

Historicizing 9/11

Credit: U.S. Department of Homeland Security

Editors' Introduction

It is both a profound truth and a common cliché that the terrorist attacks of September 11, 2001, had great historical impact, traumatizing masses of people in the United States and beyond. Astounding in their audacity and in their success, these attacks literally brought down two of the largest buildings in the world — symbolic and actual centers of U.S. financial power — and directly hit the Pentagon, the center of U.S. military power. Thousands were killed or grievously wounded. And in the midst of the massive destruction, there was real heroism — from the passengers of United Airlines Flight 93 who revolted against the hijackers of their plane, causing it to crash into a Pennsylvania field rather than finding a target in Washington, D.C., to the first responders at the attack sites who mounted rescue operations at great peril to themselves. These attacks and their aftermath were the stuff of historical mythology, and the mythologizing process of what became known as "9/11" began at once, dominated by the Bush administration and the U.S. political establishment.

As the tenth anniversary of the September 11 attacks approaches, the dominant mythologies of 9/11 have been weakened by a decade of unending war, attacks on civil liberties, and a pernicious xenophobia, largely in the name of responding to the attacks. Nevertheless, the planned, official tenth anniversary commemorations of these attacks threaten to revive these declining mythologies. The editorial collective (EC) of *Radical History Review* believes that this tenth anniversary must become an occasion to critically investigate and discuss the meanings of 9/11, not an occasion to resanctify official explanations. The EC therefore decided to produce an *RHR* issue that questions and challenges dominant 9/11 mythologies, not by dissecting the historical causes of the attacks, but by focusing on the many ways in which the attacks have been *historicized* — that is, historically defined, represented, symbolized, and used — in numerous social and cultural spheres. Hence this special issue, *RHR* 111, "Historicizing 9/11."

Radical History Review
Issue 111 (Fall 2011)   DOI 10.1215/01636545-1268659
© 2011 by MARHO: The Radical Historians' Organization, Inc.

In the call for proposals for this issue, we aimed for contributions on many different topics related to our theme, so we cast a wide net. We indicated that we welcomed participation not only by those who identify as historians but also from intellectuals and artists of a range of different backgrounds. This we got. Proposals came in from researchers into and practitioners of literature, media, journalism, communications, popular culture, theater, international relations, personal testimony, and visual art. Only a minority of the proposals came from "historians," narrowly defined. This disciplinary diversity is retained in the contributions selected for this issue. We have divided these contributions into several thematic sections.

Our first section, "Historical Reflections," is perhaps the most classically historical of the issue. In the opening piece, "The Contested Meaning of September 11," the issue's coeditor Jim O'Brien explores the development of the Bush administration's interpretation of 9/11, its use to justify this administration's foreign policy over much of the ensuing decade, and the oppositional interpretations it engendered. Next, in an *RHR* interview with Paul Atwood, the historian and U.S. foreign policy specialist Andrew Bacevich discusses the "perpetual warfare" initiated by the United States in the wake of 9/11, resulting in a crisis of civilian control over military matters. Closing this section, Ivan Greenberg traces the post-9/11 restrictions on domestic dissent to their origins in the earlier practices of the FBI and analyzes the transformation and amplification of these practices during the so-called war on terror.

In our second section, "Public Spaces," two articles consider the processes of 9/11 historicizing at public memorial sites. Micki McElya focuses on the Arlington National Cemetery memorial to the September 11 attack on the Pentagon. She argues that the historical linkages and meanings of this monument are not fixed but have shifted and continue to shift with developments in U.S. foreign and domestic policy. Linda Levitt addresses the yet-to-be-completed reconstruction of the World Trade Center site in New York—popularly dubbed "ground zero"—and examines the roles played by members of victims' families in the ongoing struggle to shape the memorial aspects of the reconfigured site.

In "Testimonies and Archives," our third section, three articles deal with the collecting and archiving of oral histories and digital materials concerning the 9/11 attacks and their aftermath. Mary Marshall Clark, the director of the Oral History Research Office at Columbia University, reports on the September 11, 2001, Oral History Narrative and Memory Project, which has collected interviews from hundreds of "ordinary" people from various racial and ethnic communities in New York City who were eyewitnesses to, or deeply impacted by, the attacks. In a complementary article, Ann Cvetkovich discusses the interviews with people of Afghani background in the same Columbia University project. Both Clark and Cvetkovich emphasize the critical importance of the diverse testimony contained in the project archive to our historical understandings of 9/11. Following this, Stephen Brier and Joshua Brown, two former *RHR* editors, describe the creation and functioning of the gigantic September 11 Digital Archive, one of the world's largest digital repositories of historical materials on the 9/11 events. Along with describing the project's history, they raise important questions about the need for historians to function as archivists and preservationists in an era of fragile and ephemeral digital communications.

Our "Curated Spaces" section features an introduction to, and striking images from, the Index of the Disappeared project of artists Chitra Ganesh and Mariam Ghani, which transforms documents from the war on terror into subversive artistic images. The following section also emphasizes the visual, as its name, "Visual Representations," indicates, but understood in a variety of ways. First, Jaclyn Kirouac-Fram explores the historical implications of the famous "Falling Man" photo and other images of the so-called jumpers from the World Trade Center, and of the public reactions to these. Kent Worcester follows with an examination of the often oppositional depictions of 9/11 in comics and graphic art, many of which were produced by New York City artists who witnessed the attacks and their aftermath. Art Spiegelman's remarkable *In the Shadow of No Towers* (2004) is among the works covered.

Two of the essays in this section concern movies. Thomas Riegler traces the changing ways in which television and cinema addressed 9/11; he argues that these media were the primary cultural means of giving popular historical meanings to the terrorist attacks, and he provides numerous examples of the themes that emerged. James Stone also considers film and 9/11, focusing on a single, recent movie, *Cloverfield* (dir. Matt Reeves, 2008). He argues that *Cloverfield*, by deploying footage of a gigantic monster attack on New York City reminiscent of documentary images of street scenes after the World Trade Center attacks, elicits viewer pleasure and thereby undermines the sanctified meanings of the 9/11 mythology.

From visual representations of 9/11, we turn to literature in our section "Literary Resonances." Bob Batchelor opens the section with an analysis of how two American "literary lions," the novelists John Updike and Don DeLillo, offer contrasting yet politically potent interpretations of the meanings of 9/11 and of the post-9/11 United States. Next, Sonia Baelo-Allué argues that, in the direct aftermath of the September 2001 attacks, literature had little to add to the journalism of the day. Yet by the middle 2000s, she writes, important novelists began creating intermedial works—incorporating other media such as photographic images, newspaper articles, radio transcripts, phone messages, e-mails, and interviews with eyewitnesses—thereby offering effective if complicated (even contradictory) representations and accounts of the 9/11 experience and its traumas. In the final article of this section, Matthew Schneider-Mayerson proposes that the surprising success of Dan Brown's *The DaVinci Code*, and, subsequently, of his other novels, can be largely explained by the growth of "conspiracism" as a popular reaction to the 9/11 attacks.

In our "UK Reflections" section, we offer two pieces. First, Jeffrey R. Kerr-Ritchie considers the U.S. and British reactions to 9/11 and to the terrorist bombings of the London Underground on July 7, 2005; similarities and differences in historicizing terrorist attacks in the two countries are probed. Then, in a passionate and personal narrative, Amir Saeed, a cultural studies scholar and British citizen of Pakistani origin, describes how his identity was transformed under the impact of increased Islamophobia in the post-9/11 United Kingdom.

In our section "Teaching 9/11," Jeffrey Melnick discusses his students' responses to the confrontational nature of David Rees's *Get Your War On* cartoons, which the students consistently found challenging but for different reasons as the decade wore on. He argues that the changes show a significant shift in the place of 9/11 in U.S. popular culture. In this same section, Magid Shihade reviews his mixed experiences teaching a course that critically addressed the broadly accepted historical meanings of 9/11 at several universities in the United States and at one in Pakistan.

Finally, we present a selection of the historian and cartoonist Joshua Brown's online series of *Life during Wartime* cartoons, begun shortly after the March 2003 invasion of Iraq and continuing into 2011. His cartoons convey the flavor of U.S. government policies in the decade that followed September 11, 2001, often carried out in the name of responding to that day's events.

In this issue, then, our authors and we seek to complicate understandings of how the September 11 attacks have been rendered into history, to take our inquiries into areas of society and culture not usually considered in this regard, and to give another shake to the already shaken 9/11 interpretive orthodoxy.

—Andor Skotnes and Jim O'Brien

The Contested Meaning of 9/11

Jim O'Brien

How we respond to this catastrophe will define our patriotism, shape the
century, and memorialize our beloved dead.
—James Carroll, September 15, 2001

The terror attacks of September 11, 2001, have been a recurrent theme — sometimes implicit, often front and center — of U.S. politics throughout the past decade.
How to interpret and understand them has been a crucial question. In the tragedy's
immediate aftermath, the George W. Bush administration struck a theme that resonated with the American public: the attacks constituted an out-of-the-blue declaration of war against an unsuspecting and entirely innocent victim, namely, the United
States. "America was targeted for attack because we're the brightest beacon for freedom and opportunity in the world," the president told the nation on the evening of
the attacks, as he promised a "war against terrorism."[1] This initial historicizing of the
9/11 attacks soon became embedded in other official speeches and documents and
in the public mind. It possessed not only a congenial explanatory power but also an
enormous power to mobilize. It fueled a war in Afghanistan and subsequently, with
leaps of logic, the invasion and occupation of Iraq.

Powerful as it has been, the official instant-history understanding of the
attacks of 9/11 was never without its challenges. A segment of the population has at
times contested even the basic facts of the events. Partisan divide has arisen over the
extent to which the Bush administration failed to heed warnings of an impending
attack. And most persistently, the claim that the terror attacks constituted acts of

Radical History Review
Issue 111 (Fall 2011)   DOI 10.1215/01636545-1268668
© 2011 by MARHO: The Radical Historians' Organization, Inc.

"war," demanding a seemingly endless military response, had critics from the start. Even as the original definition stays intact and constrains the decisions of American policy makers, the experiences of the past decade have rekindled concern about the overreach of the U.S. military. Before long, even in the United States, 9/11 may symbolize the perils of imperial pride at least as much as it evokes the death and destruction of that traumatic day.

Days of Definition, September 11 – October 7, 2001

As the administration moved rapidly and decisively to define the September 11 attacks within the framework of its "war on terrorism," other frames of reference also offered themselves; the administration would have to subsume these if its interpretation were to prevail. Perhaps the most immediately obvious take on the events was that U.S. security safeguards had failed miserably. Even before the most damning facts became known — the FBI had ignored warning signals from its branch offices; the CIA and the FBI had failed to share pertinent information with each other; the White House had tuned out repeated warnings from its so-called counterterrorism czar, Richard Clarke — something was obviously wrong when four sets of young men could walk onto planes at different airports with metallic weapons. As Clarke later said, speaking specifically to family members of 9/11 victims and including himself in the blame, "Your government failed you."[2]

Richard Clarke. Credit: Wikipedia Commons

For obvious reasons, the administration steered clear of this framework as the primary focus in defining the 9/11 attacks. It would have risked endless finger-pointing, and the immediate sense of shared national shock, grief, and anger could have given way to partisan divide. Bush, a relatively unpopular president at that point in his term, would likely have driven his ratings further down (instead of way up, as in fact happened). Enhanced security precautions — and, very soon, expanded powers for the FBI — were part of the administration's response to 9/11, but a look back at what had gone wrong in the preceding months was never given priority.

A third hypothetical framing of the events would have meant focusing and trying to build on the extraordinary generosity and heroism shown on that day — notably, by New Yorkers in and near the twin towers and by the passengers of United Airlines Flight 93, whose struggle with the hijackers caused the plane to crash well short of its intended target. As Rebecca Solnit has written, "Far more people could have died on September 11th if New Yorkers had not remained calm, had not helped each other out of the endangered buildings and the devastated area, had not reached out to pull people from the collapsing buildings and the dust cloud."[3] But from the government's point of view, this framework, too, could only be a secondary concern, for it implied no special role for the government itself and indicated no obvious way forward. The president heaped praise on the way that individual Americans had acted in the crisis, but that praise occurred in the context of showing national resolve.

A much less sunny interpretation—one that responsible politicians of both parties shunned at the beginning—was that "the Muslims," as opposed to a tiny, particular group, had attacked the United States. This view made Muslims world-wide the enemy, including those Muslims who lived in the United States. Indeed, countless Muslims (and people who looked Arabic or Middle Eastern or South Asian) suffered insults and/or physical violence throughout the country in the aftermath of the attacks.[4] But the president took pains to distinguish between the 9/11 attackers and the mass of followers of Islam. From the standpoint of U.S. foreign policy and the country's international image, any appearance of pitting the U.S. government against the world's billion-plus Muslims would have proven a disaster. It would, in fact, have played into the hands of those who plotted the attacks. Still, a miasma of distrust remained.

Another option, potentially the most persuasive of the rejected choices, would have been to treat the attacks as a crime—one momentous in scale, but a crime nonetheless—rather than as an act of war. By putting together evidence whose implications had eluded the administration before September 11, the government quickly pinned the attacks on the small extreme Islamist network known as al-Qaeda, which intelligence agencies had blamed for previous bloody attacks against the U.S. embassies in Kenya and Tanzania in 1998 and against the USS *Cole* in 2000. Its leader, Osama bin Laden, had issued a fatwa in 1998 calling on believers to kill Americans and their allies at any opportunity. Given the group's small size, the attacks might have served as the grounds for internationally coordinated law enforcement to root out bin Laden and al-Qaeda members. But for a conservative administration, distrustful of international bodies, this approach would have risked limiting American freedom of action. And by the nature of law enforcement, it would have involved long periods in which nothing seemed to be happening. The very scale of the attacks seemed to call for dramatic action.

At the heart of the Bush administration's framing of the attacks, after all, was the word *war*. This framework made the attacks an act of war, not a crime. The Pearl Harbor attack of December 7, 1941, which had united the nation behind a declaration of war against Japan, served as the pervasive analogy for the events of September 11, 2001. A military assault, as the 9/11 attacks were now held to be, called for a military response, with a central command located in the White House.

An important corollary to the new framework was that no distinction was to be made between terror groups and countries that aided or harbored them. This point was crucial to the administration's ability to respond to the attacks with actual wars. On September 18, one week after the attacks, with only the California Democratic representative Barbara Lee voting "no," Congress passed a resolution stating "that the President is authorized to use all necessary and appropriate force against those nations, organizations, or persons he determines planned, authorized, committed, or aided the terrorist attacks that occurred on September 11, 2001, or harbored such organizations or persons, in order to prevent any future acts of international terrorism against the United States by such nations, organizations or persons." The resolution most obviously endorsed war on Afghanistan, where al-Qaeda ran

training camps. But Afghanistan was not mentioned by name; the terms of the resolution remained so general, so broad, that it gave maximum discretion to the president. Bush's rhetorical naming of the enemy as "terrorism," or soon, "terror," underlined the ominous vagueness of the administration's goals.

The president's speech to a joint session of Congress on September 20 elaborated, quite eloquently, on his address to the nation nine days earlier. He praised Americans' heroism, announced the appointment of the governor of Pennsylvania, Tom Ridge, as the head of the dramatically named new office of Homeland Security, identified al-Qaeda by name as the source of the attacks and briefly

Barbara Lee. Credit: United States Congress

sketched the group's history, and promised success in the struggle against al-Qaeda and any similar groups. He reaffirmed the righteousness of the United States: "They hate our freedoms." He spoke of the "war on terror" and warned, underlining the congressional resolution, "From this day forward, any nation that continues to harbor or support terrorism will be regarded by the United States as a hostile regime."[5]

In those early weeks, the power of the official 9/11 interpretation was all but overwhelming. Conspicuous dissent in a national forum was both rare and vilified. One example was Susan Sontag's brief contribution to a symposium in the *New*

Yorker of September 24, in which she castigated the mainstream responses to the attacks: "The voices licensed to follow the event seem to have joined together in a campaign to infantilize the public. Where is the acknowledgement that this was not a 'cowardly' attack on 'civilization' or 'liberty' or 'humanity' or 'the free world' but an attack on the world's self-proclaimed super-power, undertaken as a consequence of specific American alliances and actions?"[6] Sontag wrote, "In the matter of courage (a morally neutral virtue): whatever may be said of the perpetrators of Tuesday's slaughter, they were not cowards." This point was also made by ABC-TV late-night host Bill Maher, who, in agreeing with his conservative guest Dinesh D'Souza on September 26 that the attackers were not "cowardly," went on to say, "We have been the cowards. Lobbing cruise missiles from two thousand miles away. That's cowardly." Sontag faced vehement criticism for her *New Yorker* piece, and resentment at Maher's comments was widely believed to be responsible for the nonrenewal of his popular *Politically Incorrect* show.

More politely than Sontag, and much less prominently, some other voices also questioned the administration's claim that U.S. policies had nothing to do with the attacks. On a number of college campuses, faculty members began planning courses in Middle Eastern history, at least some of which were bound to bring up U.S. partisanship in the Israeli-Palestinian conflict and the U.S. encouragement of militant Islam in its arming of opponents of the Soviet-backed government of Afghanistan in the 1980s. By coincidence, a book by Chalmers Johnson, a onetime establishment historian of East Asia, had been published (and largely ignored) in 2000, with the title *Blowback: The Costs and Consequence of American Empire*.[7] Johnson claimed that often clandestine U.S. actions worldwide had weakened U.S. security by provoking terrorism. Reissued soon after 9/11, the book quickly achieved best-seller status.

From the start, the Bush administration clearly intended to go after the Taliban regime in Afghanistan. Scattered voices in op-ed pieces, fliers, listserv messages, and publications like the *Nation* and the *Progressive* warned against a cycle of violence. The historian Howard Zinn, in a widely distributed essay, issued a heartfelt appeal against war, concluding: "We should take our example not from our military and political leaders shouting 'retaliate' and 'war' but from the doctors and nurses and medical students and firemen and policemen who have been saving lives in the midst of mayhem, whose first thoughts are not violence, but healing, not vengeance but compassion."[8] The columnist James Carroll, four days after the attacks, wrote with some prescience, "How we respond to this catastrophe will define our patriotism, shape the century, and memorialize our beloved dead."[9]

Dissent from the march to war also took the form of small-scale vigils and rallies across the country.[10] "Our Grief Is Not a Cry for War" was a typical slogan on posters and buttons, as were other such pleas as "Don't Turn Tragedy into War." Perhaps ten thousand people took part in a hastily organized demonstration in

Washington, D.C., on September 26, called by the left-wing ANSWER ("Act Now to Stop War and End Racism") coalition.[11] But a war against Afghanistan had become a logical conclusion of the administration's framing of 9/11. The intensely nationalistic atmosphere of the early autumn of 2001 never left any hope of heading off the war. Less than a month after the attacks, on October 7, bombs began falling on Afghanistan, marking the start of what has since become the longest war in U.S. history.

The New Reality, October 2001 — January 2002

With the commencement of bombing in Afghanistan, the United States was at war, not only metaphorically against "terror" but also militarily against a particular nation-state. The war enjoyed overwhelming domestic support, giving little incentive for opponents to speak out. U.S. casualties remained slight, and the fanatically fundamentalist Taliban regime in Afghanistan ranked among the least popular governments in the entire world with the American public. Only with the new year 2002, when the Bush administration began slowly to make public its goal of invading Iraq, a much more ambitious (and ambiguous) target, would a sizeable antiwar movement begin to take shape.

Besides the war in Afghanistan, the new reality included dramatically greater surveillance powers for the government, embodied in the USA PATRIOT Act, which Congress passed overwhelmingly (357–66 in the House, 98–1 in the Senate) on October 24. That sixty-seven legislators voted "no" signaled that the issue of domestic civil liberties had become more divisive, at least in the short run, than was the military engagement in Afghanistan. Even so, with memories and images of the 9/11 attacks still fresh, there was little all-out protest against the omnibus provisions of the Patriot Act, whose supporters claimed that it would help prevent new attacks.

U.S. Special Forces troops with Afghan allies, November 2001. Credit: U.S. Army

Meanwhile, the Justice Department and local police forces drew protests for rounding up nearly a thousand Muslims, Arabs, and South Asians on flimsy grounds, often holding them indefinitely.

Constantly hovering in the background during that period were reminders of the 9/11 attacks, especially of the destruction of the World Trade Center towers, captured on camera and often replayed. The clearing of the site went on for months, with the accompanying search for bodies and body parts among the ruins.[12] Beginning in September, the *New York Times* for months ran a widely reprinted series called "Portraits of Grief," which in time depicted nineteen hundred of the September 11 victims in warmly appreciative ways that underlined the tragedy of lives cut short—and kept 9/11 firmly in the minds of readers. The English professor and literary critic David Simpson wrote of the series, "One tends of course to speak only good things of the dead, but even within the expected bounds of memorial decorum, the notices seem formulaic. They seem regimented, even militarized, made to march to the beat of a single drum."[13]

The portraits had only positive things to say about the deceased, who became surrogates for a victimized United States. The media's instant use of the term *ground zero* for the World Trade Center site deepened the sense of victimization by appropriating a term usually linked to the atomic bombing of Hiroshima in 1945, which had killed on a vastly greater scale. The image of American righteousness carried over to the nation itself, with criticisms of U.S. foreign policy scorned as providing justification for terrorism. On October 11, Mayor Rudolph Giuliani of New York refused a $10 million donation from a Saudi prince to a 9/11 relief fund because the prince had accompanied the check with a statement criticizing U.S. policies in the Middle East.[14]

Beginning a week after September 11, the so-called anthrax scare exacerbated the edginess of the political atmosphere. Packages with anthrax powder began showing up in government and media offices, resulting in five deaths and stepped-up security precautions in postal facilities. The case was not closed until the 2008 suicide of the government scientist who had become the prime suspect. Notes accompanying the powder used phrases like "DEATH TO AMERICA," "DEATH TO ISRAEL," and "ALLAH IS GREAT," but the government and the mainstream media, to their credit, avoided the easy but false conclusion that Muslims were behind the mailings.

By the end of 2001, the Bush administration seemed to have carried the day with its historicizing of the events of 9/11 and with the lessons it drew from them. A suddenly popular president using new powers in foreign policy had initiated a war that by November, with almost no loss of American life, had claimed at least a mixed success: Osama bin Laden had escaped, but his Taliban hosts had fled from Afghanistan's cities and from governmental power. Congress had served up an ambitious menu of surveillance tools. President Bush's decision in December to declare the U.S. military base in Cuba, Guantánamo Bay, a site for the indefinite storing of "enemy combatants"—inmates explicitly deprived of prisoner-of-war rights in what was a thumb in the eye of the Geneva Convention—aroused protest but not enough to derail the plan. In the two years that followed, the administration was to play its 9/11 hand in a more daring fashion, with mixed results.

The Selling of the Iraq War, January 2002 — December 2003

As the events of 9/11 receded into the past chronologically—though not politically—the Bush administration had both defensive and offensive terrains on which to act. Defensively, it faced lingering, even growing, doubts about how seriously it had taken pre−9/11 warning signs that al-Qaeda might be planning a major operation inside the United States. Demands grew for the appointment of an independent commission to investigate the attacks and the government's actions. Leading the charge were widows of 9/11 victims, including the four "Jersey Girls" (Kristen Breitweiser, Patty Casazza, Lorie Van Auken, and Mindy Kleinberg), who kept constant pressure on Congress despite the Bush administration's initial opposition. At length, after the elections of November 2002, Congress voted to create the commission, whose hearings and final report were to play out over the following year and a half. In the meantime, a far more significant battle had begun taking shape.

As early as September 12, 2001, high-ranking administration officials had vainly sought evidence that linked Saddam Hussein's government of Iraq to the attacks.[15] None was found, but the ambition of toppling Saddam's regime—removing a thorn in the side of the United States and going decisively beyond the achievement of Bush's father in the 1991 Gulf War—remained. George W. Bush's State of the Union address in January 2002 publicly launched an extended sales pitch. In this speech Bush briefly unveiled the term *axis of evil*, bizarrely lumping together three discrete regimes linked only by their hostility to the United States: Iraq, Iran, and North Korea.[16] Of the three, it was clearly Iraq—already then subjected to damaging economic sanctions and sporadic aerial bombing, and moreover in possession of tempting oil reserves—that was being put on notice.

The word *evil* perhaps constituted the key to the administration's coming campaign to gain support for the invasion of Iraq. In the wake of 9/11, the question "Why do they hate us?" was typically fended off with the claim that the attackers were evil. This term could readily be transferred to the Iraqi dictator, who had already been amply demonized to Americans before and during the Gulf War. In fact, a survey taken two days after the September 11 attacks found that while only 6 percent of respondents named Saddam when asked an open-ended question about the instigator of the attacks, 78 percent responded to an explicit question about Saddam's possible involvement by calling it either "very" or "somewhat" likely that he had been involved.[17]

President Bush with Secretary of Defense Donald Rumsfeld and Vice President Dick Cheney.
Credit: Cherie A. Thurlby, Department of Defense

The reservoir of ill feeling toward Saddam gave the Bush administration a valuable head start in its gradual buildup to war with Iraq. During the winter and spring of 2001–2, the name "Osama" gradually faded from the president's speeches, replaced by "Saddam Hussein."[18] In June the president made a major foreign policy address at the U.S. Military Academy's commencement ceremony, eschewing the Cold War doctrines of containment and deterrence and claiming the right to attack preemptively in the interest of stopping terror attacks: "If we wait for threats to fully materialize, we will have waited too long. We must take the battle to the enemy, disrupt his plans and confront the worst threats before they emerge."[19] The president clearly had his sights on Iraq,[20] but the 9/11 attacks were now being used to provide an all-but-blank check for wars of choice anywhere that a U.S. administration might wish to unleash one.

In the buildup to the March 2003 invasion, the administration tried in two ways to link Iraq to the 9/11 attacks. One was to claim, or sometimes to insinuate, Iraq's involvement. For example, an unconfirmed report that an Iraqi intelligence official had been seen together in Prague with Mohammed Atta, the lead pilot of the September 11 hijackers, received much publicity, though the 9/11 Commission (officially named the National Commission on Terrorist Attacks upon the United States) later decisively refuted this claim.[21] Bush himself, unlike his vice president, Dick Cheney, mostly avoided claiming a specific Iraqi connection with the attacks,[22] but the fog of innuendo undoubtedly helped reinforce the public's predisposition to believe anything bad about Saddam Hussein.

A more consistent and explicit use of 9/11 imagery in the sales campaign was the claim that Iraq had, or was developing, weapons of mass destruction (WMDs) that, if placed in the hands of terrorists, could replicate the 9/11 attacks on a much grander scale. As the deputy secretary of defense, Paul Wolfowitz, a leading architect of the administration's Iraq policy, later put it, "For reasons that have a lot to do with the U.S. government bureaucracy we settled on the one issue that everyone could agree on which was weapons of mass destruction as the core reason."[23] An all-out propaganda assault focused on WMDs began with Sunday television talk shows in early September 2002. (As the White House chief of staff, Andrew Card, famously said, "From a marketing point of view, you don't introduce new products in August.")[24] The national security advisor, Condeleezza Rice, railing against excessive caution in weighing evidence that Iraq had WMDs, warned, "We don't want the smoking gun to be a mushroom cloud."[25] Likewise, the president claimed, "We need to think about Saddam Hussein using Al Qaeda to do his dirty work, to not leave fingerprints behind."[26] The fancied threat of another, bigger 9/11 loomed over the discussion and obscured that United Nations (UN) weapons inspectors, whose work the Bush administration sought strenuously to discredit, were finding no evidence of WMDs in Iraq. In early October, by votes of 296–133 in the House and 77–23 in the Senate, Congress passed a resolution supporting diplomatic efforts but authorizing the president to use armed force against Iraq "as he deems to be necessary and appropriate." Politically ambitious Democratic senators (notably John Kerry, John Edwards, Hillary Clinton, and Joe Biden) voted with the majority.[27]

Soon afterward, Republican candidates achieved unexpected success in the midterm elections, gaining enough seats in the closely divided Senate to become the majority party. With war drums beating, the Republican campaign played 9/11 for all it was worth. The two-term Georgia Democrat Max Cleland, a multiple amputee from the Vietnam War who had voted for the Iraq resolution but favored giving employees of the new Department of Homeland Security the right to unionize, was subjected to a TV commercial in which the face of Osama bin Laden gradually morphed into his own.[28]

The minority votes in Congress against the Iraq resolution—this time Barbara Lee was joined by 132 other House members and 23 senators—owed much to the fact that public opinion was far more divided than it had been over the war with Afghanistan in 2001. A section of elite opinion, including some former Republican policy makers, expressed this reluctance to war, but a grassroots antiwar movement had also, slowly, taken shape during 2002. For this movement, resistance to the administration's militarized definition of 9/11 became an important theme. An eight-page English-Spanish tabloid newspaper named *War Times/Tiempo de Guerras*, produced by independent Bay Area activists, connected many local groups, which distributed the free paper in their communities. The first (January–February) issue featured a trip to Afghanistan by family members of 9/11 victims. In February a new activist group called September 11 Families for Peaceful Tomorrows emerged on the East Coast. When the White House campaign for war began in earnest in the fall, however, the antiwar movement genuinely began to build momentum, with new and bigger groups entering the field. The women's group Code Pink (its name mocking the Department of Homeland Security's color-coded alert levels) formed in October and established itself as a leading force through its imaginative and confrontational tactics. Later that month, more than seventy national and local organizations came together in a coalition called United for Peace and Justice (UFPJ). After the November elections, the online activist group MoveOn.org, formed in 1998 to oppose the impeachment of President Bill Clinton, threw much energy into opposing the drive to war.

The Bush administration experienced the months between the congressional vote and the invasion of March 2003 as a time of military preparation, on the one hand, and as an uphill struggle for international support, on the other. Denied approval by the UN Security Council, the administration brandished a "coalition of the willing" that included Britain but notably not Germany or France—"Old Europe," as the secretary of defense, Donald Rumsfeld, sneeringly put it.[29] In mid-February, as the invasion drew closer, millions of people—an antiwar outpouring that dwarfed anything seen in the Vietnam era—took to the streets in cities throughout the world.[30] Turnout proved especially high in Britain, Spain, and Italy, whose governments supported the planned invasion. New York City had one of the biggest protests, with hundreds of thousands of participants, and the UFPJ claimed to have coordinated nearly eight hundred protests nationwide.[31] Patrick E. Tyler of the *New York Times* wrote, in a much quoted piece, "The huge anti-war demon-

New York City demonstration, February 15, 2003, part of a worldwide effort to stop the impending U.S.-led invasion of Iraq. Credit: Meade/Skotnes

Part of the
demonstration
of February 15,
2003, in New
York City.
Credit: Meade/
Skotnes

Part of the demonstration of February 15, 2003, in New York City. Credit: Meade/Skotnes

strations around the world this weekend are reminders that there may still be two superpowers on the planet: the United States and world public opinion."[32]

As had happened to the much smaller movement that sought to avert the Gulf War of 1991, the antiwar movement peaked before the war began, though it never collapsed and proved a persistent reminder in later years that the Bush administration had invaded Iraq without a united country behind it. Once the war began on March 20 — or more specifically, after the capture of Baghdad and the defeat of the Iraqi army — protest demonstrations decreased in size. The swift collapse of Saddam's regime seemed to many to show that the war, even as it flouted international law, was at least a military success — a crime, as the French statesman Talleyrand might have put it long ago, but not a blunder. On May 1, 2003, Bush stood on the deck of a military transport returning from the war zone and proclaimed the end of "major military operations." "We have not forgotten the victims of September the eleventh, the last phone calls, the cold murder of children, the searches in the rubble," he intoned. "With those attacks, the terrorists and their supporters declared war on the United States, and war was what they got."[33]

Behind the president as he spoke a giant banner proclaimed "Mission Accomplished." The banner made for a stunning photo op, seeming to mark a happy climax to the administration's long sales pitch for the Iraq invasion. Yet as the incisive blogger Tom Engelhardt soon pointed out, it was not clear whose photo op it would eventually turn out to be.[34]

Occupation, War, and Growing Mistrust, 2003–2006

The period between the early summer of 2003 and the congressional elections of 2006 was marked by a growing frustration of U.S. goals in Iraq and a rearguard action by the Bush administration (successful in the 2004 presidential campaign) to defend its expanded definition of the meaning of 9/11. Even the bare-bones consensus definition—that 9/11 was an unexpected attack by Muslim extremists—came under attack on the political fringes, as inside-job conspiracy theories emerged to blame U.S. officials for either allowing or orchestrating the attacks.

By the end of 2003, even after the capture of Saddam Hussein on December 13, it had become clear that the lightning-fast invasion had been only the opening act in a protracted conflict. In the ensuing years, turning points came and went, with no clear-cut American victory in sight. Opponents of the war, while no longer mounting rallies on the scale of those in February 2003, kept pressing their point. The failure of U.S. inspectors to find the notorious weapons of mass destruction that had served as the war's chief rationale dampened popular enthusiasm

Members of Iraq Veterans Against the War (IVAW) at a Boston antiwar march.
Credit: Jonathan McIntosh

for the conflict, even as politicians spoke of the need to "support the troops." By 2004 new organizations called Iraq Veterans against the War (IVAW) and Military Families Speak Out had joined the array of groups seeking an end to the war and to the occupation. The revelation of the widespread torture of American-held Iraqi detainees at Baghdad's Abu Ghraib prison in April 2004, documented with vivid photographs, created a serious embarrassment to the occupying forces.

Much antiwar sentiment in the United States played out in the 2004 Democratic presidential primaries, which witnessed a groundswell of support for the vehement war critic Howard Dean and the eventual nomination of Senator John Kerry, who also called the war a mistake. Kerry in the fall campaign accused Bush of having diverted resources from the fight against the 9/11 perpetrators to pursue a war of choice in Iraq. The Republican Party, for its part, ratcheted up its claim to the heritage of 9/11, hammering the theme that the Democrats could not be trusted to prevent future terror attacks. The Republican Party held its 2004 National Convention in early September in New York City to put the "terror threat" front and center. (At the same time, with the Republican Michael Bloomberg holding the mayor's office, police hemmed in and harassed antiwar demonstrators, who were denied a permit for what would have been a huge rally in Central Park.) By combining its national security mantra with an appeal to social conservatives on domestic issues, the Bush-Cheney ticket squeaked through to victory in November.

Outside the realm of electoral politics, the growing mistrust of the Bush administration opened the door wider than ever before for the spread in the United States of so-called conspiracy theories on the nature of the 9/11 events.[35] Asking, "Who benefits?," these theories pounced on scattered bits of evidence to claim that the government itself may have planned, or at least deliberately allowed, the attacks. Such theories had originally been more common in Europe than in the United States, but they began spreading in this country in 2004. A retired theology professor, David Ray Griffin, became their best-known proponent, starting with his book published in the spring of that year, *The New Pearl Harbor: Disturbing Questions about the Bush Administration and 9/11*.[36] Although the inside-job theories ranged far and wide, the most commonly touted beliefs were that the World Trade Center towers had been felled by controlled demolition and that the Pentagon and Flight 93 had both been hit by missiles.

Ironically, the publication of the 571-page report of the 9/11 Commission in July 2004 did as much to fuel the conspiracy theories as to bury them.[37] The commission's well-written report quickly achieved best-seller status, but for those prepared to be skeptical, the report only deepened suspicion of a cover-up. Critics pointed to the role of Philip Zelikow, a close associate of Rice and a former member of the Bush transition team, as the staff director of the commission. They

9/11 Truth banner at a Los Angeles antiwar demonstration. Credit: Damon D'Amato

complained that leads turned up by inside-job theorists had not been investigated. In truth, the commission had not undertaken to refute every claim about 9/11. The claims of controlled demolition and missile attacks were not considered worthy of comment.

Aware of the spread of conspiracy theories, *Popular Mechanics* stepped in where the 9/11 Commission had declined to go. The magazine published a special issue in February 2005, which it subsequently expanded into a book under the title *Debunking 9/11 Myths: Why Conspiracy Theories Can't Stand Up to the Facts.*[38] Much more elaborately, in October 2005 the National Institute of Standards and Technology (NIST) produced a forty-three–volume report on its investigation of the twin towers' collapse, again concluding that the impact of the planes, and the subsequent weakening of the buildings' structures, had been enough to bring down the towers.[39] On the political left, the best-known unrelenting critic of U.S. foreign policy, Noam Chomsky, dismissed the conspiracy theories as implausible and devoid of convincing evidence. Still, the inside-job beliefs grew, no doubt fed by the deteriorating U.S. military effort in Iraq. A poll reported by Scripps-Howard in the summer of 2006 found that 36 percent of Americans found it either "very likely" or "somewhat likely" that federal officials had assisted in the attacks or had let them happen "because they wanted the U.S. to go to war in the Middle East."[40]

Cindy Sheehan, 2005. Credit: Jacob Appelbaum

The Democrats' failure to oust President Bush in the narrowly decided 2004 election proved discouraging to many opponents of the war. In the following summer, the antiwar movement got a shot in the arm from the initiative taken by Cindy Sheehan, a thirty-eight–year-old mother of a soldier killed the previous year while serving in Iraq. In August 2005, at the outset of Bush's stay at his vacation home near Crawford, Texas, Sheehan set up a makeshift camp nearby, demanding to see the president. The camp swelled to well over a thousand people at times. The publicity helped dramatize that growing numbers of Americans were unhappy about the war: a *Newsweek* poll in August showed that only 34 percent approved of Bush's handling of Iraq.[41] The two main antiwar coalitions, UFPJ and ANSWER, drew well over a hundred thousand protesters to a September 24 march and rally in Washington, D.C.[42]

By 2006, costs and casualties had reached unacceptable levels, and it was obvious that, as a 2006 National Intelligence Estimate found, the war in Iraq had worsened the U.S. position in the struggle against terrorism.[43] If one issue dominated the congressional elections of 2006, it was the war in Iraq. Candidates of the Democratic Party, often without making specific promises regarding how they would vote on war-related issues, hammered the Bush administration for having embroiled the United States in an unwinnable war—in a "quagmire," as it was now called, vividly evoking a label given the Vietnam War. Democrats regained control of the House for the first time since 1994 and, narrowly, of the Senate for the first time in four years. Meanwhile, the blue-ribbon Iraq Study Group, headed by the Republican former secretary of state James Baker and the Democratic former congressman Lee Hamilton, prepared to recommend a gradual disengagement from Iraq.[44] Events that fall seemed to herald the repudiation of the administration's grand definition of 9/11.

Downed U.S. helicopter in Iraq. Credit: U.S. Air Force photo by Airman First Class Jeff Andrejcik

The New Normal?

Events following the 2006 elections can be quickly recounted. Sidelining the Baker-Hamilton commission completely, Bush replaced Rumsfeld with a consummate Washington insider, Robert Gates, as secretary of defense. He put General David Petraeus in charge of U.S. forces in Iraq with a new strategy called the "surge," increasing troop levels and soon benefiting from a dampening down of the Iraq insurgency. The latter occurred less because of the new troops than because of decisions by many Iraq militants—the so-called Awakening Councils—to accept American payments and turn their weapons against the most extreme elements of the insurgency. Meanwhile, the new Congress under Democratic leadership, fearful of appearing not to support the troops, continued to fund the war. In effect, Bush avoided explicit defeat in Iraq.

Antiwar hopes were soon pinned on the presidential candidacy of Senator Barack Obama, who had spoken out against the war in Iraq when it was first proposed in 2002 and who had strongly criticized it in his campaign, pledging to end it expeditiously should he gain the presidency. At the same time, wary of being savaged by Republicans as soft on "national security," Obama promised a more strenuous war effort in Afghanistan, where the U.S. position had turned ever more precarious. True to his word, Obama as president ended direct U.S. combat in Iraq, and Afghanistan soon replaced Iraq as the primary site of U.S. military (and, on a larger scale, local civilian) casualties.

U.S. soldiers stuck in sand in southern Afghanistan. Credit: U.S. military staff

In embracing the Afghan war, Obama has, in a sense, reenacted the experience of Lyndon Johnson, who inherited a war in Vietnam that was impossible to win but nearly impossible to withdraw from. He has tried to set a time limit on the U.S. combat role, but the target date has slipped—at first, operations were to wind down in the summer of 2011, but as that date approached, it was replaced by often contradictory talk about 2014. As of this writing, the war gives few grounds of hope for a face-saving result. The war that Congress authorized all but unanimously a mere week after the 9/11 attacks had become (on June 7, 2010) the longest war in U.S. history.

All the while, the 9/11 connection to the war has become increasingly remote. Al-Qaeda, whose presence in Afghanistan was the casus belli, currently scarcely operates in the country, though it does flourish elsewhere. Yet that reality has not deterred the ongoing war effort. Nor has the loss of majority support for the war among the U.S. population, shown by repeated polls in the winter of

2010–11.[45] The war threatens to become an endless embodiment—perhaps a caricature—of the "war against terrorism" pronounced so blithely by George W. Bush following September 11. President Obama, in his speech accepting the Nobel Peace Prize in December 2009, said that the United States and its coalition partners were in Afghanistan "in an effort to defend ourselves and all nations from further attacks."[46]

Meanwhile, the underground theme that showed itself in insults and beatings after 9/11, the theme that "the Muslims" did it, has reemerged with a vengeance. In the summer of 2010, when New York City's Lower Manhattan Community Board endorsed a proposal for an Islamic cultural center two blocks away from the World Trade Center site (and invisible from it), protests immediately arose. Too close, critics claimed. This time, influential political figures joined the attack—the former House speaker Newt Gingrich, for example, charged that the cultural center would symbolize Muslim "triumphalism" and "would be like putting a Nazi sign next to the Holocaust Museum."[47] The controversy over the "ground zero mosque," as it was labeled by its foes, served as a reminder that the meaning of 9/11 will continue to be an object of often fierce contention.

Conclusions

From the start, the Bush administration seems to have seen the 9/11 attacks as not just a challenge but also as an opportunity. The "war president" would lead a united country in a muscular, primarily military response that would cripple the ability of terrorists to take American lives or damage American interests. It sought first a quick and decisive victory over al-Qaeda in its Afghan lair by overthrowing the Taliban regime. The victory when it came proved at best Pyrrhic: al-Qaeda was sent fleeing but was not destroyed, while the overthrow of the Taliban committed the United States to a lengthy and increasingly costly stay in a country that has been called the "graveyard of empires."

Likewise, when the administration shifted its focus to Iraq, it saw an opportunity to use the 9/11 attacks as the occasion for vastly increasing U.S. influence in the entire Middle East. The war in Iraq soon became an even more obvious fiasco than that in Afghanistan, as both the public and the private rationales melted in the desert heat.

For all its failures, the Bush response to the 9/11 attacks has set parameters for "responsible" discourse by U.S. politicians throughout the past decade. The United States is always to be hailed as a beacon of idealism and freedom in the world, erring—when it does err—only because of good intentions gone awry. As a presidential candidate, Obama hedged his disdain for the war in Iraq by promising a fresh start through victory in Afghanistan. Overall, the military-based foreign policy given renewed momentum by the 9/11 attacks has held up in the face of challenges. The United States currently has an unknown number—more than one thousand—military bases around the world.[48] When President Obama asked the Pentagon for alternatives in regard to the Afghan war, he was given a narrow range of options—all calling for escalation—and he dared not choose from outside the menu given to him.[49]

Still, with an economic crisis that began toward the end of Bush's second term and has brought record budget deficits among many other problems, the ability of the economy to sustain military spending at the current level is doubtful. As Andrew Bacevich, a military historian and former Marine officer, pointed out in early 2011, "U.S. military outlays today equal that of every other nation on the planet combined, a situation without precedent in modern history."[50] Estimates of the long-term costs of the wars in Iraq and Afghanistan range in the trillions at a time of record budget deficits.[51]

In the summer of 2002, as the administration was preparing for its high-pressure drive for a congressional vote authorizing war with Iraq, a high-ranking Bush official (likely the political strategist Karl Rove) made a telling remark to a journalist in a private conversation. "We're an empire now," he said, "and when we act we create our own reality."[52] It was a wise remark, but perhaps not in the way the speaker intended. As the attacks of September 11, 2001, recede into the past, memories of the trauma will remain, but so will the legacy of the way in which the U.S. government used it.

Notes

I received valuable suggestions on earlier drafts of this article from Andor Skotnes, a coeditor of this *RHR* issue, and from several other friends and colleagues, notably Jonathan Cobb, Max Elbaum, James Green, Kevin Murphy, Nick Thorkelson, and Mary Ann Wynkoop.

1. "A Day of Terror: Bush's Remarks to the Nation on the Terrorist Attacks," *New York Times*, September 12, 2001.
2. Clarke went on to say, "Those entrusted with protecting you failed you. And I failed you. We tried hard. But that doesn't matter. Because we failed." Philip Shenon, *The Commission: An Uncensored History of the 9/11 Investigation* (New York: Twelve, 2008), 282. Shenon covered the 9/11 Commission for the *New York Times*.
3. Rebecca Solnit, "How 9/11 Should Be Remembered: The Extraordinary Achievements of Ordinary People," September 10, 2009, www.tomdispatch.com/post/175132. She contrasts the New York events with Hollywood disaster films in which the mass of ordinary, stupid people are rescued by heroes. See also her book *A Paradise Built in Hell* (New York: Viking, 2009).
4. See, e.g., the articles by Mary Marshall Clark and Ann Cvetkovich in this issue.
5. "A Nation Challenged," *New York Times*, September 21, 2001.
6. Susan Sontag, "A Mature Democracy," *New Yorker*, September 24, 2001, 32.
7. Chalmers Johnson, *Blowback: The Costs and Consequence of American Empire* (New York: Metropolitan Books, 2000).
8. Howard Zinn, "The Old Way of Thinking," *Progressive*, November 2001, 8–9.

9. Reprinted in James Carroll, *Crusade: Chronicles of an Unjust War* (New York: Metropolitan Books, 2004), 21.

10. It should be kept in mind that there was very little by way of a preexisting antiwar movement in September 2001. The Clinton administration's aerial bombing campaign in Serbia in 1999 had been supported by many liberals and drew little protest in the United States. The predominantly youthful antiglobalization movement had far more energy, as evidenced by large demonstrations that disrupted a meeting of the World Trade Organization in Seattle in late 1999.

11. Elizabeth Becker, "Marchers Oppose Waging War against Terrorists," *New York Times*, October 1, 2001.

12. See William Langewiesche's gripping *American Ground: Unbuilding the World Trade Center* (New York: North Point Press, 2002).

13. David Simpson, *9/11: The Culture of Commemoration* (Chicago: University of Chicago Press, 2006), 23.

14. Jennifer Steinhauer, "A Nation Challenged: The Donations," *New York Times*, October 12, 2001.

15. Richard A. Clarke, *Against All Enemies: Inside America's War on Terror* (New York: Free Press, 2004), 32.

16. "The State of the Union: President Bush's State of the Union Address to Congress and the Nation," *New York Times*, January 30, 2002.

17. Scott L. Althaus and Devon M. Largio, "When Osama Became Saddam: Origins and Consequences of the Change in America's Public Enemy #1," *Political Science and Politics* 17 (2004): 795–96.

18. Ibid.

19. Elisabeth Bumiller, "U.S. Must Act First to Battle Terror, Bush Tells Cadets," *New York Times*, June 2, 2002.

20. By the following month, British intelligence officials meeting with their U.S. counterparts in Washington found that the Bush administration, even while denying publicly that any decision had been made, was bent on waging war in Iraq. "The Secret Downing Street Memo," *Sunday Times* (London), May 1, 2005.

21. Walter Pincus and Dana Milbank, "Al Qaeda-Hussein Link Is Dismissed," *Washington Post*, June 17, 2004. This article provides a succinct recounting of the administration's efforts to connect Iraq to al-Qaeda. Cheney's trumpeting of the alleged Prague meeting is traced in Frank Rich, *The Greatest Story Ever Sold: The Decline and Fall of Truth from 9/11 to Katrina* (New York: Penguin, 2006), 40, 58, 59, 65.

22. A more typical Bush statement was this, in October 2002: "This is a man that we know has had connections with al Qaeda. This is a man who, in my judgment, would like to use al Qaeda as a forward army." Pincus and Milbank, "Al Qaeda-Hussein Link Is Dismissed."

23. U.S. Department of Defense News Transcript, July 23, 2003, www.defenselink.mil/transcripts/transcript.aspx?transcriptid=2594.

24. Elisabeth Bumiller, "Bush Aides Set Strategy to Sell Policy on Iraq," *New York Times*, September 7, 2002.

25. Todd S. Purdum, "Threats and Responses," *New York Times*, September 9, 2002.

26. Elisabeth Bumiller, "Threats and Responses," *New York Times*, October 15, 2002.

27. Alison Mitchell and Carl Hulse, "Congress Authorizes Bush to Use Force against Iraq, Creating a Broad Mandate," *New York Times*, October 12, 2002.

28. This episode is recounted in, among other places, Shenon, *The Commission*, 28–29.

29. Steven R. Weisman, "U.S. Set to Demand That Allies Agree Iraq Is Defying U.N.," *New York Times,* January 23, 2003.

30. The BBC News estimated 6 to 10 million participants over the weekend of February 15–16. "Millions Join Global Anti-war Protests," February 17, 2003, news.bbc.co.uk/2/hi/europe/2765215.stm.

31. UFPJ, "History and Accomplishments," www.unitedforpeace.org/article.php?list=type&type=16 (accessed February 25, 2011).

32. Patrick E. Tyler, "A New Power in the Streets," *New York Times,* February 17, 2003.

33. Rich, *Greatest Story Ever Sold,* 90.

34. Tom Engelhardt, "Drip, Drip, Drip," August 10, 2003, www.tomdispatch.com/blog/879.

35. Of course the mainstream account is a conspiracy theory too, but one that fits many more of the known facts. See, for example, Lawrence Wright, *The Looming Tower: Al Qaeda and the Road to 9/11* (New York: Knopf, 2006).

36. David Ray Griffin, *The New Pearl Harbor: Disturbing Questions about the Bush Administration and 9/11* (Northampton, MA: Olive Branch Press, 2004). The book's title picked up on a term used in a report of 2000 by the Project for a New American Century (PNAC), whose members soon came to dot the upper reaches of the Bush administration. A PNAC report titled "Rebuilding America's Defenses" had noted that the process "is likely to be a long one, absent some catastrophic and catalyzing event—like a new Pearl Harbor." PNAC, "Rebuilding America's Defenses: A Report from the Project for a New American Century," September 2000, 51, www.Newamericancentury.org/RebuildingAmericasDefenses.pdf.

37. *9/11 Commission Report: Final Report of the National Commission on Terrorist Attacks upon the United States* (New York: Norton, 2004). An example of the inside-job theorists' rejection of the report is David Ray Griffin, *The 9/11 Commission Report: Omissions and Distortions* (Northampton, MA: Olive Branch Press, 2005).

38. David Dunbar and Brad Reagan, eds., *Debunking 9/11 Myths: Why Conspiracy Theories Can't Stand Up to the Facts* (New York: Hearst Press, 2006).

39. The NIST subsequently produced a more manageably sized document, "Answers to Frequently Asked Questions," August 30, 2006, wtc.nist.gov/pubs/factsheets/faqs_8_2006.htm.

40. Thomas Hargrove, "Third of Americans Suspect 9/11 Government Conspiracy," Scripps-Howard News Service, August 1, 2006, www.scrippsnews.com/911poll.

41. Rich, *Greatest Story Ever Sold,* 195.

42. Petula Dvorak, "Antiwar Fervor Fills the Streets: Demonstration Is Largest in Capital since U.S. Military Invaded Iraq," *Washington Post,* September 25, 2005.

43. Karen DeYoung, "Spy Agencies Say Iraq War Hurting U.S. Terror Fight," *Washington Post,* September 24, 2006.

44. *The Iraq Study Group Report* (New York: Vintage, 2006).

45. See, e.g., Amanda Terkel, "Sixty-Three Percent of Americans Oppose War in Afghanistan," *Huffington Post,* December 30, 2010, www.huffingtonpost.com/2010/12/30/63–percent-of-american-public-opposes-war-afghanistan_n_802765.html.

46. Full text of Obama's Nobel Peace Prize speech, www.msnbc.msn.com/id/34360743/ns/politics-white_house (accessed April 8, 2011).

47. Edward Wyatt, "Three Republicans Criticize Obama's Endorsement of Mosque," *New York Times,* August 14, 2010.

48. Nick Turse, "Empire of Bases 2.0: Does the Pentagon Really Have 1,180 Foreign Bases?" January 9, 2011, www.tomdispatch.com/blog/175338.

49. Andrew Bacevich, *Washington Rules: America's Path to Permanent War* (New York: Metropolitan Books, 2010), 213–21.

50. Andrew J. Bacevich, "Cow Most Sacred: Why Military Spending Remains Untouchable," January 27, 2011, www.tomdispatch.com/post/175347.

51. See, e.g., Joseph E. Stiglitz and Linda J. Bilmes, *The Three Trillion Dollar War: The True Cost of the Iraq Conflict* (New York: Norton, 2008). Stiglitz is a former chief economist of the World Bank.

52. Ron Suskind, "Faith, Certainty, and the Presidency of George W. Bush," *New York Times Magazine*, October 17, 2004, 51.

Andrew Bacevich

September 11, the War on Terror,

and Perpetual Warfare

An *RHR* Interview with Andrew Bacevich

Paul L. Atwood

Andrew J. Bacevich, a professor of international relations and history at Boston University, has emerged over the past decade as a leading critic of U.S. foreign policy, and particularly of the U.S. wars in Iraq and Afghanistan. This graduate of West Point and veteran of the Vietnam War has written numerous books and articles and appears frequently on news programs and op-ed pages. In his conversation with *Radical History Review*, he affirmed, "I do call myself a conservative," adding, however, that "we should be wary of these labels. Political conviction shouldn't simply be a bunker, a place to find sanctuary. To say that politics simply consists of a right and a left is a vast oversimplification. I think people on the left represent a set of truths, but I think there are truths on the conservative side of the spectrum as well." Bacevich was interviewed in his office at Boston University on November 5, 2010, by Paul L. Atwood, who teaches in the American Studies Program at the University of Massachusetts, Boston, and who, like Bacevich, is a veteran of the Vietnam War.

RHR: *What was your immediate personal reaction to the awful events of September 11, 2001? Has your perspective shifted in any way since?*

Bacevich: I suspect my immediate reaction mirrored the reaction of most of our fellow citizens. I was afraid, I was angry, and I was confused. I remember vividly a

Radical History Review

Issue 111 (Fall 2011)   DOI 10.1215/01636545-1268677

© 2011 by MARHO: The Radical Historians' Organization, Inc.

sense of foreboding that the attacks that happened were not the end of things. My views have changed considerably since. Specifically, I've come to believe that the attacks of 9/11 succeeded in large part not because the attackers were so smart, but because we were so stupid. The agencies of government responsible for aviation security had simply failed to meet any kind of minimal standards. I've come to believe that the jihadist threat, if we can call it that, is not nearly as great as it was portrayed by the Bush administration in the immediate wake of the attack. I do believe that there is such a threat, but that it falls well short of being existential. It certainly makes no sense whatsoever to think that protracted war provides the proper response to the actually existing threat.

You said that you were fearful at first—of what, if not the existential threat?

At the time I didn't know how to gauge the threat. I didn't know if the attacks were going to be followed by more attacks on September 12, September 13. I felt a great personal confusion of the sort that awakens you from your worst nightmares. Again, that was entirely exaggerated, but I didn't have the access to intelligence information that insiders presumably had.

In your new book you state that Bush "dishonestly turned attention to Iraq after 9/11." For what purpose?

I take seriously the comment that Paul Wolfowitz made in his famous *Vanity Fair* interview that the weapons-of-mass-destruction argument for the Iraq war served chiefly to provide an explanation that most of the bureaucracy could agree to. In other words, the weapons of mass destruction do not provide a complete or adequate explanation for why we went to war. I think that among the small circle of people who made the decision for war, different people had different motives in mind. To my mind, the closest thing to an adequate explanation is this: that in order to prevent a reoccurrence of 9/11, senior officials in the Bush administration decided that they would eliminate the conditions giving rise to violent anti-Western jihadism. In order to do that, they had to undertake a vast project of transforming the Middle East. Lending this project plausibility in their minds was their belief that American military power was unstoppable. To put it another way, they thought that a determined use of American military power in the Islamic world would either coerce or persuade governments across the region to change their ways such that the jihadist threat would be suppressed. A particular challenge was finding the right place to initiate this massive project. Iraq provided the right venue in their minds.

Why?

Because Saddam Hussein was a bona fide bad guy. Because despite the claims that Saddam posed a real threat, the fact was that he was militarily very weak. We had battered his army back in 1991, and the sanctions imposed in Iraq ever since had effectively prevented him from rebuilding his forces. The architects of the war imagined incorrectly that Iraqi society possessed qualities that would facilitate Iraq's transformation; they thought the population was largely secular. For all those reasons, they felt Iraq was the place to begin the project. They thought it was going to be easy. They thought this easy triumph would set the stage for the second and the third and the fourth and the fifth steps that would ultimately lead to a greater Middle East that would be profoundly changed. Whether one would call the result "U.S. hegemony" or whether one would call the result "freedom prevailing everywhere" probably would be an interesting argument. But it's an argument that's never going to happen because the project turned out to be misguided from the very outset. American military power turned out to be far less effective than people in the Bush administration imagined. The willingness of allies to assist us turned out to be less than they expected. The malleability of Iraqi society turned out to be all but nonexistent. And the capacity of those opposing this project to resist turned out to be much greater than anyone anticipated. We have to remember that the Iraq war was conceived as a conventional war, but it ended up being an ugly, protracted, thoroughly unconventional war. That fact testifies to the level of miscalculation by the people who conceived the war in the first place.

Your new book's title, Washington Rules, *seems to possess a double entendre by referring to a set of rules enforced by Washington, as well as the rule of Washington elites over much of the planet. Was this intentional?*

Absolutely. I intended *rules* to be both a noun and a verb. Using *rules* as a noun in the title indicates that the book describes the precepts that national security elites have adhered to for more than a half century, precepts defining the basic continuities of U.S. national security policies across decades and across administrations. And using the word *rules* as a verb indicates that these precepts provide the basis whereby the national security elites have tried to govern and police the so-called American Century.

You state in your book that "the adherents of the Washington consensus believe that the US has a unique obligation of leadership." Some feel such statements are cynical camouflage for public consumption by the decision makers, hiding deeper goals that they know the public would not be willing to accept. To what extent do you think American policy is fashioned on the basis of such idealism?

I don't think we should accept such statements at face value, nor do I think we should simply dismiss them as cynical. Henry Adams—a very shrewd observer of politics—makes a statement in *The Education of Henry Adams* to the effect that people believe what is expedient for them to believe. I think he's on to something. I am a college professor. I really believe that the best way for young people to acquire an education is by spending four years attending classes in a college or university listening to people like me. I really do believe that. But of course it's really convenient for me to believe it because I make my livelihood participating in this enterprise called college education.

Something of the same applies to George W. Bush. Prior to 9/11 he would have mocked the notion of the United States pursuing a freedom agenda. Yet as a result of 9/11 Bush underwent what in religious terms we would call a conversion. He really came to believe, with all the sincerity of Woodrow Wilson (who also believed what was expedient) that America is called upon to spread freedom and democracy to parts of the world where there hasn't been much freedom and democracy. That said, he never would have embraced the freedom agenda for the greater Middle East if this did not serve a variety of other, far more substantive American interests. Neither Bush nor anybody else is willing to expend resources to pursue a freedom agenda in sub-Saharan Africa, because we don't have many interests there. Frankly, it would be a lot easier to take on the proponents of our militarized, quasi-imperial foreign policy if they were simply power-crazed cynics. The fact that at least some of them truly believe that this is an enterprise consistent with American ideals makes it more difficult to unseat these tendencies in our diplomacy.

President Obama campaigned on a promise to end the war in Iraq, and recently declared it at an end, but we both know otherwise. Some time ago the president declared that forces in Afghanistan would begin withdrawing next July [2011], but all signs indicate that his subordinates are in virtual mutiny over this, and it is likely that the mutiny will spread. Why can't or won't President Obama assert his legitimate constitutional authority as commander and live up to what he promised those who voted for him?

This is one of the dirty little secrets that people in Washington are in on but about which the rest of us remain in the dark. The dirty little secret is this: civil-military relations in this country are dysfunctional if not entirely broken. To the extent that they think about these things at all, ordinary people assume that the principle of civilian control is sacrosanct. They assume that officers advise, the commander in chief decides, and then officers implement. That's not how the system actually works in Washington. There is rampant dishonesty, mutual manipulation, privileging parochial concerns above the national interest. The whole rigmarole preceding President Obama's decision to escalate the war in Afghanistan provides a classic example of what really goes on.

Put simply, Obama asked General [Stanley A.] McChrystal, then U.S. commander in Afghanistan, to undertake a strategic analysis. McChrystal reached a set of conclusions about how the war should be fought. The game began when the famous McChrystal report was leaked through (of all people) Bob Woodward in the *Washington Post*; in essence, this hijacked Obama's attempt to reassess the Afghanistan war. From that point until the president announced his so-called decision in December 2009, the military exerted itself to ensure that McChrystal's views would prevail. Or to put it another way, they maneuvered Obama into a position where he would simply endorse what McChrystal, the field commander, wanted.

There is plenty of evidence that this is what happened, most vividly the Woodward book, which quotes President Obama—and these are quotes that nobody denies—in conversation with Admiral [Michael] Mullen, the chairman of the Joint Chiefs of Staff, saying in effect: I want options but you guys have given me only one. And that's all he ever got. In effect, the Pentagon asked, "Mr. President, tell us if you want to escalate with ten thousand troops, or twenty thousand troops, or thirty thousand troops." The real decision had been made before the issue ever got to the president's desk. This is not new, of course. It's not as if President Obama is in a uniquely weak position relative to his military. This struggle for control can be traced to the immediate wake of World War II. Sometimes the civilians have the upper hand, sometimes the military has the upper hand. But the tussle never ends. The upshot is that civilian control has been deeply compromised, and the policies that have resulted have been, more often than not, deeply flawed. This is a huge problem, to which most Americans remain blind. Again, people in Washington understand the reality, but they choose to keep the rest of us in the dark.

During the recent midterm campaign, public concerns about the war came in almost dead last, most citizens believing that the economy and jobs trump such matters. Yet Nobel economist Joseph Stiglitz and Harvard professor Linda Bilmes have shown that the 4 trillion–and-growing price tag [for the wars] has contributed mightily to the stillborn recovery. Yet none of this seems to have entered into debate during the election. Why?

The electorate is focused on problems that cause immediate pain, and it tends to be oblivious to the real cause of the illness. It's the 9.5–, 9.6–point unemployment rate that grabs people's attention, not the catastrophic deterioration of our economic relationship with the rest of the world, not the probable effect on both future economic growth and on the ability to make good on commitments to future generations in matters like Social Security and medical care. The politicians in Washington, who one might hope would take a long view, prove themselves incapable of doing so. Or, to put it another way, they show themselves to be utterly obsessed with ensuring their own reelection. So we end up where we are. I think we're sort of stumbling down the road to bankruptcy. The Tea Party is to my mind likely to be at best a passing phenomenon. But we should at least credit members of that movement with being somewhat aware of the long-term issues that are at stake. I don't hear them offering any solutions that would pass the common-sense test. But at least they know that trillion-dollar deficits can't be sustained indefinitely.

In your book, you sound notes of frustration and disappointment about the dearth of civic responsibility today. What might it take for "we, the people" to live up to the democracy we claim and to save ourselves from a future fraught with perpetual war?

Well, I'm very pessimistic on this score. But let us set aside the by-no-means-trivial reality of our permanent war, where approximately half of 1 percent of our citizens bear the burden of service and sacrifice. Let's focus simply on the fiscal issues. I think the global war on terror is a wrongheaded enterprise. But if you believe in the global war on terror, if you believe that the wars being fought in our name in places like Iraq and Afghanistan are necessary, should we not pay for them? Should not our tax bill be increased so as to cover the cost? Or should we not accept some decrement in the benefits that we get from the government to cover the cost? The reality is, and we all know this, that the wars being fought in our name, in the name of the present generation, are being funded with borrowed money, so that the burden of paying for these wars will fall on future generations. That's wrong, that's just utterly wrong. I think future generations will curse us when they realize that we've stuck them with this bill. So, what could be done? We could behave responsibly. We could insist that we pay for policies undertaken supposedly on our behalf. You know and I know that's never going to happen. And it's that very fact that makes me so pessimistic about citizens taking steps to bring Washington back to a course of common sense.

The FBI and the Making of the Terrorist Threat

Ivan Greenberg

When the administration of George W. Bush proclaimed a war on terror after the 9/11 attacks, the Federal Bureau of Investigation (FBI) found itself with widened powers. Bush's FBI operated under a revised legal framework for investigations based on the official goal of "prevent, preempt, and disrupt." New FBI guidelines, as well as congressional legislation such as the USA PATRIOT Act and advanced surveillance technologies, empowered the bureau to conduct political policing on a previously unknown scale. Recently declassified government records are beginning to document how the FBI, using its expanded powers, played a major role in threatening the rights of free speech and assembly after 9/11.

To be sure, the FBI's role was not new. Through much of its history, the bureau had waged systematic campaigns to chill progressive and radical viewpoints.[1] Even the specific focus on "terrorism" was not completely new, building on more than twenty-five years of threat mongering. While the events of 9/11 elevated and expanded the nature of the threat, prior efforts by the FBI dating to the 1970s already equated many forms of peaceful and legal political activity with violence. Whereas J. Edgar Hoover, who ran the FBI from 1924 to 1972, had framed the domestic threat in terms of "subversion," his successors at the FBI developed a new paradigm of "terrorism" to characterize most domestic security investigations. The significance of this change proved enormous. It helped demonize dissent by blurring meaningful distinctions between nonviolent and violent political activity. It helped undermine popular social movements by smearing opposition as uncivilized, repugnant, and abnormal. The terrorist became the most feared figure in contemporary society.

Radical History Review

Issue 111 (Fall 2011)   DOI 10.1215/01636545-1268686

© 2011 by MARHO: The Radical Historians' Organization, Inc.

J. Edgar Hoover, the head
of the FBI from 1924 to
1972, saw domestic threats
as "subversion," but his
successors shifted their focus to
"terrorism"—a change of great
significance. Credit: Federal
Bureau of Investigation

Following the 9/11 attacks, the bureau drew on past methods and continued interpreting dissent as terrorism. However, the U.S. Department of Justice and the FBI pushed the issue further by developing a so-called preventative approach, which viewed well-nigh all street protest as suspect. The FBI began monitoring public spaces and deployed increasingly sophisticated technological surveillance. For example, intrusive cyberspace surveillance extended to the Internet and e-mail. The extensive use of data mining and watch lists became part of the new goal of "total information awareness."[2] The FBI operated as the leading control agency in what scholars and popular writers term the new "surveillance society." The bureau's director, Robert S. Mueller III, articulated the surveillance goal in a November 10, 2008, speech: "In the FBI, we have a mantra: 'Know Your Domain.' Knowing your domain means understanding every inch of a given community—its geography, its populations, its economy, and its vulnerabilities."[3]

An event like 9/11, characterized by a large attack on U.S. soil, is unprecedented in the post–World War II period. Perhaps after only ten years it is difficult to determine if the U.S. government's reaction to the attacks has led us closer to a police state. Yet the policies and practices carried out by the FBI with apparent sanction from the executive branch certainly raise troubling questions about the evolution of democratic society. It seems well to recall the comments of the retired Supreme Court justice Sandra Day O'Connor from a 2006 speech about partisan attacks on an independent judiciary: "It takes a lot of degeneration before a country falls into dictatorship, but we should avoid these ends by avoiding these beginnings."[4]

The "Urban Guerrilla"

The FBI category of subversion had denoted radical efforts by political actors to undermine or transform the government. But it did not imply violent methods to achieve these goals. During the early 1970s, domestic terrorism emerged as a major public policy and law enforcement issue for the first time since the Palmer Raids

(1919–20). The bureau believed violence had become part of a generalized challenge to constituted legal and political authorities. In public speeches and private communications, FBI leaders purported that the country faced the beginnings of a domestic revolution led by "urban guerrillas" such as the Black Liberation Army (BLA) and the Weather Underground Organization (WUO). On November 22, 1972, L. Patrick Gray III, the recent successor to Hoover as the bureau's director, defined his policy in a secret memo to all agents and supervisors.

> These are not normal times. We are in an age of terrorism. The tactic of the urban guerrilla, often used in Latin America, Algeria, the Middle East and elsewhere in the world, was introduced into the U.S. about five years ago and we have seen ample evidence of it in the form of ambushed police officers and terrorist bombings which have included the U.S. Capitol and the Pentagon. We now accept the existence of urban guerrilla terrorism and the fact that the urban guerrilla's philosophy of terrorism has made it necessary for law enforcement to adopt new standards and adapt to the constant threat of terrorist attack.[5]

About a year later, a new director, Clarence M. Kelley, told the International Association of Police Chiefs: "Ten or fifteen years ago urban guerrillas and violence-prone extremists were peripheral in law enforcement concern. This is no longer true. Riots, demonstrations, mass rallies, the general unrest of recent years suddenly deposited this new born baby, so to speak, on our doorstep."[6] Of course, Kelley could not acknowledge that in many cases revolutionary groups formed in response to the official repression of political activity, which prompted radicals to turn to violence.[7] By 1975, the FBI had gathered about ninety thousand pages on the WUO, and Kelley felt certain that "the gospel of violent revolution and insurrection had to be halted."[8] The urgency to protect the government from radical challenges included safeguarding the police. "Officers are today, as never before, targets of terrorist groups which deliberately seek to ambush patrol cars, to bomb precinct stations, to kill our personnel. They chatter a constant stream of abuse against law enforcement. They encourage others to disobey the law and hurl epithets against the men in blue. Who are these terrorists?"[9] The FBI had begun to misapply the terrorist label. For example, when the U.S. Senate Church Committee hearings provided details of COINTELPRO (Counter Intelligence Program), which led to a public outcry against civil liberty violations, FBI leaders falsely justified the program in terms of the fight against terrorism. In fact, COINTELPRO had begun in 1956 to combat the U.S. Communist Party and investigated tens of thousands of people who had no ties to political violence. As in later years, touting the threat of violence served as a public justification for monitoring progressive opposition.[10]

In 1976, the U.S. Justice Department imposed a new terrorism framework for FBI investigations in what was conceived, ironically, as an effort to limit secret surveillance. The first Attorney General Guidelines for the FBI, known as the Levi Guidelines, limited FBI investigations to violations of the law and direct threats of political violence to end a long history of political policing by the government.[11] Under the Ford (1974–77) and Carter (1977–81) administrations, the FBI dramatically reduced the number of security investigations, describing its new approach as one that stressed "quality over quantity."[12] Compared to 21,414 active investigations in 1973, the FBI allegedly conducted only 4,868 investigations in 1976, a decline of more than 400 percent.[13] By 1978, the FBI claimed that only 102 investigations were conducted nationwide and conservatives decried the success of the "anti-intelligence lobby." For the first time in its history, the FBI rejected congressional attempts to increase its budget for spying.[14]

But robust FBI spying soon reemerged under President Ronald Reagan within a revitalized terrorism framework. Reagan cited an alleged global Soviet terror conspiracy to justify spying on Americans, and he began to expand the meaning of what constituted a terrorist act. The FBI director William Webster told the new U.S. Senate Subcommittee on Security and Terrorism in 1982: "The question is whether words, unaccompanied by conduct, can be the subject of an investigation. We must be careful, of course, to preserve the right of free speech and to insure that investigations are not used in a way that would inhibit statements that present no serious threat to society. That is not to say that statements alone, particularly statements that advocate criminal violence, or indicate an apparent intent or ability to engage in violence, are protected against investigation."[15]

In 1983, new FBI guidelines incorporated the violent words and speech criteria to justify investigations.[16] As a result, without sound evidence, the FBI claimed a broad range of individuals and groups advocated violence and supported terrorism, including critics of U.S. policy in Central America, environmental activists, the antinuclear and peace movement surrounding the nuclear freeze, animal rights advocates, gay organizations, anti-apartheid groups, and Arab Americans. Peaceful street protests could activate surveillance.[17] One of the largest investigations targeted the Committee in Solidarity with the People of El Salvador (CISPES), with surveillance in twenty-two cities. The CISPES file totals about 142,500 pages.[18] A Senate committee concluded that the probe resulted "in the investigation of domestic political activities that should not have come under governmental scrutiny."[19] By the end of the 1980s, the FBI had come to apply the terrorist label so loosely that a Senate Intelligence Committee report concluded that spying on peaceful protests, including the use of undercover informers, had become a "fairly routine practice."[20]

With the end of the Cold War, a "peace dividend" might have decreased FBI spying. Instead, the Clinton administration responded to the first World Trade Center bombing (1993) and the Oklahoma City bombing (1995) with one of the largest expansions of the FBI in U.S. history. The terrorist threat grew in magnitude. In addition to nearly doubling the FBI budget during the 1990s,[21] the president also set in motion a series of institutional changes at the bureau, establishing a new Counter-terrorism Center as well as the National Infrastructure Protection Center (NIPC). The bureau also spoke of the threat of cyberterrorism for the first time, viewing a nonlethal threat, largely unconnected to protest movements, through a prism of political violence. Moreover, city police worked in conjunction with the FBI in new Joint Terrorism Task Forces (JTTFs). The Red Squads of the past were reorganized and renamed utilizing the new keyword—*terrorism*. Meanwhile, Congress passed the Antiterrorism and Effective Death Penalty Act (1996), continuing the trend of treating nonviolent activity as subject to discipline if it could be linked to terrorism. It focused on immigrants, whose membership in alleged terrorist groups became the basis for exclusion and deportation and included a broader provision making it a federal crime to provide "material support" (including financial contributions) to a group designated as terrorist by the government.[22] As one example of a major political policing initiative, Clinton's FBI placed antiglobalization protests under its terrorist rubric even though no acts of violence were linked to the movement apart from select petty street vandalism.[23]

The Politics of Fear

The 9/11 attacks initially brought attention to the FBI's intelligence failure prior to September 11. The revelation of an internal FBI memo from early August 2001, "Bin Laden Determined to Attack in the United States," embarrassed the bureau as did other pre-attack indicators: a July 2001 FBI report of potential terrorist interest in aircraft training in Arizona and the August 2001 arrest and release of the plotter Zacarias Moussaoui while he attended a flight school in Minnesota.[24] Many critics believed the bureau had enough prior warning to stop the attacks. Yet the Bush administration, promoting an aggressive "wartime" posture, gave the FBI even greater secret spying capabilities. The popular refrain, "nothing will ever be the same," seemed to give new legitimacy to government efforts to sacrifice rights under the banner of national security. The so-called war on terror necessitated a reduction in civil liberties not only for select high-profile targets but also for the general domestic population whose e-mail, phone calls, and other communications were data-mined and collected. Bush and his vice president, Dick Cheney, engaged in exaggerated rhetoric, looked for scapegoats, and demonized opponents.[25] Dissenting voices were accused of disloyalty. When the presidential candidate Senator John Kerry said he hoped to reduce the threat of terrorism to a "nuisance," similar to gambling and prostitution, Cheney charged that Kerry's comments were "naïve and dangerous, as was Senator Kerry's reluctance earlier this year to call the war on terror an actual war." Cheney went on to predict a national catastrophe if Kerry won: "The terrorists will escalate their attacks, both at home and overseas, and the likelihood will increase that they will acquire weapons of mass destruction to use against us."[26] The invocation of a terrorist threat dominated almost every speech at the 2004

Republican Convention, and as Tom Ridge, the former head of the Department of Homeland Security, recalled, Bush tried to manipulate terror alerts before the 2004 election to enhance his chances of victory.[27] In many respects, an uncritical mass media left unchallenged state propaganda promoting the administration's construction of the universal threat of terror.[28]

Both Bush and Congress expanded the legal framework for FBI investigations. When the president signed the Patriot Act six weeks after 9/11, what once had been the executive branch's loose and broad view of terrorism now received sanction throughout the government. Section 802 of the act created the federal crime of "domestic terrorism" to cover "acts dangerous to human life that are in violation of the criminal laws of the United States or of any State." A terrorist act consisted of any effort "to intimidate or coerce a civilian population" or "to influence the policy of government by intimidation or coercion." What is intimidation? What is coercion? Demonstrators who disobey a police officer might be viewed as engaging in terrorist activity. Indeed, the government equated most peaceful civil disobedience with terrorism. Acts of disorderly conduct, once considered violations of local law, were transformed into transgressions of federal statutes.[29]

Moreover, gathering vast amounts of information on Americans became a top priority. The Patriot Act lowered the standard for obtaining third-party records (medical, financial, educational) without a warrant by expanding the use of special National Security Letters (NSLs).[30] The further loosening of restrictions on spying occurred with the imposition of new Attorney General Guidelines for the bureau. In a major change, the guidelines, issued on May 30, 2002, empowered the FBI to monitor public spaces (lectures, religious meetings, college classes, or the Internet) independent of any ongoing investigation. The Justice Department reported: "Under the old guidelines, FBI field agents were inhibited from visiting public places, which are open to all other citizens. Agents avoided them not because they were barred by the Constitution, or any federal statute, but because of the lack of clear authority under administrative guidelines issued decades ago. . . . The new guidelines clarify that FBI field agents may enter any public space that is open to other citizens."[31] By 2003, almost all civil liberty and human rights groups in the United States criticized the changes in the law. The Lawyers Committee for Human Rights, Human Rights Watch, the Center for Constitutional Rights, the American Civil Liberties Union (ACLU), the National Lawyers Guild (NLG), and Amnesty International issued reports decrying human rights violations under the terror scare.[32] Moreover, some observers noted serious problems with the "war" metaphor itself. When does it end? The amorphous nature of the enemy did not lend itself to an easy resolution.[33]

By 2003, the FBI also had begun to take action against street demonstrations. In what has been referred to as the "Miami model," the bureau and local police organized preemptive, suppressive tactics to curtail public expressions of political activity. When in November 2003 trade ministers from the western hemisphere met in Miami for the Free Trade Area of the Americas (FTAA) meetings, police in riot gear violently attacked groups of demonstrators by firing rubber bullets, tear gas, and pepper spray, as well as wielding batons and electronic shields. Legal observers described this "indiscriminate, excessive force" as inhibiting the right of hundreds of people to engage in assembly and free speech. Law enforcement unlawfully detained, searched, and falsely arrested protestors to curtail activism. From the police perspective, convictions were less important than clearing the streets from opposition during the FTAA meetings. Notably, only 4 of the 219 people arrested by the Miami police were convicted of crimes.[34]

Similar heavy-handed methods of protest suppression also regularly occurred elsewhere. Backed by FBI intelligence, city police engaged in nonlethal violent attacks against protestors who posed no threat to public safety. The law professors David Cole and Jules Lobel noted the new development of a "very troubling form of anticipatory state violence — undertaken before any wrongdoing has actually occurred and often without good evidence for believing that any wrongdoing will in fact occur. Such preventive coercion places tremendous stress on the rule of law."[35] The public space for free speech seemed to shrink. In large cities like Boston or New York, police developed free speech ghettoes resembling prisons, restricting rallies and demonstrations to highly regulated spaces — "militarized spaces," Timothy Zick calls them — and courts upheld their imposition in the name of "security."[36]

A case study of surveillance in Denver, Colorado, illustrates the practices of a JTTF. The ACLU had sued the Denver police department and uncovered broad First Amendment monitoring by the bureau of the activities of peaceful protestors who had no connection to terrorism or any other criminal activity. In 2002, the JTTF's "active case" list included the American Friends Service Committee, Colorado Campaign for Middle East Peace, Denver Justice and Peace Committee, Colorado Native American Indian Movement, Rocky Mountain Independent Media Center, and the Human Bean Company, which imported coffee from indigenous people in Mexico. Again, monitoring street demonstrations became a high priority. The JTTF trained the Denver police on the alleged "criminal tactics of protest extremists." On one occasion, the JTTF recorded the names and license plate numbers of environmental and conservation activists at a peaceful demonstration against the lumber industry's threats to endangered old-growth forests. It monitored a person who distributed leaflets promoting a documentary film critical of the FBI. The JTTF intercepted e-mail from several local organizations, which provided intelligence on an upcoming protest by animal rights activists, on a pro-Palestine rally, on plans for a Transform Columbus Day rally, and on a several-day festival billed by local activists as the "Flying Circus."[37]

As in earlier decades, civil disobedience sent the FBI into a monitoring mode.[38] In 2004, the JTTF conducted surveillance against Food Not Bombs (FNB), a group described as embracing anarchist politics. The anarchists liked to ride bicycles, so the FBI surveyed the Derailer Bicycle Collective, which some FNB members had joined. Neither FNB nor the Derailer Bicycle Collective organized street protest. FNB became known for distributing free vegetarian food to the homeless in public parks and the collective fixed old bikes that it then donated to the poor. One young activist, Sarah Bardwell, was put under twenty-four-hour surveillance. She recalled a visit by FBI agents to her home, where she refused to answer their questions. "They did say that since we weren't giving them the information that they wanted, they were taking that as non-cooperation and they were going to have to therefore take more intrusive effort in the future to find out what they needed to know, but they wouldn't specify what they needed to know specifically or what those more intrusive efforts were, she said."[39] More than 150 FNB chapters exist in the United States. Elsewhere, the FBI closely watched a small number of individuals and groups described as anarchist. From 2002 to 2004, the alleged anarchist threat surfaced in several FBI reports, including during protests at the Republican Convention in New York City. But no criminal charges for violence resulted from any of these investigations.[40]

The October Plan

The FBI invoked the 9/11 attacks during the 2004 presidential election campaign to justify surveillance. Six weeks before voting, the FBI announced the so-called October Plan that included "aggressive — even obvious — surveillance" to fight potential terrorism before Election Day.[41] In a recently declassified memo, an agent in Charlotte, North Carolina, explained the historical reasoning used by the bureau to monitor Arabs and Muslims in America: "According to the Islamic Lunar calendar, November 2, 2004 is the anniversary of the Battle of Badar [*sic*]. This battle was the first battle fought in the name of Islam. It was fought against the enemies of Allah. Mohammed, the prophet and his forces, battled in the holy city of Mecca. Of course, November 2, 2004 is the U.S. election day."[42] A special FBI 04 Threat Task Force indicated no advance intelligence on any plot, but CNN reported, "The FBI is putting together an aggressive plan that includes rousting people suspected of supporting violent extremists. Federal lawmen may jail some who have committed minor crimes or immigration violations and question or tail others if only to let them know the government can find them."[43] The Islamic Center of San Francisco (ICSF) was among the organizations targeted by the bureau. The FBI tried to interview its leadership but reported resistance.

On 10/21/2004, [text redacted], DOB [text redacted], telephone number [text redacted], contacted SA [text redacted]. [text redacted] is a [text redacted] of the ICSF. [text redacted] advised that the board members at ICSF are worried about the FBI's interest in talking to them. They believe the interviews are really interrogations, and that an interview with the FBI could lead to further investigation and ultimately deportation from the United States. They have been advised by the ACLU not to talk to the FBI.[44]

```
                                              DECLASSIFIED BY 60324 uc bau/sab/rs
                                              ON 05-17-2010
                              SECRET
                        ---- Working Copy ----                    Page      1


     Precedence:  ROUTINE                      Date:  10/29/2004

     To: Counterterrorism          Attn:   2004 Threat Task Force

     From:  San Francisco
            Squad 17A
            Contact:  SA [                              ]

     Approved By: [                        ]

     Drafted By:  [              ]:jc

 (U) Case ID #:  (S)   315N-HQ-C1463271-PREVENT   (Pending)

 (U) Title:   (S)  2004 Threat Task Force - Prevention Plan

     Synopsis:  (U)  Liaison with the Islamic Center of San Francisco
     (ICSF).

            (U) (S)       Derived From :  G-3
                          Declassify On:  X1

     Details:  (U) . SA [        ] contacted [              ] to arrange a
     meeting with the leadership of the Islamic Center of San
     Francisco (ICSF), 400 Crescent Street, San Francisco, California.
     [      ] is the subject of 315N-SF-135174, and was previously
     interviewed by SA [        ] on 10/06/2004. [      ] advised SA
     [      ] that he talked to [        ] board members about meeting
     with SA [      ], but that they preferred to contact SA [        ]
     themselves.

            (U)  On 10/21/2004, [            ] DOB [              ]
     [        ], telephone number [            ], contacted SA
     [      ]. [    ] is a [        ] of the ICSF. [    ] advised that the
     board members at ICSF are worried about the FBI's interest in
     talking to them.  They believe the interviews are really
     interrogations, and that an interview with the FBI could lead to
     further investigation and ultimately deportation from the United
     States.  They have been advised by the ACLU not to talk to the
     FBI.

            (U) [      ] stated that he himself is being investigated
     by the FBI. When asked why [    ] believes he is under FBI
     investigation, [    ] stated he was told that his application for
     U.S. citizenship has been pending for almost two years because of
     a pending FBI investigation on him.

            (U) (S) [      ] is the subject of [              ]

     ------------------------------------------------------------------
     Case ID : 315N-HQ-C1463271-PREVENT          Serial : 896
     [                              ]                     [      ]
                              SECRET
```

This declassified FBI document details efforts to interview the leaders of the Islamic Center of San Francisco. It was obtained from the FBI under the Freedom of Information Act after filing an administrative appeal with the Office of Information at the U.S. Justice Department.
Source: October Plan FBI document, in the author's possession

The October Plan continued into November after the Bush victory. On November 4, the president opened his first postelection press conference with a prepared statement: "We are fighting a continuing war on terrorism." Bush intensified efforts against the terrorist threat during his second term. On November 18, 2004, he issued three separate presidential directives giving even greater power to the CIA and the FBI. The FBI's power would increase with the goal to "strengthen further the FBI's ability to prevent, preempt, and disrupt terrorist threats to and attacks against the United States." At last, we had the new keywords for the FBI role after 9/11 — "prevent, preempt and disrupt" — which reappeared in a Bush memorandum to the attorney general on November 23, 2004 ("Further Strengthening Federal Bureau of Investigation Capabilities").[45] Who were the targets? The FBI investigated under the terrorism framework groups such as the Thomas Merton Center, Greenpeace USA, People for the Ethical Treatment of Animals, Code Pink, the American-Arab Anti-Discrimination Committee, the antiwar coalition United for Peace and Justice, the Raging Grannies, and the ACLU.[46]

From July 2004 through November 2007, the FBI investigated almost 108,000 potential terrorism-related threats, as well "reports of suspicious incidents."[47] The FBI began to equate "suspicious activity" with the threat of political violence. The bureau's definition of *suspicious* remains unclear. But fighting the threat included the recruitment of private companies into so-called Watch programs. As one example, boat fishermen were called on to function as the FBI's "eyes on the water" and to report "unusual behavior when you see it." Truck drivers also were recruited as part of highway Watch efforts to serve as a "potential army of eyes and ears to monitor for security threats." In some cities, the police trained real estate agents and residential building doormen to report to the authorities. In Florida, police trained emergency personnel and cable and utility workers to report anything out of the ordinary as they visited private homes. Members of the U.S. Air Force, in the Eagle Eyes program, were enlisted to report to police if they noticed "people who don't seem to belong in the workplace, neighborhood, business establishment or anywhere else. . . . If a person just doesn't seem like he or she belongs, there's probably a reason for that."[48]

The misapplication of "terrorism" to protest activity was written into law in the Animal Enterprise Terrorist Act (AETA) of 2006. The FBI now considers animal rights activity a major terrorist threat, even though no deaths have been associated with such activism. The government views property sabotage or vandalism as a form of terrorism, as well as any effort to "physically disrupt" the functioning of a business or research center related to animals. Two groups—the Animal Liberation Front (ALF) and the Earth Liberation Front (ELF)—are identified as leading "ecoterrorists" responsible for hundreds of criminal acts.[49]

The FBI in the Surveillance Society

The making of the threat occurred as the information society morphed into the surveillance society. Past practices persisted with the unaccountable imposition of political policing: the amassing of large dossiers on political subjects and the use of counterintelligence disruptive acts. The FBI's conduct continued to raise the question, how speech and assembly can be considered "protected" when federal law enforcement secretly tracks and fights its practitioners? The attacks of 9/11 prompted the FBI to expand significantly its information collection with vast new databases.[50] For example, the FBI began to rely on biometrics—records of palm prints, scars and tattoos, iris eye patterns, and facial shapes—and also broadly scrutinized financial activity by compelling financial institutions to report to the special U.S. Treasury agency termed FinCen. In 2008, FinCen shared more than 1.2 million "suspicious activity reports" with the bureau.[51] The FBI deployed cyber "worms" or robots, whereby a computer code migrates across the Internet and places itself into the hard disks of computer users without causing any damage, transmitting information back to the bureau. Cell phones not only functioned as tracking devices via their connection to a Global Positioning System (GPS) but were also used as eavesdropping tools remotely activated.[52] Outdoor video surveillance in the form of Closed Circuit TV (CCTV) dramatically expanded in urban areas.[53] Leading critics such as Simson Garfinkel evoked George Orwell's *1984*. "Orwell thought the ultimate threat to privacy would be the bugging of bedrooms and offices. Today, an equally large threat to freedom is the systematic monitoring of public places through microphones, video cameras, surveillance satellites, and other remote sensing devices, combined with information processing technology. Soon it may be impossible to escape the watchful outdoor eye."[54]

Before Bush left office, the Justice Department issued another set of FBI guidelines expanding spying power. The new guidelines, which took effect on December 1, 2008, lowered the standard to authorize surveillance, prompting civil liberty concerns about profiling based on race, religion, or ethnic background. Bureau agents had begun collecting intelligence on businesses, behaviors, lifestyle characteristics, and cultural traditions in ethnic communities.[55] Moreover, the new guidelines allow agents in local field offices to conduct physical surveillance, recruit informers, and interview friends of subjects without higher approval. The FBI began to investigate people simply to determine if they would make effective informants. The FBI General Counsel stated that the new guidelines "are the culmination of prior efforts to revise the FBI's operating rules in the wake of the September 11 terrorist attacks." The FBI will "proactively look for threats within the country . . . moving beyond a reactive model (where agents must wait to receive leads before acting)."[56]

How will "proactive" spying differ from "reactive" spying? The Bush administration asserted that to "connect the dots" and prevent another 9/11, it needed spying both inside and outside existing laws. While Barack Obama as president has shed the overblown rhetoric of the war on terror, he has not placed any new limits on FBI practices. Rather, he supported the renewal of provisions of the Patriot Act and advocated the collection of Internet use records without warrants.[57] All efforts have been directed at expanding the surveillance state. The widespread misapplication of the terrorist label continues to challenge the very existence of a rights-based democratic society.

Notes

My thanks to Nancy C. Carnevale and Richard Greenwald for comments on an earlier draft. This article is loosely adapted from my book *The Dangers of Dissent: The FBI and Civil Liberties since 1965* (Lanham, MD: Lexington Books, 2010).

1.   The literature on FBI spying includes Athan G. Theoharis, *The FBI and American Democracy: A Brief Critical History* (Lawrence: University of Kansas Press, 2004); Richard Gid Powers, *Broken: The Troubled Past and Uncertain Future of the FBI* (New York: Simon and Schuster, 2004); David H. Price, *Threatening Anthropology: McCarthyism and the FBI's Surveillance of Activist Anthropologists* (Durham, NC: Duke University Press, 2004); David Cunningham, *There's Something Happening Here: The New Left, the Klan, and FBI Counterintelligence* (Berkeley: University of California Press, 2004); Regin Schmidt, *Red Scare: FBI and the Origins of Anticommunism in the United States, 1919–1943* (Copenhagen: Museum Tusculanum Press, 2000); Kenneth O'Reilly, *Hoover and the Un-Americans: The FBI, HUAC, and the Red Menace* (Philadelphia: Temple University Press, 1983); O'Reilly, *"Racial Matters": The FBI's Secret Files on Black America, 1960–1972* (New York: Free Press, 1989); Ward Churchill and Jim Vander Wall, *The COINTELPRO Papers: Documents from the FBI's Secret War against Dissent in the United States* (Boston: South End Press, 1990).

2.   Total Information Awareness is a Pentagon program developed by Bush in 2002. See Peter Galison and Martha Minow, "Our Privacy, Ourselves in the Age of Technological Intrusions," in *Human Rights in the "War on Terror"*, ed. Richard Ashby Wilson (New York: Cambridge University Press, 2005), 258–68; Shane Harris, *The Watchers: The Rise of America's Surveillance State* (New York: Penguin, 2010).

3.   Robert S. Mueller III, speech before the International Association of Chiefs of Police, San Diego, California, November 10, 2008, www.fbi.gov/news/speeches/using-intelligence-to -protect-our-communities.

4.   Quoted in Howard Ball, *Bush, the Detainees, and the Constitution: The Battle over Presidential Power in the War on Terror* (Lawrence: University Press of Kansas, 2007), 1.

5.   FBI Director, "Memorandum to All Bureau Officials and Supervisors," November 22, 1972, L. Patrick Gray III FBI File. The FBI released the Gray file, as well as the file on Clarence M. Kelley, as a result of civil litigation, *Greenberg v. FBI* (2008).

6.   Clarence M. Kelley, "Receptiveness to Change," speech before the International Association of Chiefs of Police, San Antonio, Texas, September 25, 1973, Clarence M. Kelley FBI file.

7.   Akinyele Omowale Umoja, "Repression Breeds Resistance: The Black Liberation Army and the Radical Legacy of the Black Panther Party," in *Liberation, Imagination, and the Black Panther Party: A New Look at the Panthers and their Legacy*, ed. Kathleen Cleaver and George Katsiaficas (New York: Routledge, 2001), 3–19; Curtis J. Austin, *Up against the Wall: Violence in the Making and Unmaking of the Black Panther Party* (Fayetteville:

University of Arkansas Press, 2006); Jeremy Varon, *Bringing the War Home: The Weather Underground, the Red Army Faction, and Revolutionary Violence in the Sixties and Seventies* (Berkeley: University of California Press, 2004).

8.   In May 1972, an FBI official summarized the bureau's WUO efforts. "Our investigation of the revolutionary Weatherman group centers on approximately 280 people throughout the country. Included in that number are the 26 Weatherman fugitives. Also included is a group of about 40 individuals, all non-fugitives, whose whereabouts are unknown and who are believed active in the Weatherman underground." Francis J. Martin to Paul V. Daly, *United States v. Felt*, June 8, 1979, Gray FBI file; R. L. Shackelford to Mr. E. S. Miller, "Weatherfug," May 8, 1972, Gray FBI file; Clarence M. Kelley, "The FBI's Role in Protecting America," speech at the University of Kansas, Lawrence, March 28, 1974, Kelley FBI File.

9.   Kelley, "Receptiveness to Change."

10. The FBI continues to view COINTELPRO in these terms. The bureau recently wrote on its Web site that during the 1960s it "used both traditional investigative techniques and counterintelligence programs ("Cointelpro") to counteract domestic terrorism and conduct investigations of individuals and organizations who threatened terroristic violence." See the FBI Web site, www.fbi.gov/libref/historic/history/vietnam.htm (accessed April 7, 2010, www.fbi.gov/about-us/history/brief-history).

11. The FBI investigated the U.S. Communist Party under the category of "foreign counterintelligence."

12. U.S. Attorney General, "Material Regarding the FBI for Consideration in Conjunction with the President's State of the Union Address," November 12, 1976, Gerald R. Ford FBI File.

13. Office of the Inspector General, U.S. Justice Department, "The Federal Bureau of Investigation's Compliance with the Attorney General's Investigative Guidelines," September 2005, www.justice.gov/oig/special/0509/final.pdf; U.S. Senate Subcommittee on Security and Terrorism, *Impact of Attorney General's Guidelines for Domestic Security Investigation (The Levi Guidelines)* (Washington, DC: U.S. Government Printing Office, 1984), 5, 9.

14. W. Raymond Wannall, "The FBI's Domestic Intelligence Operations: Domestic Security in Limbo," *International Journal of Intelligence and Counterintelligence* 4 (1990): 452; Brent L. Smith, *Terrorism in America: Pipe Bombs and Pipe Dreams* (Albany: State University of New York Press, 1994), 8–9.

15. Quoted in Eve Pell, *The Big Chill: How the Reagan Administration, Corporate America, and Religious Conservatives Are Subverting Free Speech and the Public's Right to Know* (Boston: Beacon Press, 1984), 192–93.

16. A federal appeals court in a six-to-one ruling upheld the Smith Guidelines. Geoffrey R. Stone, "The Reagan Administration, the First Amendment, and FBI Domestic Security Investigations," in *Freedom at Risk: Secrecy, Censorship, and Repression in the 1980s*, ed. Richard O. Curry (Philadelphia: Temple University Press, 1988), 276–83; "FBI Spying Is Permitted," *Washington Post*, August 11, 1984. See also Ivan Greenberg, "Reagan Revives FBI Spying," in *The 1980s: A Critical and Transitional Decade*, ed. Kimberly Moffitt and Duncan Campbell (Lanham, MD: Lexington Books, 2011), 43–64.

17. Nat Hentoff, "Someone to Watch Over Us," *Washington Post*, June 19, 1984; Sanford Unger, "The FBI on Defensive Again," *New York Times Magazine*, May 15, 1988, 78; James X. Dempsey and David Cole, *Terrorism and the Constitution: Sacrificing Civil Liberties in the Name of National Security* (New York: New Press, 1992), 48–49; Natalie Robins, *Alien Ink:*

The FBI's War on Freedom of Expression (New York: William Morrow, 1992), 360–61; "At FBI, a Traitor Helps in Search for Subversives," *Los Angeles Times*, July 29, 2001.

18.   FBI memo, "Transfer of Records to the National Archives and Records Administration (NARA)," February 22, 1991, National Archives FBI File. See also Dempsey and Cole, *Terrorism and the Constitution*, 29–30.

19.   Quoted in Whitfield Diffie and Susan Landau, *Privacy on the Line: The Politics of Wiretapping and Encryption* (Cambridge, MA: MIT Press, 1998), 147–48.

20.   Dempsey and Cole, *Terrorism and the Constitution*, 55; Ward Churchill and Jim Vander Wall, *Agents of Repression: The FBI's Secret Wars Against the Black Panther Party and the American Indian Movement* (Boston: South End Press, 1988), 376–78; "Report Cites F.B.I.'s Following of Terrorist Suspects," *New York Times*, October 9, 1990.

21.   Federal Bureau of Investigation, "Ensuring Public Safety and National Security under the Rule of Law: A Report to the American People on the Work of the FBI, 1993–1998," 1999, 5, available for purchase at bookstore.gpo.gov/actions/GetPublication .do?stocknumber=027–001–00077–7; Athan G. Theoharis, ed., *The FBI: A Comprehensive Guide* (Phoenix: Oryx Press, 1999), 4–5.

22.   Dempsey and Cole, *Terrorism and the Constitution*, 117–26.

23.   National Lawyers Guild, "Waging War on Dissent: A Report by the Seattle National Lawyers Guild WTO Legal Group," November 2000, 2, www.ratical.org/co-globalize/NLG -REPORT.pdf; Associated Press, "Ohio Braces for World Bank Protests," October 29, 2000; Abby Scher, "The Crackdown on Dissent," *Nation*, February 5, 2001, 23. See also Luis A. Fernandez, Policing Dissent: Social Control and the Anti-globalization Movement (New Brunswick, NJ: Rutgers University Press, 2008).

24.   *The 9/11 Commission Report: Final Report of the National Commission on Terrorist Attacks upon the United States* (Washington, DC: U.S. Government Printing Office, 2004), 347.

25.   John Mueller, *Overblown: How Politicians and the Terrorism Industry Inflate National Security Threats, and Why We Believe Them* (New York: Free Press, 2006), 1. See also Michael Welch, *Scapegoats of September 11: Hate Crimes and State Crimes in the War on Terror* (New Brunswick, NJ: Rutgers University Press, 2006); Susan Faludi, *The Terror Dream: Fear and Fantasy in Post–9/11 America* (New York: Metropolitan Books, 2007); and David Cole, "The New McCarthyism: Repeating History in the War on Terrorism," *Harvard Civil Rights–Civil Liberties Law Review* 38 (2003): 1–30.

26.   "Bush Slams Kerry for Anti-terror Comments," *New York Times*, October 11, 2004; Associated Press, "Cheney Calls Kerry 'Naïve' on Terrorism," October 11, 2004.

27.   "Will Terror Alert Level Show Its True Colors?" *Washington Post*, October 13, 2004; "Bush Official, in Book, Tells of Pressure on '04 Vote," *New York Times*, August 21, 2009. On the waning of public support for the war on terrorism, see Darren W. Davis, *Negative Liberty: Public Opinion and the Terrorist Attacks on America* (New York: Russell Sage Foundation, 2007).

28.   Anthony R. DiMaggio, *Mass Media, Mass Propaganda: Examining American News in the "War on Terror"* (Lanham, MD: Lexington Books, 2008).

29.   Jules Boykoff, *Beyond Bullets: The Suppression of Dissent in the United States* (Oakland, CA: AK Press, 2007), 293–95; Nancy Chang, *Silencing Political Dissent: How Post–September 11 Anti-terrorism Measures Threaten Our Civil Liberties* (New York: Seven Stories Press, 2002), 112; DeMond Shondell Miller, Jason David Rivera, and Joel C. Yelin, "Civil Liberties: The Line Dividing Environmental Protest and Ecoterrorists," *Journal for the Study of Radicalism* 2 (2008): 109–23.

30. "Law Creates Intelligence Behemoth," *Washington Post*, November 4, 2001.

31. "Government Will Ease Limits on Domestic Spying by FBI," *New York Times*, May 30, 2002; U.S. Department of Justice, "Attorney General's Guidelines: Detecting and Preventing Terrorist Attacks," September 21, 2002, www.justice.gov/archive/ag/speeches/2002/53002factsheet.htm.

32. These reports include Lawyers Committee for Human Rights, "Imbalance of Powers: How Changes to U.S. Law and Security Since 9/11 Erode Human Rights and Civil Liberties," 2003, www.voiceoffreedom.com/archives/imbalanceofpowers/powers.pdf; Chang, *Silencing Political Dissent*; Human Rights Watch, "'We Are Not the Enemy': Hate Crimes against Arabs, Muslims, and Those Perceived to Be Arab or Muslim," November 2002, www.hrw.org/en/reports/2002/11/14/we-are-not-enemy; American Civil Liberties Union, "Freedom under Fire: Dissent in Post–9/11 America," 2003, www.aclu.org/national-security/freedom-under-fire-dissent-post-911–america.

33. See, for example, Philip B. Heymann, *Terrorism, Freedom, and Security: Winning Without War* (Cambridge, MA: MIT Press, 2003).

34. Boykoff, *Beyond Bullets*, 262–66.

35. David Cole and Jules Lobel, *Less Safe, Less Free: Why America Is Losing the War on Terror* (New York: New Press, 2007), 1–2.

36. Timothy Zick, *Speech Out of Doors: Preserving First Amendment Liberties in Public Spaces* (Cambridge: Cambridge University Press, 2009), 220–58.

37. ACLU of Colorado, "The Denver Police Spy Files: FBI's Joint Terrorism Task Force," 2006, www.aclu-co.org/our-work/litigation-legal-advocacy/the-denver-police-spy-files/read-files-from-jttf.

38. ACLU, "Denver Police Keeps 'Spy Files' on Peaceful Protesters," June 20, 2003, www.aclu.org/national-security/denver-police-keeps-spy-files-peaceful-protesters.

39. ACLU, "Documents Obtained by ACLU Expose FBI and Police Targeting of Political Groups," May 18, 2005, www.aclu.org/national-security/documents-obtained-aclu-expose-fbi-and-police-targeting-political-groups; Democracy Now!, "The Return of COINTELPRO: FBI Launches Nationwide Surveillance of Activists Ahead of GOP Convention," August 19, 2004, www.democracynow.org/2004/8/19/the_return_of_cointelpro_fbi_launches.

40. Democracy Now!, "Secret FBI Unit Detained War Protestors in 2002," April, 5, 2007, www.democracynow.org/2007/4/5/secret_fbi_unit_detained_war_protesters; "Police Log Confirms FBI Role in Arrests," *Washington Post*, April 3, 2007.

41. American Civil Liberties Union, "FBI's New Surveillance Plan Chills Religious and Political Activity, Bay Area Civil Rights Groups Warn," October 5, 2004, www.aclu.org/print/national-security/fbis-new-surveillance-plan-chills-religious-and-political-activity-bay-area-civil-.

42. Raleigh Resident Agency, SA [text redacted] to Counterterrorism, Charlotte, "FBI National Initiatives," October 5, 2004, October Plan FBI file.

43. "Election Heightens Terrorism Offensive," *Washington Post*, September 27, 2004; "FBI Pursues a Tough New Anti-terror Strategy in the Runup to November," CNN.com, September 27, 2004 (no longer online); "FBI's Anti-terror 'October Plan,'" CBS News, September 17, 2004, www.cbsnews.com/stories/2004/09/17/eveningnews/main644096.shtml.

44. San Francisco Squad 17A, SA [text redacted] to Counterterrorism, "2004 Threat Task Force—Prevention Plan," October 29, 2004, October Plan FBI File.

45. Memorandum for the Attorney General, "Further Strengthening Federal Bureau of Investigation Capabilities," November 23, 2004, http://www.fas.org/irp/news/2004/11/wh112304ag.html; Reuters, "With Reform Stalled, Bush Orders Changes at CIA, FBI," November 24, 2004.

46. American Civil Liberties Union, "FBI Is Keeping Documents on ACLU and Other Peaceful Groups," July 18, 2005, www.aclu.org/national-security/fbi-keeping-documents-aclu-and -other-peaceful-groups.

47. U.S. Department of Justice, Office of Inspector General, "Report to Congress on Implementation of Section 1001 of the USA PATRIOT Act," February 2009, 9–10, www .justice.gov/oig/special/s0902/index.htm.

48. American Civil Liberties Union, "The Surveillance-Industrial Complex: How the American Government Is Conscripting Businesses and Individuals in the Construction of a Surveillance Society," August 2004, 4–6, www.aclu.org/FilesPDFs/surveillance_report.pdf.

49. Department of Homeland Security, *Domestic Terrorist Newsletter* 1 (2006): 1–2; "Eco-Terrorists, Too, May Soon Be on the Run," *Christian Science Monitor*, February 15, 2002.

50. Electronic Frontier Foundation, "EFF Sues for Information on Huge FBI Database of Personal Information," October 17, 2006, www.eff.org/press/archives/2006/10/17.

51. "FBI Prepares Vast Database of Biometrics," *Washington Post*, December 22, 2007; "Lockheed Secures Contract to Expand Biometric Database," *Washington Post*, February 13, 2008; Robert O'Harrow Jr., *No Place to Hide* (New York: Free Press, 2005), 98–102, 260, 262, 266; American Civil Liberties Union, "Reclaiming Patriotism: A Call to Reconsider the Patriot Act," March 2009, 13, www.aclu.org/pdfs/safefree/patriot _report_20090310.pdf; "FBI to Build Data Warehouse," *Federal Computer Week*, June 3, 2002, fcw.com/articles/2002/06/03/fbi-to-build-data-warehouse.aspx?sc_lang=en; Charles J. Sykes, *The End of Privacy: Personal Rights in the Surveillance Society* (New York: St. Martin's Press, 1999), 66. See also Christian Parenti, *The Soft Cage: Surveillance in America, from Slavery to the War on Terrorism* (New York: Basic Books, 2004).

52. Declan McCullagh, "FBI Taps Cell Phone Mic as Eavesdropping Tool," CNET, December 1, 2006, www. news.cnet.com/2100–1029_3–6140191.html; "This Goes No Further . . . ," BBC News, March 2, 2004, news.bbc.co.uk/2/hi/uk_news/magazine/3522137.stm.

53. Mayor's Office, District of Columbia, "Mayor Fenty Launches VIPS Program: New System Will Consolidate City's Closed-Circuit TV Monitoring," April 8, 2008, www.dcwatch.com/mayor/080408.htm.

54. Simson Garfinkel, *Database Nation: The Death of Privacy in the Twenty-first Century* (Cambridge, MA: O'Reilly, 2001), 11.

55. American Civil Liberties Union, "ACLU Seeks Records about FBI Collection of Racial and Ethnic Data in 29 States," July 27, 2010, www.aclu.org/national-security/aclu-seeks-fbi -records.

56. Valerie Caproni, statement before the Senate Select Committee on Intelligence, September 23, 2008, 1–2, www.centerforinvestigativereporting.org/files/FBItestimonySept23.pdf; "Terror Plan Would Give F.B.I. More Power," *New York Times*, September 13, 2008; "Justice Dept. Completes Revision of F.B.I. Guidelines for Terrorism Investigations," *New York Times*, October 4, 2008; "Rule Changes Would Give FBI Agents Extensive New Powers," *Washington Post*, September 12, 2008.

57. "Obama Signs Patriot Act Extension without Reforms," *Christian Science Monitor*, March 1, 2010; Michelle Richardson, "FBI's Latest Power Grab Is a Bold and Unnecessary Move," August 4, 2010, American Civil Liberties Union, www.aclu.org/blog/national-security -technology-and-liberty/fbis-latest-power-grab-bold-and-unnecessary-move.

Remembering 9/11's Pentagon Victims and Reframing History in Arlington National Cemetery

Micki McElya

With the passage of time it may come to appear that 9/11 did not blow away our past in an eruption of the unimaginable but that it refigured that past into patterns being made into new and often dangerous forms of sense.
—David Simpson, *9/11: The Culture of Commemoration*

This is our nation's most sacred military shrine and bears silent witness to the whole of American history.
—Arlington National Cemetery current official map

On September 12, 2002, the defense secretary, Donald H. Rumsfeld, presided over the burial with full military honors of a single casket in Arlington National Cemetery containing both unidentified and identified remains representing all 184 victims of the 9/11 attack on the Pentagon, a group that included civilian and military personnel on the ground and the crew and passengers of American Airlines Flight 77. Military spokespeople had taken great pains to ensure the public that none of the hijackers' remains were among those in the coffin.

Before the interment, Rumsfeld addressed a crowd of more than one thousand mourners in the Memorial Amphitheater at the Tomb of the Unknowns; it

Radical History Review
Issue 111 (Fall 2011)   DOI 10.1215/01636545-1268695
© 2011 by MARHO: The Radical Historians' Organization, Inc.

was the first funeral of its kind since services for the unknown soldier of the Vietnam War in 1984. With special reference to the five people killed who were never identified, including a three-year-old girl aboard the hijacked plane, the defense secretary stood next to the flag-draped coffin and said, "Today, these five join the unknown of past wars even as we pursue the war that is still unfolding."[1] Rhetorically linking the dead of a terrorist incident, many of whom were civilians and some of whom were children, to the lost uniformed soldiers, disembodied martial manhood, and nationalism represented by the Tomb of

Memorial Service for the Unidentified Victims of the 9/11 Pentagon Attack, Memorial Amphitheater, Arlington National Cemetery, September 12, 2002. Credit: defenseimagery.mil. Use does not imply or constitute Department of Defense endorsement.

the Unknowns, Rumsfeld's eulogy suggested the radical reimagining of war and of who constitutes a hero, a warrior, an enemy, a combatant, or an innocent under way in the formulation of the war on terror and the Bush Doctrine, one that mirrored the logic and aims of terrorism itself—a war "still unfolding," indeed.[2]

The first-anniversary ceremonies at the Pentagon and the next day's group burial at Arlington further solidified the Bush administration's position that the attacks of September 11, 2001, were acts of war demanding—and justifying—an expansive, global military response that would include the invasion of Iraq. President George W. Bush and several members of his national security team, most of whom had long records of experience with conservative administrations reaching back to Nixon and long histories with one another, quickly absorbed the events of

9/11 into already extant military goals. Chief among them ranked "finishing the job" that George H. W. Bush had left incomplete in the first Gulf War (when he left Saddam Hussein in power) and enacting Rumsfeld's vision of a transformed military.[3] Because of the cemetery's unique purchase on the American imagination and on nationalist self-conception, one known to most Americans whether or not they have ever been there, the service and monument dedication at Arlington proved especially powerful in popularizing these aims.

Today the September 11 memorial, more commonly known as the Pentagon Group Burial Marker, is linked both in official and unofficial discourses to a set of monuments and graves scattered throughout the cemetery related to incidents of terrorism in the post-Vietnam era. These include the Iran Rescue Mission Memorial dedicated in 1983, the memorial to servicemen killed in the Beirut Marine barracks bombing of the same year dedicated in 1984, and the Lockerbie Memorial Cairn for the victims of the 1988 bombing of Pan Am Flight 103 dedicated in 1995.[4] Imbued with fresh urgency as markers for casualties from the current war on terror, these monuments are freighted with new historical meanings and claims to legitimacy. They are knit together in official cemetery materials, on tours, and in popular histories and guidebooks in a pattern designed to make "dangerous forms of sense"; a pattern that uses Arlington's memorial landscape to popularize a longer story of American victimization, Islamic aggression, reluctant empire, and triumphant U.S. nationalism and military virtue.

As Rumsfeld spoke from Arlington that day, President Bush was addressing the United Nations General Assembly in New York outlining his early case against Iraq, capitalizing on the first-year anniversary of 9/11 to lay the groundwork for invasion and to make claims that Iraq constituted a legitimate front in an expansive war against terrorism in general and against al-Qaeda in particular. The president had made his intent clear the day before during the first-year anniversary ceremonies at the Pentagon. There, struggling with heavy winds and construction dust on an otherwise clear September morning not unlike the day of the attacks the previous year, Bush proclaimed that "as long as terrorists and dictators plot against our lives and our liberty, they will be opposed." There was no doubt that the dictator in question was Saddam Hussein. The nephew of Rhonda Rasmussen, a civilian budget analyst for the U.S. Army who would be honored the next day in Arlington as one of the five unidentified Pentagon victims, expressed his dismay at Bush's speech to a reporter from *USA Today*. "It was prepping for what's going to happen in Iraq," he said. "It was inappropriate for a memorial service."[5] Memorial events for the Pentagon in particular, orchestrated entirely as they were by Rumsfeld's Department of Defense and the Bush White House, were as obviously political and militaristic as they were sorrowful and patriotic. This held true for the speeches and stagecraft as well as for the forms of their commemorations, and in particular it rang true of the decision to hold a military

The Pentagon Group Burial Marker (middle distance). The side of the Pentagon struck by Flight 77 is visible behind the trees. Credit: Micki McElya

funeral for all 184 victims at the Tomb of the Unknowns and to bury their representative remains just down the hill in eyesight of the building where they had died.

Flight 77 had come in low at Arlington's edge before striking the Pentagon's west side at 9:37 a.m. on September 11, 2001. Cemetery employees and visitors used to seeing the constant flow of air traffic into nearby Reagan National Airport higher overhead witnessed the approach and crash.[6] Two planes had already been flown into the World Trade Center in New York; another would be brought down soon after by passengers over Shanksville, Pennsylvania, en route to Washington. The plane and the destruction and intense fire its impact generated tore through the outer three of five concentric rings that comprise the building complex, killing all aboard — 54 passengers, 5 crew members, and 5 hijackers — and 125 people on the ground. A year later, the anniversary memorial took place at a Pentagon that appeared fully restored, a monument in itself, thanks to a grueling construction schedule and the round-the-clock work of crews, lauded as "hard-hat patriots" by General Richard Myers, the chairman of the Joint Chiefs of Staff. With this day and monumental vision in mind, the reconstruction, Project Phoenix, had moved from the outside inward, creating, quite literally, a brave face. "It says much about our nation and the fierceness of the American people that were we not here now in this solemn ceremony, a visitor passing would see no hint of the terrible events that took place here but one year ago today," Rumsfeld marveled, standing in a place he had just minutes before called a "battlefield." Despite appearances, the project would not be internally complete until February 2003.[7]

The next day at the graveside service, Myers accepted on behalf of the victims' families the precisely folded American flag from the casket holding the cremated remains. This part of the military funeral was a purposeful adaptation of the traditional service for an unknown soldier in which the president of the United States would receive the flag.[8] A large procession had moved from the Tomb of the Unknowns to Section 64 near the Pentagon for the interment. Mourners followed honor guards from each branch of the service and a horse-drawn caisson carrying the casket. Sixty-four active and retired service people were individually buried in Arlington in the months following the attack, most together in three rows in Section 64. The group burial site was nestled beside them and marked by a four-and-a-half-foot-high, pentagonal monument of solid Vermont granite, a smaller version of an intact, but forever changed, Pentagon. It is inscribed around the top in relief letters: "Victims Of/Terrorist/Attack On/The Pentagon/September 11, 2001." The rest of each of the five sides is covered almost entirely by large, aluminum plates that together carry the names of all 184 victims in alphabetical order. A system of symbols defined at the bottom of the last plate designates those whose remains were never identified and the passengers and crew of Flight 77.

The Pentagon Group Burial Marker. Credit: Micki McElya

In some ways Arlington made for an obvious place to honor those who died in the Pentagon given its proximity to the building that symbolizes and houses the highest U.S. military authority and the qualifying status of several victims. But controversy had erupted within days of 9/11 when the families of several civilian Pentagon employees sought to have their loved ones honored with burial in Arlington as well, despite the deceased's lack of uniformed service. They had been integral to the functioning of the military as electronics and communications specialists and as budget analysts, among other things, and should be honored as "part of the military community," the family members urged.[9] Arguably, this very notion helped facilitate the diminished place of the Pentagon and its victims in popular perceptions of 9/11 over time, a place overwhelmed by New York's staggering human loss, physical destruction, the televisual record, and event-framing language like *ground zero*, but also one symptomatic of difficulties to absorb those who worked and died in the Pentagon into the narratives of innocence assigned the victims at the World Trade Center and aboard the four doomed flights. The army ultimately denied the petitions, citing the rules and ongoing space concerns, as well as the fact that they had previously denied waiver requests from the families of civilian Defense Department employees who died in the Oklahoma City bombing of 1995. By this time, however, Rumsfeld was already considering a symbolic group burial inclusive of the civilians in the national cemetery—an act contradicting the intent of the army's specific ruling and one running contrary to the site's history as a shrine to military service.[10] This intervention seemed unsurprising in the context of Rumsfeld's persistent rejections of traditional military authority and of his marked unpopularity and ongoing struggles with uniformed leadership at the Pentagon.

The national cemetery satisfied deeper emotional and political registers for a stunned and distraught population, one hungry for solace, strength, triumph, and revenge. Both those in official capacities and the general public were drawn to the site's solemnity, nationalism, and expressly hallowed ground. Washington-area papers reported spontaneous collections of people in the cemetery in 9/11's immediate aftermath, perhaps seeking to be surrounded by death framed through honor and patriotism as much as to get a clear sight line on the devastation at the Pentagon. Arlington National Cemetery "is even a more hallowed ground since September 11," explained one of the cemetery's historians, Tom Sherlock, less than two months after the attacks. "That is reflected in the mood of the people who visit."[11]

Arlington is a small portion of land meant to represent the whole of the nation and its history. It is intensely managed and constantly changing, but it is designed to seem inevitable, uniform, and eternal, producing a version of an enduring United States ennobled by sorrow and sacrifice, made strong and heroic through vulnerability, and always triumphant in the face of loss. There is no other place in the United States invested with this particular kind of symbolic weight, and because of this, there is perhaps no other terrain so deeply political in its development and role in the wider culture. In Arlington the symbols and narratives of what actions and values and which people best represent the United States are condensed and writ large through the gears of the official and state power. Yet so are their inconsistencies, contests, and failures, despite best efforts to craft a unified and impenetrable story of heroism and U.S. exceptionalism. From its inception as a cemetery during the Civil War, Arlington has been the scene of pitched struggles over the use and shape of the land — struggles that have always been about the larger meanings of freedom, sacrifice, citizenship, honor, state authority, and the nation itself, and about which bodies, alive and dead, are most representative, most capable and valuable, and most painful to lose.

In addition to being an active cemetery with an average of thirty interments and inurnments every weekday, Arlington is also a busy tourist destination visited by more than 4 million people each year. These visitors move through a complex terrain of nationalism, history, and mourning punctuated by the central presence of an antebellum plantation house reflecting the cemetery's Civil War origins. They discover quickly that this house was the home of the Confederate general Robert E. Lee, its rooms the scene of his wedding to the daughter of George Washington's adopted grandson and later of Lee's penning of his resignation from the U.S. Army. Fewer realize that before the federal government began carving Union graves out of the land surrounding Arlington House, the War Department made the plantation the site of a model community for the formerly enslaved, called Freedman's Village. Several residents, including some of the community's organic leadership, had been enslaved by Lee or his family. When Arlington was designated a federal cemetery in

A panoramic view of Freedman's Village, Arlington, Virginia, in the 1860s. *Harper's Weekly*, May 7, 1864. Courtesy of Library of Congress

1864, many contemporaries understood both uses of the land to be fitting, appropriately linked, and poetically just. Yet in the contexts of Reconstruction and reunion, Freedman's Village would come to be seen as a public nuisance and a barrier to cemetery operations. Attempts to disband the community began as early as 1868. Resistance from residents made the efforts unsuccessful until the late 1880s, when the village was finally dismantled and its cultivated lands turned over to cemetery expansion and a government experimental farm. Today, a Pentagon parking lot covers land once farmed by Freedman's Villagers.[12]

What began with Union military exigency forged out of crushing sadness, loss, and rage was transformed within a few decades into a potent scene for sectional reconciliation, triumphant white supremacy, and imperial might with the creation of a Confederate section and the burial of dead from the Spanish-American War (and the much longer Philippine-American War) at the turn of the century. It was only in this context that burial at Arlington came to carry the kind of gravitas it has now. That meaning was produced in a time of overseas empire building, the celebration of white martial manhood, and the Progressive Era growth of the liberal state.[13] This new official nationalism found its clearest expression in the creation of the Tomb of the Unknowns and the interment of the Unknown Soldier of the First World War in 1921, "saturated," Benedict Anderson has argued, "with ghostly national imaginings."[14] These imagined affective ties and the unknown's ability to represent the national whole are made possible by the remains' lack of identity and individual history, and by taking for granted, as did historical contemporaries and as does Anderson, their presumed masculinity, whiteness, and valor. Three more unknowns would be entombed there, one each for World War II, the Korean War, and Vietnam. The last of these was identified through DNA testing in 1998 as Air Force First Lieutenant Michael J. Blassie, who was subsequently disinterred to be buried near his family and childhood home in St. Louis. Most assumed that advances in forensic science and military organization meant that there would never be another unknown.[15] This notion shifted in 2002 with the Pentagon group burial.

The official category of military unknown did not make for an easy fit for the unidentified victims of the Pentagon attack. While no remains could be found, all five were known and known to be lost. Only two were members of the armed services, and one of them was retired and working as a civilian employee at the time of his death. One was a child. None had died in a conventionally defined act of war on a clearly established battlefield. But in a clear indication of the historical frames to which the Bush administration appealed through its orchestrations of mourning on September 12, 2002, the victims' memorial service was designed to suggest that each was, in fact, a kind of soldier and hero in the new war on terror. Constituting a near perfect inversion of the concept of the military unknown, the Pentagon group burial has begotten new ghosts and new national imaginings. If the notion of a "hero" had become slippery in the context of 9/11's losses, burial in

Arlington and a service at the Tomb of the Unknowns for all the Pentagon victims sought to ground them, literally, in earth that defined honorable death and service to the nation. Rather than making hallowed the ground where they were buried, the civilian victims' collective burial in Arlington made them honorable — it made them into warriors.

This definitional expansion in the cemetery not only persists but has grown over time. In 2009, Arlington began distributing a new guide map that replaced the one in use since the late 1980s, which had remained largely unchanged and was terribly outdated. Like the old one, the new map is available for free at the Visitors Center and distributed in the millions each year. Most visitors employ it as their primary source of information about Arlington. It was adapted from a popular book about the cemetery published in 2007 by the National Geographic Society and is reproduced in a new narrative history of Arlington, both of which are available for purchase in the Visitors Center's large gift shop and in two smaller bookstores at memorial sites in the cemetery.[16] The old version of the map lifted the cemetery out of geographic space, isolating it from surrounding buildings and from most Virginia landmarks. It appeared visually busy, dominated by a tight grid overlaying the entire image that was designed to facilitate the location of individual graves. The new map dispenses with this grid, resulting in a less obscured representation of the total space that encourages the viewer to read it as a whole visual plane. The new map settles the cemetery within the wider environment, locating the surrounding buildings, sites, and roadways beyond its borders; the Pentagon stands the most prominent among them. Given its wide circulation, this map has an impact on popular understandings of the cemetery, its monuments, and their meanings. A comparison of the old and new versions that pays particular attention to what has been removed and what newly added illuminates recent processes of reimagining Arlington's memorial landscape to provide greater historical contexts and a sense of horrible inevitability to the events of 9/11 to validate the wars that followed and continue.

As one opens the new map, one first encounters a short narrative history of the cemetery framing the image within the brochure. A section near the end titled "Remembering Our Heroes" advances a narrative arc for the current war on terror that starts with the explosion and sinking of the USS *Maine* in Havana Harbor in 1898. After describing the Tomb of the Unknowns, the brochure notes:

Other memorials and monuments are located throughout the 624 acres of the cemetery. In 1915, the mast of the battleship *USS Maine* was relocated to Arlington to honor the 260 men who were killed when the ship was sunk off of Cuba in 1898. The Maine memorial significantly raised Arlington National Cemetery in the national consciousness. There are now memorials to all branches of the military, to nurses and chaplains who were killed in the line of duty, and to the people who lost their lives in the September 11, 2001 attack on the Pentagon and in the Global War on Terror.[17]

Conjuring the Spanish-American War's historical battle cry, "Remember the *Maine!*" while sliding across the still-unclear and commonly presumed accidental (or conspiratorial) source of the ship's explosion through the passive voice, this passage telescopes over a hundred years to push the USS *Maine* and the attacks of 9/11 into romantic historical proximity as precipitating events for justified military responses and reluctant overseas empire building.[18]

Given that no monument other than the Pentagon Group Burial Marker is listed in relation to the country's current wars, the text's reference to memorials for those lost "in the Global War on Terror" actually points back to markers for several events in the 1980s, similarly suggesting historical depth for current events.[19] This is clearest with the inclusion of the memorial for the 241 service people killed in their sleep in Lebanon in 1983 when attackers drove an explosives-laden car into their barracks. Dedicated in 1984, the memorial consists of a cedar planted above a plaque reading, in part, "'Let Peace Take Root'—This cedar of Lebanon tree grows in living memory of the Americans killed in the Beirut terrorist attack and all victims of terrorism throughout the world." Although it was already in existence, this memorial was not deemed a "Point of Interest" significant enough to include for visitors using the old map. Today, the Beirut Barracks Memorial joins three other sites—the Iran Rescue Mission Memorial, dedicated in 1983 for the eight servicemen killed in the failed 1980 attempt to free the hostages in Tehran and included on the old map; the Lockerbie Cairn, dedicated in 1995; and the Pentagon Group Burial Marker—in a "terrorist cluster" defined by the logic of the map.[20]

Marking as areas of interest all the memorials connected to incidents of terrorism, the new Arlington guide map is also notable for what it no longer includes. The four thousand–plus Civil War–era graves of the Freedman's Village and of U.S. Colored Troops in Section 27 are not identified and carry only a brief mention in the brochure's historical narrative. The new national geography of valor and remembrance evoked by the map gains momentum through the idea that some stories are no longer worth dwelling on, that some graves are less worthy of visiting. It encourages people to understand the losses of September 11, 2001, as part of a longer, more conventional war with decades of mounting casualties, while at the same time broadening the scope of honorable martial death in unconventional ways to include all those who might be victims of terrorism, whether or not they wear the uniform. Where nonmilitary visitors were once guided to feel awed respect for the sacrifice of others, all are now encouraged to paranoia, to see themselves making that sacrifice, ennobled and emboldened by their fear. This deliberately vague narrative of vulnerability and victimization simultaneously frames the wars in Afghanistan and Iraq as unavoidable and necessarily just, absolving individual complicity and national responsibility for the wars' conduct. This distance from accountability and from reckoning with difficult histories and their ongoing effects is mirrored in the map's

failure to identify the graves of Section 27 and the injustices of slavery and segrega-
tion, struggles for citizenship, and the variable forms of honor they represent. This
most recent iteration of the cemetery's official story and of the nation it embodies
releases Americans from a shameful past while implicating us all in a triumphant,
paranoid future of limitless war.

Notes

I would like to thank Jim O'Brien, Andor Skotnes, and the two anonymous readers. As always, my
thanks to Alexis Boylan for her sharp critical eye and support.

1. Donald H. Rumsfeld, "Arlington National Cemetery Funeral Service for the Unidentified
    Victims of the Attack on the Pentagon Remarks," September 12, 2002, United States
    Department of Defense, www.defenselink.mil. For general information about the attack
    on the Pentagon of September 11, 2001, see Alfred Goldberg et al., *Pentagon 9/11*
    (Washington, DC: Department of Defense, 2007); Steve Vogel, *The Pentagon, a History:
    The Untold Story of the Wartime Race to Build the Pentagon—and to Restore It Sixty
    Years Later* (New York: Random House, 2007). On the memorial events of September 12,
    2002, at Arlington National Cemetery, see Frank J. Murray, "Pageantry to Mark Pentagon
    Goodbyes," *Washington Times*, September 4, 2002; Mary Otto, "A Single Coffin, But Many
    Tales of Lives Lost; Service to Honor the Pentagon Dead," *Washington Post*, September
    12, 2002; Alan Pusey, "Final Service Honors Victims of Pentagon Attack," *Dallas Morning
    News*, September 13, 2002; and Steve Vogel, "Lost, and Sometimes, Never Found: Pentagon
    Families Bury Their Dead Together and Mourn Five Not Identified," *Washington Post*,
    September 13, 2002.
2. Many have analyzed the emergence and cultural work of 9/11's particular idiom; see Judith
    Butler, *Precarious Life: The Powers of Mourning and Violence* (New York: Verso, 2004);
    Marc Redfield, "Virtual Trauma: The Idiom of 9/11," *diacritics* 35, no. 1 (2007): 55–80; and
    Simpson, *9/11*.
3. For a detailed accounting of these histories, interconnections, and aims, see Lloyd C.
    Gardner, "Mr. Rumsfeld's War," in Gardner and Marilyn B. Young, eds., *Iraq and the
    Lessons of Vietnam; or, How Not to Learn from the Past* (New York: New Press, 2007),
    174–200; and James Mann, *The Rise of the Vulcans: The History of Bush's War Cabinet*
    (New York: Viking Penguin, 2004).
4. As another memorial to civilian victims of terrorism, the Lockerbie Cairn, a gift from
    Scotland, is distinct among these monuments in its history and effects. Surviving family
    members struggled for years to find a location. Seeking a site within Arlington, they
    were denied by cemetery officials and the army and failed to get a waiver from President
    George H. W. Bush. In the aftermath of the 1993 World Trade Center bombing, Congress
    unanimously passed a joint resolution dedicating a "small, vacant plot of land, unsuitable
    for gravesites" within the national cemetery for the monument. There are no remains at the
    site. Daryl Britton, "Elegies of Darkness: Commemorations of the Bombing of Pan Am 103"
    (PhD diss., Syracuse University, 2008), 121–37.
5. Andrea Stone, "Mourners Shaky But Present Strong Face," *USA Today*, September 12,
    2002. For a concise history of the path to war in Iraq from the 9/11 attacks, see Nicolaus
    Mills, "Run-up: The Road to Iraq," *Dissent* 56 (2009): 15–24.
6. Poole, *On Hallowed Ground*, 251–54; Vogel, *Pentagon*, 423–27; Arlington National
    Cemetery Tourmobile guide narrative, April 25, 2010.

7. Vogel, *Pentagon*, 492.

8. Murray, "Pageantry to Mark Pentagon Goodbyes."

9. Raymond Hernandez, "Pentagon Deaths: Pleas to Bury Civilian Victims at Arlington Spark Debate," *New York Times*, September 21, 2001.

10. "No Arlington Burial for Civilian Victims," *New York Times*, November 2, 2001. On Rumsfeld's consideration, see Steve Vogel, "Remains Unidentified for Five Pentagon Victims; Bodies Were Too Badly Burned, Officials Say," *Washington Post*, November 21, 2001.

11. Karen Goldberg Goff, "Field of Honor: Veterans Receive Final Tribute at Arlington National Cemetery," *Washington Times*, November 4, 2001. On gatherings in Arlington National Cemetery in the days just after 9/11, see also Laura Bly, "Tourism Suffers in Wary Washington," *USA Today*, September 21, 2001; David Cho and Jamie Stockwell, "Pentagon Wreckage Lures Thousands," *Washington Post*, September 16, 2001; Stephan Dinan and Margie Hyslop, "Hush Prevails as Citizens Remember, Grieve," *Washington Times*, September 15, 2001.

12. Joseph P. Reidy, "Coming from the Shadow of the Past: The Transition from Slavery to Freedom at Freedman's Village, 1863–1900," *Virginia Magazine of History and Biography* 95 (1987): 403–28.

13. Cecelia Elizabeth O'Leary, *To Die For: The Paradox of American Patriotism* (Princeton, NJ: Princeton University Press, 1999), chaps. 11–12.

14. Benedict Anderson, *Imagined Communities: Reflections on the Origin and Spread of Nationalism*, rev. ed. (New York: Verso, 1992), 9. For critical reconsiderations of Anderson's analysis of the role of death and mourning in modern nationalism as exemplified in the creation of an Unknown Soldier and the national cemetery, especially in relation to the particularities of gender and race, see Sharon Patricia Holland, *Raising the Dead: Readings of Death and (Black) Subjectivity* (Durham, NC: Duke University Press, 2000), 22–28; Dana Luciano, *Arranging Grief: Sacred Time and the Body in Nineteenth-Century America* (New York: New York University Press, 2007), 219–27; and Mark Redfield, "Imagination: The Imagined Community and the Aesthetics of Mourning," *diacritics* 29 (1999): 58–83.

15. Steven Lee Myers, "'Unknown' Vietnam Soldier Now Has a Name," *New York Times*, June 30, 1998. We currently face the horrifying reality that thousands of unknowns may be scattered throughout Arlington National Cemetery due to decades of mismanagement, the misrecording of graves, and the misplacing of bodies. The military and congressional investigations continue, but by June 2010 they had already confirmed 211 misidentified bodies and/or graves. See "Special Defense Department Briefing on the Army Inspector General's Review of Management and Operations at Arlington National Cemetery," June 10, 2010, United States Army, www.army.mil.

16. Rick Atkinson, *Where Valor Rests: Arlington National Cemetery* (Washington, DC: National Geographic Society, 2007); and Poole, *On Hallowed Ground*. There are smaller gift shops at the Women in Military Service for America Memorial and housed within the slave quarters behind Arlington House.

17. Current Arlington National Cemetery map, dated 2009.

18. In the 1970s, Admiral Hyman G. Rickover spearheaded a new official investigation into the *Maine*'s destruction, finding that it was an accident, probably started by a coal bunker fire. The findings were published in Rickover, *How the Battleship Maine Was Destroyed* (Washington, DC: Department of Defense, 1976). Peggy and Harold Samuels challenged

the Rickover investigation and argued for a Spanish mine in their *Remembering the Maine* (Washington, DC: Smithsonian Institution Press, 1995). A National Geographic Society study commissioned in 1998 for the one hundredth anniversary of the *Maine*'s sinking and the Spanish-American War remained inconclusive. Thomas B. Allen, "Remember the *Maine*?" *National Geographic*, February 1998, 92–111. For a comparative discussion of the manipulation of U.S. public opinion in the drives for war in 1898 and 2001–3, see Christopher Sharrett, "9/11, the Useful Incident, and the Legacy of the Creel Committee," *Cinema Journal* 43 (2004): 125–27. For an example of conspiracy theories claiming the McKinley administration's responsibility for the *Maine*'s destruction to facilitate public support for war, a so-called "False Flag Operation" argument linked to 9/11 conspiracy claims, see www.seattle911visibilityproject.org/RC_wseattlehtm.htm (accessed November 15, 2010).

19. The current Arlington map mistakenly lists the Pentagon Group Burial Memorial's dedication year as 2005. It was, in fact, 2002.

20. David Simpson's notion of an emergent "terrorist cluster" near the World Trade Center site is a concept most illuminating in relation to the historical and political work of the guide map's official version of Arlington's memorial landscape. He argues that disparate and already extant sites of remembrance made a newly coherent group downtown, "unified by the negatively charismatic circulation of 9/11 as the summum of previous events." Simpson, *9/11*, 80.

Mourners hold portraits of departed loved ones during the 9/11 Memorial Service, September 11, 2007.
Credit: Andrea Booher/Federal Emergency Management Agency

Speaking Memory, Building History

The Influence of Victims' Families at the World Trade Center Site

Linda Levitt

O n the fourth anniversary of the September 11 terrorist attacks, several hundred relatives of 9/11 victims protested at the site of the former World Trade Center, wanting their voices to be heard regarding its future. The protestors rallied against the International Freedom Center (IFC), one of four institutions selected as part of the cultural core at the site. Despite broad and respectable sponsorship, the IFC had come under fire from conservatives for potentially diluting the memorial site's focus on the 9/11 attacks and on American patriotism. Two weeks after the protest, New York's then governor George Pataki announced that the IFC would no longer be part of the rebuilding plans. "There remains too much opposition, too much controversy over the programming of the I.F.C. and we must move forward with our first priority, the creation of an inspiring memorial," Pataki said.[1] The governor and others readily attributed this decision to the outspoken protests of victims' families.

When individuals have a personal stake in a public memorial, to what degree should their memories, sentiments, and aesthetic aims influence how cultural memory will be determined? Stories of dissent in the memorial planning processes at the World Trade Center (WTC) site recall the design competition for the Vietnam Veterans Memorial, a conflict reaching such fervor that a representative statue of three soldiers was added to the site to placate those unhappy with Maya Lin's more abstract design for the memorial. The Vietnam Veterans Memorial marked a sig-

Radical History Review

Issue 111 (Fall 2011) DOI 10.1215/01636545-1268704

© 2011 by MARHO: The Radical Historians' Organization, Inc.

The Statue of the Three Servicemen, added after some controversy, is located above the original Vietnam Veterans Memorial on the Mall in Washington, D.C. Credit: Chief Warrant Officer Seth Rossman

nificant shift in memorialization in that individuals with a personal interest were involved in the planning of a sanctioned national monument. How veterans understood the experience of Vietnam, and chose to articulate that understanding in a memorial, differed from the traditional heroic perspective presented in war memorials, leading to a bitter, broadly publicized conflict. In the wake of these disputes, finally resolved, family members, survivors, and other individual voices are now more commonly heard in decisions about commemoration.

This essay looks closely at the role and influence of victims' families in decision making at the WTC site. In the immediate aftermath of the attacks, those who lost loved ones came together to share their grief, to work toward healing, and to participate in commemorating the events of September 11. In confusing circumstances in which many tried to make sense of the events, victims' family members had the firsthand experience to articulate the emotional consequences that reverberated throughout the nation. Their emotional authority evolved into what Christy Ferer, the widow of the Port Authority director Neil Levin, described as moral authority, indicating in late 2002 that "the families are still regarded as having the moral authority on what goes on" at the WTC site.[2]

Victims' family members constitute an ideal profile of what makes news in the media age: they offer narratives that allow the media to craft emotional, dramatic, and personalized stories of September 11. Because a national audience readily identifies with victims' families, the latter have enormous persuasive power. We should not underestimate Ferer's understanding that family members have moral authority over the site. As various media outlets give voice to the personal perspectives of victims' families, the public embraces those points of view, making it difficult to ignore the wishes of those whose voices have been privileged. While the views of family members were distinctly heard in the rebuilding process, the diverse needs for the site to serve commerce, culture, and commemoration have meant that family members' wishes are not uniformly privileged over other needs.

Rebuilding, Reconsidering

As clearing the disaster site continued into late 2001, it became possible to consider what, if anything, should be built where the twin towers had once stood. Two weeks after the terrorist attacks, the *New York Times Magazine* asked several prominent architects for their opinions. Philip Johnson and Robert A. M. Stern initially suggested that the towers be rebuilt precisely as they were. The architects Elizabeth Diller and Ricardo Scofidio argued that the site should remain vacant: the silence of emptiness, they wrote, was the most powerful statement to be made. Richard Meier's musings were most in line with what followed: "It should be rebuilt. We need office space, though we don't want to build the same towers—they were designed in 1966 and now we live in 2001. What has to be there is an ensemble of buildings that are as powerful a symbol of New York as the World Trade towers were."[3] Rebuilding at the site is both symbolic and material: as Meier pointed out, Lower Manhattan not only needs office space but also retail, entertainment, and public space, along with an appropriate memorial to commemorate the events of September 11.

In July 2002, ten months after the attacks, the Lower Manhattan Development Corporation (LMDC) and the Port Authority of New York and New Jersey unveiled six rebuilding designs; the two organizations share public responsibility for the site. The Port Authority owns the land on which the World Trade Center complex was built, and it also owned the buildings until leasing them to the real estate investor and developer Larry Silverstein shortly before the September 11 attacks. The LMDC, created in the aftermath of the attacks by Governor Pataki and Mayor Rudolph Giuliani, had the task of overseeing the rebuilding of Lower Manhattan. The public meeting was held at the Jacob Javits Center, and more than five thousand people from surrounding New York and New Jersey responded to the open invitation to participate. Furnished with electronic instant-polling devices, they flatly rejected all six proposals. Paul Goldberger, the architecture critic for the *New Yorker*, noted that "when the participants were asked to select the features of the plans that bothered them the most, the highest number of votes went to 'Schemes not ambitious enough.'"[4] (The second most common criticism was that all the plans included too much office space.) Considering the demands placed on the site and the conflict inherent in creating a significant memorial in a lively commercial and public center, it comes as little surprise that the initial designs fell short of consensus.

The LMDC and the Port Authority then decided to hold a design competition, yielding more than four hundred entries. In February 2003 a panel including representatives of the LMDC, the Port Authority, the state, and the city selected Daniel Libeskind's master plan, "Memory Foundations." Where the other plans aimed to "ultimately replace the Twin Towers," Libeskind's included several buildings that "ascend gradually in a pattern," circling the memorial site — the footprints of the twin towers — and culminating in what he coined the Freedom Tower, designed to be the world's tallest building at a deliberately calculated 1,776 feet.[5] The guiding principle of Libeskind's master plan was to "create a link between memorial experience and resurgent urban life."[6] The plan envisioned a below-ground museum, while calling for an international competition for a memorial design for the WTC site. The Libeskind plan called specifically for preserving an element of the WTC site that had survived the catastrophe, the so-called slurry wall. Libeskind wrote: "The great slurry wall is the most dramatic element which survived the attack, an engineering wonder constructed on bedrock foundations and designed to hold back the Hudson River. The foundations withstood the unimaginable trauma of the destruction and stand as eloquent as the Constitution itself asserting the durability of Democracy and the value of individual life."[7] Because it went down to bedrock, where thousands of victims' remains had been found, the slurry wall had special emotional resonance for many family members.

Although Libeskind's master plan was chosen for the site, Silverstein chose the architect David Childs to design the Freedom Tower. At the design unveiling, the *New York Times* reported, "it was clear that Mr. Childs's vision had prevailed."[8] Yet Libeskind fought for, and retained, what he likely deemed the two most significant elements of the design: the building, now called 1 World Trade Center, remains at 1,776 feet (Childs proposed extending the structure to 2,000 feet), and the offset spire topping the building is still present, echoing the arm of Lady Liberty. Some aspects of Libeskind's plan, including a "Park of Heroes," were dropped, but the principle of trying to "balance memorial experience and resurgent urban life" remained alive. From the point of view of family groups, the desire for balance would bring both conflict and accommodation as the design process unfolded.

The Emergence of Family Groups

The human loss and physical devastation on September 11 was shocking and difficult to comprehend. As victims' family members sought out each other for solace and compassion, and in some instances to provide a unified voice, more than a dozen official groups emerged. Some groups formed around common affiliations, like widows and family members of Cantor Fitzgerald employees, firefighters, or airline families. Voices of September 11th, for example, was founded by Mary Fetchet, whose son Brad had died at the World Trade Center, and Beverly Eckert, who lost her husband in the attack. Voices of September 11th hosts the 9/11 Living Memorial digital archive and conducts workshops across the nation. The Marriott WTC Survivors Group is also a nonprofit organization, founded by survivors from the Marriott WTC Hotel, including employees, guests, first responders, and family members.[9]

Although most groups initially intended to provide support and community, in November 2002 the *New York Times* aptly described the family groups as "one of the most potent political forces to rise from the aftermath of the attack on the World Trade Center."[10] Family groups were vocal from the beginning. After all, a small group of victims' family members calling themselves the 9/11 Family Steering Committee pressured the White House and Congress to create the 9/11 Commission, a goal achieved in late 2002.

With regard to the overall political lessons to be drawn from the 9/11 attacks, no one expected consensus among the diverse groups of family members. Most of the family groups had politically diverse memberships and kept their purposes limited. Among the exceptions was the September Eleventh Families for Peaceful Tomorrows, formed in early 2002 with a perspective that challenged the Bush administration's appropriation of the attacks. Over time it opposed the wars in Afghanistan and Iraq, the USA PATRIOT Act, and wiretapping without warrants, among other Bush administration policies.[11]

Another family group, 9/11 Families for a Safe and Strong America, prominently used its members' familial connections to support the Bush administration's responses to the attacks. The organization was founded by Tim Sumner, whose brother-in-law Joseph Levy had been a firefighter, and Debra Burlingame, whose brother Charles was the captain of the American Airlines plane that crashed into the Pentagon. Sumner and Burlingame both write frequently for the conservative and mainstream press, and Burlingame, a former producer for Court TV, appears often on television news programs, commenting on conservative issues far beyond the realm of 9/11.

Seeking Input but Curtailing Impact

As planning moved forward, the LMDC organized several groups, including a thirty-member Families Advisory Council, for stakeholders to have a say in redevelopment plans. Several members of the council represented existing family groups, including Voices of September 11th, the WTC United Family Group, Families of September 11, the September 11th Widow's and Victims' Families Association, and the Cantor Fitzgerald Relief Fund.[12] On its Web site, the LMDC publicly reinforced its commitment to involving family members in the recovery and rebuilding: "From the very beginning, victims' family members have played a critical role in this process. Family members have participated and voiced their opinions by responding to our outreach mailings, by attending public meetings, and by sending thousands of letters and emails to the LMDC. It is a priority of the LMDC to continuously reach out to family members to keep them informed of our initiatives and events."[13] The

LMDC frequently sent mailings to more than three thousand family members, with the stated intention of seeking input. Yet many mailings were primarily informative, keeping this constituency aware of ongoing decisions and plans. On occasions when meetings were opened to direct input from family groups and other stakeholders, unhappiness became evident. Issues arose in particular at two public meetings called by the LMDC-created Memorial Competition Jury, whose mission was to choose a plan for the memorial aspects of the site. Marian Fontana, the founder of the 9–11 Families Association and a member of the Families Advisory Council, said she and others "all experienced some frustration" at feeling their "views have not been heard completely." She "felt that the families started out with a powerful voice and have been marginalized for economic concerns and stakeholders who have overrode the dignity of what happened and the poignancy of what happened to our loved ones."[14] Complaints of this nature voiced by Fontana and other family members led to a sense of both urgency and anger.

At a May 27, 2003, joint meeting of the Memorial Competition Jury and the Family Advisory Council, family members wanted to ensure that the jury would uphold the principles of the memorial mission statement drafted by the advisory council.[15] Family members spoke to their vested interest in providing a memorial that would not only take into account the need to appropriately commemorate both the devastation and heroism of September 11 but would also reflect their personal needs for memorialization.

Issues of accommodating infrastructure raised at the meeting were reiterated at another meeting two weeks later, when the memorial jury met with all of the LMDC advisory councils. The need for a bus garage pitted local residents against family members: residents wanted the garage below ground, thus minimizing noise, air pollution, and interference with pedestrian and vehicular traffic.[16] Family members did not want the bus garage below ground, where it would intrude on what had readily been termed "sacred ground."[17]

Victims' family members, after all, have a unique relationship to the site of the former World Trade Center: many think of that space as the final resting place of their loved ones. Elisabeth Kubler-Ross has argued that the families and friends of those whose bodies have not been recovered struggle with their grief. They have "no body around on which to focus and express their grief and they are vulnerable to the temptation to deny the reality of the death."[18] Where cemeteries often function as a space to commune with the memory of a loved one, many victims' family members have no such place to visit. Rather, as the site of death, it becomes "sacred ground."

The LMDC's "guiding principles" for the memorial site, based on the Family Advisory Council's draft, call for a memorial that will "respect and enhance the sacred quality of the overall site and the space designated for the memorial."[19] That the entire sixteen–acre site should have a "sacred quality" presents a challenge for the needs of commerce and government in Lower Manhattan, yet the memorial design selected responds to the guiding principles generally. Chosen by the LMDC's memorial jury in January 2004, Michael Arad and Peter Walker's Reflecting Absence provides an exceptional variety of opportunities for mourning. Within the vast, tree-covered Memorial Plaza, visitors will encounter two pools of flowing water set into the footprints of the twin towers. Adjacent to the Memorial Plaza, the Museum Pavilion will lead visitors to the museum below grade. In addition to a variety of exhibits and the Survivors Stairs, used by hundreds to escape the twin towers on September 11, the museum will enable access to the slurry wall, which family members consider "ground zero" since so many human remains were found there.

Also at bedrock, as part of the Family Advisory Council's guiding principles, will be a private room for family members, adjacent to the office of the city medical examiner where the DNA analysis will continue in hopes of identifying remains that can be returned to families. This space exists in addition to the Family Room set aside for private reflection in the museum.

Whose Idea of Freedom?

As plans for the site continued to move slowly forward, a firestorm over the International Freedom Center was set off in June 2005 by a *Wall Street Journal* op-ed piece by Burlingame. She opens "The Great Ground Zero Heist" with the image of three Marines who, on returning from Iraq, visit the WTC site for a Memorial Day wreath-laying ceremony. She brings to bear the image of these soldiers, and her assumptions about their definition of "freedom," to launch her attack on the IFC:

> The organizers of . . . the International Freedom Center (IFC) have stated that they intend to take us on "a journey through the history of freedom"—but do not be fooled into thinking that their idea of freedom is the same as that of those Marines. To the IFC's organizers, it is not only history's triumphs that illuminate, but also its failures. The public will have come to see 9/11 but will be given a high-tech, multimedia tutorial about man's inhumanity to man, from Native American genocide to the lynchings and cross-burnings of the Jim Crow South, from the Third Reich's Final Solution to the Soviet gulags and beyond. This is a history all should know and learn, but dispensing it over the ashes of Ground Zero is like creating a Museum of Tolerance over the sunken graves of the USS Arizona.[20]

Burlingame urges her readers to join her in a display of horrified incredulity that the site and its meanings have been "stolen" from those who know its real value, as well as the value of "freedom." Her thieves are the IFC organizers, "a Who's Who of the human rights, Guantanamo-obsessed world." Among them is Eric Foner, the "radical-left history professor," whom she assails at length for his opposition to the Bush administration and the war in Iraq. She caricatured the IFC's purposes and leadership—its chairman was a former business partner of George W. Bush, for example—but she succeeded in channeling some family members' worries about the direction of the WTC planning.[21] A dozen family groups, including Burlingame's own 9/11 Families for a Safe and Strong America, organized under the banner of "Take Back the Memorial." This coalition of family groups called for the LMDC to agree to Pataki's "historic mandate that the World Trade Center Memorial and memorial quadrant be solely devoted to honoring the victims and heroes of September 11, 2001 . . . as well as the story of the first attack on the Trade Center in 1993."[22]

In the midst of the uproar, the IFC appointed five family members to its advisory board, including Nikki Stern, the executive director of Families of September 11, and Robin Theurkauf, a member of the September Eleventh Families for Peaceful Tomorrows.[23] Tom Rogér, the father of a flight attendant who died on American Airlines Flight 11, cochaired the advisory board. "I've always been supportive of having some form of what I would call a living memorial or something that engages people positively," he said. "After they've visited the site and paid their respects, to me it makes sense to take people in a sort of different direction."[24] But the voices in opposition prevailed, resulting in Pataki's withholding of approval for the IFC.

The notion of "sacred ground" fueled the opposition. In a news release of September 29, 2005, that responded to the removal of the IFC, Anthony Gardner wrote on behalf of the Coalition of 9/11 Families:

> We and the tens of thousands of supporters who fought for this memorial did so, not because we wish to turn these few acres in Lower Manhattan into a cemetery or convert the site into one of enduring sadness. We did so because of our unshakable belief that this is Sacred Ground, that the truth should be told there, and that the core values of our nation will be amply demonstrated by the lives remembered, the deeds done and the spirit reawakened.[25]

In reassuring family members that he would not allow the cultural complex to intrude on the memorial quadrant, Pataki pledged: "I view that memorial site as sacred memorial ground, akin to the beaches of Normandy or Pearl Harbor, and we will not tolerate anything on that site that denigrates America."[26]

The idea of sacred ground is also tied to the decision of the Drawing Center, an established gallery and exhibition space, not to move as planned to the cultural center. Writing for the *Nation*, the critic Alisa Solomon noted that the Drawing Center was "driven away by censorship-like demands for oversight after trumped-up accusations that several works displayed over its twenty-eight-year history were 'un-American.' "[27] The rhetorical strikes against the Drawing Center resembled those launched at the IFC, with opponents arguing that artworks or exhibitions that are not steadfastly patriotic have no place at the WTC site. Although the controversies surrounding the Drawing Center and the IFC were resolved swiftly, notions of freedom, sacred ground, and moral authority continued to circulate in public discourse as plans for rebuilding slowly moved forward.

Personal Influences on Public Memory

A study conducted for the LMDC and the Port Authority predicts 5.5 million annual visitors for the Reflecting Absence memorial once it is completed.[28] Since the September 11 attacks, the WTC site has become a popular destination for tourists; many come to try to make sense of what occurred there. Visitors are drawn there because of the need to get closer, to see, touch, and hear what they know only through mediated experiences. Millions will want to visit the memorial to affirm their tenuous connection to it.

While it is a place of personal memory for many, the WTC site also constitutes a nexus of cultural memory for millions. As the sociologist Eviatar Zerubavel notes, cultural memory is "more than just an aggregate of individuals' personal memories"; rather, it comprises what a group, culture, or nation *"collectively* considers historically eventful."[29] The many family groups that have formed since September 11 show the value of collective memory as a means of negotiating both meaning making and healing through communal practices.

But what distances are traversed between the formation of individual memory and public memory? What aspects of individual memory must be sacrificed for public memory to take shape as consensual? Elinore Hartz, who served as the family liaison to the 9/11 Commission, expressed her willingness to surrender her individual position on the meaning of the WTC site for the sake of creating a memorial meaningful to others. She did so, however, with a warning to other family members: "And for all of you who want to interpret history in this memorial, there's a lot to be considered. And I just don't want it to be trivialized."[30] Her concerns rest with the many interpretive displays that will form part of the memorial museum and that will raise similar issues as did the IFC. Many family members express their interest in the historical aspects of the memorial and museum, saying that they must tell both the individual and collective stories of September 11. Carol Ashley, a member of the Family Advisory Council, wants the memory of her daughter and of others who died on September 11 to persist when the time comes that "there is nobody to tell her story." Ashley believes that in addition to preserving memory, the memorial must "communicate the history of what happened" and "educate people too about what happened, why this happened and perhaps even things we can do to prevent it from happening again."[31] This kind of communication and education cannot take place without interpretation, and these historical interpretations will be inevitably laden with the perspectives and ideologies of those involved in creating the memorial.

Rebuilding at the World Trade Center site nine years after the 9/11 attacks. Credit: Chris Bridges

Continuing Conflicts:
Names at the Memorial and the "Ground Zero Mosque"

Museums like the IFC and sanctioned memorials like the WTC site's Reflecting Absence are inevitably shaped by multiple perspectives and circumstances: their funders, their organizers, their curators, the governments that create these structures, and the moments of their design and creation. In the original design for the Reflecting Absence memorial, Arad had intended for the names of those who died in the 2001 and 1993 attacks to be randomly arranged, because he deemed the loss of life to be circumstantial and random. Yet some family groups perceived a lack of affiliation among victims' names as unacceptable. In 2006, Patricia Reilly and Anthony Gardner, members of the Coalition of 9/11 Families who both had brothers die on September 11, wrote in the *New York Daily News* that the lack of an identifying order stripped meaning from the memorial:

The absence of identifying information also fails to convey the callous nature of the attacks. Visitors will not see that eight young children and a family of four were among those murdered on the planes. They will not know which 40 of the 3,000 names represent the heroes of United Flight 93, who together made a choice to take back the plane or die trying. Visitors to the memorial will be unaware that six of the names mixed among the hundreds were killed in 1993, during Al Qaeda's first attack on the Trade Center.[32]

A decision of the World Trade Center Memorial Foundation in December 2006 mostly met Reilly's and Gardner's demands, although the ages and relationships among those who died will not be explicit on the memorial. Nonetheless, as inscribed on the two pools, the names of the deceased will be organized into nine groups: one for each of the airliner passengers and crews, one for those who were in the North Tower and another for those in the South Tower, those who were killed at the Pentagon, those who lost their lives in the 1993 attack on the World Trade Center, and a grouping for first responders.[33] This grouping will apply even to those who happened to be visitors at the World Trade Center on that day, whose presence there was, as Arad would say, simply random. Others will be defined by their careers or by where they reported for work, regardless of their feelings of connection to their professional lives. Tombstones seldom include mention of one's profession, and for many whose remains were not recovered, the listing of names on the reflecting pools will be the facsimile of a grave marker.

By the ninth anniversary of the September 11 attacks, the early shapes of future buildings and monuments finally began to emerge: the shell of the memorial, in the footprints of the twin towers, was complete, with plans to have the waterfalls running and the names inscribed by the tenth anniversary. Trees were planted, and the two tridents originally at the base of the towers were in place at the site of the memorial museum. Yet rather than celebrating the completion of any of the core elements at the site, the nation saw yet another conflict erupt in Lower Manhattan, this time over the "ground zero mosque." Park51, a multicultural community center planned by Muslims on property they own near the site of the former World Trade Center, quickly earned this moniker, despite Park51 being neither a mosque nor located at the WTC site. With the rhetoric and moral authority of family groups established, conservatives invoked the idea of sacred ground and used victims' families to justify their opposition to the project.

The now typical ideological split among victims' families reinforces the impossibility of a unified voice in which one person could speak on behalf of all. Robert McIlvaine, who lost his son on September 11, sees the matter as an ideological struggle. "It is so sad that people would use a simple issue of religious tolerance to spew hate and anger and create fear," he said. "People who have absolutely no connection to 9/11 are using it for their own political agendas. Fear and hatred help those agendas."[34]

Burlingame once again stepped forward to allege a lack of respect for victims' families. Absent an entity like the IFC, Burlingame launched her attack at Barack Obama for defending the construction of Park51. She wrote that the "president declares that the victims of 9/11 and their families must bear another burden. We must stand silent at the last place in America where 9/11 is still remembered with reverence or risk being called religious bigots." Burlingame opposes Park51 because "building a 15-story mosque at Ground Zero is a deliberately provocative act that will precipitate more bloodshed in the name of Allah," though she cites no evidence to support her claims.[35] In a partisan media landscape, Park51—and the victims of the September 11 terrorist attacks—become fodder for pundits, paring significant cultural issues down to matters of religious intolerance.

Conclusion

The involvement of individuals with a personal interest in a public memorial is now commonplace: from the Vietnam Veterans Memorial to the Oklahoma City National Memorial, survivors and family members of those who have died participate in planning public sites of commemoration. With these precedents, victims' family members were readily called on to participate in memorial planning at the WTC site. Yet in part because of the force of their narratives in a highly mediated culture, family members' voices had much greater reach. The rhetorical power of victims' families has, at times, been used by those who seek a privileged voice in determining how Lower Manhattan will be rebuilt. The removal of the IFC from the WTC site was spearheaded by family members who already had an established media presence. The physical changes at the site reflect ideological perspectives, and those who opposed Park51 appropriated that rhetoric.

For family members, the memorial will always be personal, political, and collective. Yet the personal may overwhelm the collective: are family members too emotionally invested to know how the memorial will work for the millions with no personal connection who will come to experience it? In looking at how the memorial will speak to future generations, many family members explicitly express the desire for their children to be able to visit as a means of understanding their loss. James Young, an expert on the Holocaust and commemoration who was also a member of the LMDC memorial jury, sees broader value in the involvement of family members. In his research and writing about memorials, Young says that "the survivors of the events and the families . . . have the most visceral, actually, sometimes the most informed connections to the events and to the memory of them. And these are the kinds of memories that often get codified or put into place for eternity."[36]

Notes

The use of the term *victims' families* in this article is adopted from the Lower Manhattan Development Corporation (LMDC), which uses the term sparingly. It should be noted that naming—as a group—the individuals involved in the discourse surrounding the World Trade Center memorial constitutes a complex problem. The Take Back the Memorial Web site provides a list of fourteen different groups that include family members of those who died on September 11, and none use the word *victim* in their name. The September 11th Widows' and Victims Families Association, represented on the Families Advisory Council by its founder, Marian Fontana, has cast out *victim* from its name by becoming part of the umbrella organization, the September 11 Families' Association. Many other associations, such as Voices of September 11 and 9/11 Families for a Safe and Strong America, also mark their purpose by the significance of the date.

The LMDC cannot refer to family members as September 11 families because their grouping includes families of those killed in the 1993 attack on the World Trade Center as well. Nor does the World Trade Center stand as a possible method for naming, since the LMDC's *victims' families* also includes relatives of those killed when planes were crashed at the Pentagon and Shanksville, Pennsylvania, on September 11.

1. David Dunlap, "Marking off Sacred Ground at the Trade Center Site," *New York Times*, October 6, 2005.

2. Edward Wyatt, "Some Victims' Families Feel Influence on 9/11 Memorial Slipping Away," *New York Times*, November 6, 2002.

3. "To Rebuild or Not: Architects Respond," *New York Times Magazine*, September 23, 2001, 81; quoted in Marita Sturken, "Memorializing Absence," Social Science Research Council, www.ssrc.org/sept11/essays/sturken.htm (accessed March 11, 2011).

4. Paul Goldberger, "Designing Downtown: How Will So Many People with So Many Different Ideas Agree on the New Proposals for the World Trade Center Site?" *New Yorker*, January 6, 2003, 62–79.

5. Daniel Libeskind, *Breaking Ground: Adventures in Life and Architecture* (New York: Riverhead Books, 2004), 46.

6. Lower Manhattan Development Corporation, "Renew NYC," www.renewnyc.org.

7. Studio Daniel Libeskind, "Memory Foundations," www.daniel-libeskind.com/projects/show -all/memory-foundations/.

8. Robin Pobregin, "The Incredible Shrinking Daniel Libeskind," *New York Times*, June 20, 2004.

9. Mary Voboril, "9/11 Groups: Dedicated to the Memory," September 6, 2005, Newsday.com, available at www.peacefultomorrows.org/article.php?id=581.

10. Wyatt, "Some Victims' Families Feel Influence on 9/11 Memorial Slipping Away."

11. Bella English, "Where to Try a Terrorist Suspect," *Boston Globe*, April 17, 2010.

12. See the LMDC Web site, www.renewnyc.com.

13. Lower Manhattan Development Corporation, "Renew NYC," www.renewnyc.org.

14. Lower Manhattan Development Corporation, "Joint Meeting of Memorial Competition Jury and Families Advisory Council," May 27, 2003, transcript, 18–19, www.renewnyc.org/ content/pdfs/alladvisorycounciltranscript.pdf.

15. Lower Manhattan Development Corporation, "Memorial Mission Statement and Memorial Program," www.renewnyc.com.

16. The bus parking issue, still disputed as of early 2011, will be resolved through the Port Authority's Vehicular Security Center (VSC), an underground series of roadways and parking facilities that will provide tour bus parking for the memorial and the museum. The VSC is slated to open in 2012, despite concerns that underground parking can create circumstances similar to the 1993 bombing at the World Trade Center.

17. Lower Manhattan Development Corporation, "Memorial mission statement and Memorial Program," www.renewnyc.com/Memorial/memmission.asp. The mission statement calls for a memorial that will "respect this place made sacred through tragic loss."

18. Elisabeth Kubler-Ross, *Death: The Final Stage of Growth* (Englewood Cliff, NJ: Prentice-Hall, 1975), 46.

19. Lower Manhattan Development Corporation, "Memorial Mission Statement and Memorial Program."

20. Debra Burlingame, "The Great Ground Zero Heist," *Wall Street Journal*, June 8, 2005.

21. Sarah Baxter, "Republicans Defect to the Obama Camp," *Sunday Times* (London), May 6, 2007.

22. "Alliance of Major 9/11 Family Groups Calls on LMDC to Fulfill Gov. Pataki's Mandate," Take Back the Memorial, October 26, 2005, www.freerepublic.com/focus/f-news/1510003/posts.

23. Maki Becker, "Ground Zero Museum Adds 9/11 Kin Advisers," *New York Daily News*, September 7, 2006.

24. Jarrett Murphy, "Memorial Plots: The Clash over Exactly What Story to Tell at the Ground Zero Museum," *Village Voice*, June 14, 2005.

25. Anthony Gardner, "Family Member Group Response to the Removal of the IFC," Take Back the Memorial, September 29, 2005, web.archive.org/web/20050930212938/http://takebackthememorial.org.

26. Dunlap, "Marking off Sacred Ground."

27. Alisa Solomon, "Memorial Chauvinism," *Nation*, September 26, 2005, 26–28.

28. David Dunlap, "Matters of How Many and How Much at the Sept. 11 Memorial," *New York Times*, September 22, 2005.

29. Eviatar Zerubavel, *Time Maps: Collective Memory and the Social Shape of the Past* (Chicago: University of Chicago Press, 2003), 28.

30. Lower Manhattan Development Corporation, "Joint Meeting," 47.

31. Ibid., 50.

32. Patricia Reilly and Anthony Gardner, "Absence of Meaning: 9/11 Kin Say Memorial's Purpose Lost If Dates, ID Tossed," *New York Daily News*, August 24, 2006.

33. National September 11 Memorial and Museum, "Names Arrangement," www.national911memorial.org/site/PageServer?pagename=New_Memorial_NA (accessed March 11, 2011).

34. Bob Braun, "Ground Zero Mosque Fear, Anger Stun Families of 9/11 Victims," Newark *Star-Ledger*, August 18, 2010.

35. Debra Burlingame, "9/11 Families Stunned by President's Support of Mosque at Ground Zero," August 14, 2010, Coalition to Honor Ground Zero, stopthe911mosque.com/2010/08/14/911–families-stunned-presidents-support-of-mosque-at-ground-zero.

36. Lower Manhattan Development Corporation, "Joint Meeting," 19–20.

Herodotus Reconsidered

An Oral History of September 11, 2001, in New York City

Mary Marshall Clark

The work of historians becomes especially complex when their services are needed most, namely, when addressing the inevitable rewriting of history that takes place in the wake of catastrophic political events. Never in recent history has there been a clearer case in which the intervention of conscientious historians as guardians of memory (the future of the past) was required more than in the political aftermath of the spectacular attacks on the World Trade Center and other sites on the clear morning of September 11, 2001.

Within hours of the terrorist events in the United States on September 11, CNN selected the headline designed to frame the meaning of this historic experience, "America under Attack," which was quickly picked up by most major news outlets. This headline was quickly transformed into the ubiquitous banner "America at War." President Bush announced a global war on terrorism only days later. The nightly news channels cooperated in heightening the hysteria that defined the coverage of the attacks by supplying a soundtrack and by repeating the images of the towers collapsing again and again, as if New York City was entirely engulfed by the impact on lower Manhattan and had vaporized as a result. This media hysteria aided the state in rationalizing a wholesale war on terror that positioned Osama bin Laden as the head not only of the Taliban but also of an amorphous group of people who appeared to be the enemy, both at home and abroad. This war was named in memory of those who had tragically perished in New York, in Shanksville, in Washington, and on the planes—who became instant citizens and patriots by virtue of

Radical History Review

Issue 111 (Fall 2011)   DOI 10.1215/01636545-1268713

© 2011 by MARHO: The Radical Historians' Organization, Inc.

a sacrifice they never intended to make and could never speak about. Next in the hierarchy came those who died saving others, beginning with the firefighters, all of them persons who also could not testify to the meaning the events held.

Some of us living and working in New York raised the following question: How did the views of those most directly affected, and who therefore had something potentially valuable to say about the country's response, relate to the rollout to war? Did New Yorkers agree with the growing national consensus that government retaliation was warranted in the time frame in which it occurred? And finally, how did New Yorkers differently affected by the attacks make meaning of the events in light of the strong international community that links New Yorkers to the rest of the world? In a national context that treated September 11, 2001, as an exceptional event that resisted any serious attempts at historical analysis, how would the events of the day become history in the place where they occurred and had the greatest impact?

Our idea was simple in its intent. Like Herodotus, we placed great value on the stories of those who lived through the events that histories are written about. We believed this approach particularly important in a culture that increasingly mass-mediates memory and, therefore, the accounting of political events.[1]

Project Origins and Methodology

The first suggestion for a major urban oral history of September 11 came from the New York City historian Kenneth Jackson, who asked me as the director of Columbia University's Oral History Research Office to speak to his class on New York City. He urged his students to help the research office launch a major project to capture responses to the events. I contacted the provost of Columbia, Jonathan Cole, about the possibility of securing emergency fieldwork funding, and he enthusiastically suggested I collaborate with the interdisciplinary sociologist Peter Bearman, who used biographical analysis in his research. Together Peter and I wrote a proposal for the project and received funding from the National Science Foundation, the Rockefeller Foundation, and Columbia University to create the September 11, 2001, Oral History Narrative and Memory Project. The project was conceived longitudinally, using life history as a primary methodology that would result in three hundred interviews in the first year; the same people were to be followed up on in the months or years to come.

We wanted to allow those we interviewed to begin by telling their stories of origin, move through their life history to September 11, 2001, and construct a story of the events and their aftermath based on their own identities and values. The project's intellectual purpose, defined in the days after the attacks, was to explore the myriad ways that September 11 became history in the life stories and eyewitness accounts of those we interviewed:

The purpose of the first wave of the effort is to document the early interpretations and experiences of the event through life story interviews before "official" versions of the story defined by the media, government, and private and public institutions take hold. Oral history is founded in the knowledge that people and societies organize meaning through the construction and telling of stories, and that cultural and individual stories often revolve around events that are perceived as "turning points" in history, particularly in situations where public meaning is contested.

Because stories provide the most fundamental bases for self-understanding, contestation over the significance and meaning of the World Trade Center/Pentagon tragedy is taking place now through the generation and diffusion of stories from individuals differently positioned with respect to the tragedy. At some point, in the not too distant future, collective interpretations of the bombing will emerge that will highlight some narratives and eclipse others. It is likely that those with greatest access to media and to official channels of decision making in public and private spheres will have the greatest power to describe the lasting impact of the tragedy, repositioning not only our understanding of a quintessential city, but a nation in a time of already great transition. The purpose of this project is to extend the power of interpretation of the events of September 11, 2001 to individuals in New York City whose stories provide critical perspectives on the immediate and lasting impact of the terrorist attack and its cultural, economic and political legacy.[2]

Bearman, an heir to the intellectual legacy of Paul Lazarsfeld, a sociologist who first wrote about the impact of mass media on society, was keenly interested in the role of media in the construction and telling of stories. His expertise in training interviewers to approach people in public places to make initial contacts allowed us to find interviewees with broad and diverse networks. These networks and other contacts resulted in nearly two hundred interviews in the first six or seven weeks following the events. Among those we interviewed were people directly affected by the attacks, including about 170 eyewitnesses, survivors, rescue workers, volunteers, and others who lived or worked in relative proximity to the towers; 50 of them worked at the World Trade Center. We also interviewed people throughout New York City, at a more distal location to the events, who were affected by the economic and political aftermath.

From the perspective of creating a diverse archive that would grow over time, we also realized that we had the unique opportunity to capture the memory of New York City in a way that would reveal the particular tensions between memory and history that was already evident. As I wrote in 2002, "One of the dilemmas in the debate over whether memory or history dominates the interpretation of major events is that few opportunities exist to study how people reconstruct the past before a dominant public narrative has been created by those who have a vested interest in defining the political meaning of events. . . . As a result, debates over the relationships between memory and history, and between individual and collective memory, often remain abstract and theoretical."[3] Given the opportunity to collect such a rich and diverse set of voices, we intended to create an archive that would stand the test of time.[4]

To extend our outreach as widely as possible, we obtained funding to hire interviewers who had the knowledge and language skills to work in Latino, Muslim, and Arab communities. We also committed ourselves to interviewing those whose work was affected in the aftermath of the events: artists, public health workers, business people, psychologists, teachers, lawyers, and service workers throughout the city and its boroughs.

The thirty interviewers we directed were assigned to conduct ten interviews each, to mitigate trauma, and to encourage in-depth encounters. The interviewers were either experienced fieldworkers trained in oral history, journalism, or sociology or received training before they began their work. The interviewers exhibited skill and creativity in their interventions in the field, met weekly to encourage one another in their work, and played a significant role in defining the ways that project objectives were achieved. The interviews we conducted in the first five to six weeks after September 11 were often compressed, as people could only focus on the trauma of the event itself, but by November 2001, our interviewees often talked for two hours or more, relishing the opportunity to ascribe meaning to experiences that were complex and difficult to talk about with friends or family members. From the beginning, our work transcended the limits of pure historical research and emerged as project documenting public meaning and memory.

The September 11, 2001, Narrative and Memory Project grew in scope, and by the end of the first round of our work — roughly within a year — we had interviewed close to 450 people. We returned to 215 narrators to reinterview them beginning eighteen months later. We also used the method of life history to interview people in the second round, allowing the interviewees to choose new aspects of their lives to talk about or to return to themes and topics they had discussed earlier. Some returned to a discussion of the events of September 11, elaborating on its individual or collective impact; others used the time to talk about their lives without reference to September 11, which made for an interesting finding in itself.

By the end of our fieldwork in 2005 we had conducted 665 sessions with people in the longitudinal project and had completed three additional related projects resulting in more than six hundred full interviews totaling more than one thousand hours.[5] By the end of our work we had interviewed over fifty Muslims and sixty Latinos. With the exception of Mexico, most of the first generation immigrants we interviewed came from countries in the Middle East and South Asia. We also interviewed about thirty artists whose material conditions for work and forms of artistic expression were influenced by the events. The majority of the interviews, transcribed and edited, are now available for consultation at the Columbia University Oral History Research Office.

Everyone we interviewed received a transcript of the interview and was given ample time to review and correct it and to give open access to all or part of the interview immediately or at a future point in time. Most of our interviewees were grateful for the opportunity to reflect on their interviews before committing them to an official archive. This occasion to review and edit interviews is not given in journalistic event-centered oral history projects that are commemorative and curatorial in nature. In the oral history project directed by the National Memorial Museum, to complement and extend the number of StoryCorps interviews of September 11 that will be stored there, one of the first questions asked is "Where were you when our homeland was bombed?" This question perfectly exemplifies a leading question that defines the meaning and purpose of the interview, before the interviewee's (note, not narrator's) story begins.

Findings

"The Event"

One of the most striking findings of our work, based on a careful reading of all the interviews conducted in 2001 and 2002, was that the majority of those we interviewed across political, national, cultural, and ethnic lines of difference did not agree with the official description of their experiences, namely, that used to rationalize a war on terror. As Rameen Moshref Javid claimed, "This is not a war. This is something small. Once you are bombed on a regular basis and you are targeted as a people you know what war is."[6] Javid's life experiences, which included his training as a soldier in Kabul to fight the Taliban (then supported by the U.S. government), would understandably lead him to question the designation of a single day's attacks as a war. But we found a similar resistance to the characterization of 9/11 as an ultimate geopolitical catastrophe in many of the interviews we conducted, both before and after October 7, 2001 (when the first U.S. bombings of Afghanistan began). For our interviewees, this often meant rejecting the prominent constructions of meaning about the attacks perpetuated in the mass media, for example, the analogy with Pearl Harbor. Especially those who fled for their lives down the steps of the towers, often having to leave others behind, and who witnessed the carnage at close range were offended by a comparison between the massacre they lived through and an attack on a military base.

The majority of New Yorkers we interviewed experienced the events as an almost random civilian massacre, one that had symbolic overtones. The word *surreal* was the single term most frequently used, and it expressed the unreality of September 11 as a historic marker, even as that marker was used to legitimize the deaths of civilians in Afghanistan. The formulaic linguistic tropes contributed by the media to describe the attacks contributed to the sense, omnipresent in our interviews, that an Armageddon had occurred and had to be avenged in kind. The use of the term *ground zero* to describe the impact of the towers' explosion in Manhattan, when it originally described the horrific impact of a nuclear bomb detonated by the United States on Hiroshima, proved particularly toxic. One could read from it that the epicenter of ultimate terror had shifted to New York City. Similarly, 9/11 quickly became the shorthand for what was being treated as one of the most exceptional days in recent world history, eclipsing September 11, 1973, in Chile, for example, when Augusto Pinochet's coup led to Salvador Allende's death and the exile of more than two hundred thousand Chileans. These antihistorical terms evidenced the fusion of nationalism and patriotism under the umbrella of U.S. empire.

The towers, and their absence, became the focal point of the nationalistic imaginary about the events. The continued dissemination of images of the towers collapsing expressed injury to the nation, in which the experiences of those on the ground in New York, Shanksville, and Washington, D.C., and of those who lost loved ones on the planes were wrapped into one synchronized story. While many of the New Yorkers we interviewed mourned the destruction of the towers and the loss of life that occurred, they most feared a future in which other innocent people like them would be harmed. Concretely, they expressed despair over the probability that an expansive war on terror, fought in their names, would unleash more terror at home and abroad. This worry took two forms. First, a number of interviewees feared that Muslim citizens would suffer the same kind of internment that Japanese American citizens had suffered following Pearl Harbor. Second, and as suggested above, almost all of those we interviewed were either opposed to or ambivalent about a rush to war both in 2001 and in 2003.

One antiwar story that stands out in its nonpartisan character is that of James Dobson, a paramedic who was one of the last to leave before the second tower collapsed: "I'm more of a pacifist than ever. I said — and I'm a Republican — because what I saw that day, the devastation, I could not basically see us doing to other people. Life is too cheap then; it doesn't mean anything, and there's no reason for it. These people did not attack me, Jimmy Dobson, or the American people per se. They attacked the corporate world."[7] Dobson's perspectives on the misuse of his suffering to launch what he felt was an illegitimate war were conditioned by the general lack of respect accorded the paramedics, who were treated as second-tier rescuers in relation to the firefighters. But especially fascinating is his interpretation of the attack as corporate in nature, and his refusal to want his experiences used in the same meaningless way. While we did not specifically ask people for their political opinions on the wars in Afghanistan and Iraq, many people, like Dobson, found little personal meaning in the media and government rhetoric around sacrifice and suffering.

On a political level, many of our interviewees, including first responders, resisted the grafting of their experiences onto a highly symbolic, and narrowly patriotic, narrative focused on those who made the ultimate sacrifice. Firefighters, police, paramedics, ironworkers who helped with search and rescue, and others told complicated stories of running to survive, sometimes at the expense of others.[8] The nationalistic promotion of the ideal of citizenship as the heroic loss of life, while useful for a government preparing to recruit its soldiers for a prolonged war, did not fit into the structure of the life narratives of most people we interviewed. That so many New Yorkers actively protested the war itself in the days and weeks after September 11 seems to have escaped the rest of the country, but it constituted an active form of mourning as well as a cry for humanity on the part of those who had themselves suffered.

In sum, people in New York City contested the collective understanding disseminated by official sources that a global war on terror constituted a necessary outcome of the September 11 attacks. This became evident both during our first round of interviews and during the second, when the United States was preparing to invade Iraq.

The Aftermath

A second major finding in our work was the degree to which Muslims, Arabs, and anyone who appeared to be the "enemy," including nonnative citizens, were persecuted in the aftermath of the events of September 11.

Incidents like this August 22, 2010, demonstration against the Park 51 Islamic cultural center near the World Trade Center site in New York City have made many Muslims, Arabs, and others feel they are being cast as the enemy at home. Credit: David Shankbone

The work we did in Muslim, Arab, and Sikh communities revealed a striking level of fear about the loss of a sense of belonging in the "beloved community" that they had migrated to find. Often the parents' generation expressed this fear more directly than did the younger generations of immigrants. A case in point is two interviews we did with Pakistani immigrants: a father who worked in one of the World Trade Center towers and a son who was at an appointment in the other. Zaheer Jaffrey, the father, had to climb down seventy flights with a cane to survive. His son, Salmaan, arrived by subway at the scene to go to an appointment in the other tower, emerged, and saw the large gaping hole in the building where his father worked and believed, for several hours, that his father had died.[9] The father did not describe the event itself as tragic, but mourned his son's loss of identity in the aftermath (Salmaan shaved his beard and would not leave the house for weeks for fear of being targeted).[10] This was a typical narrative we found among older Muslim, Arab, and Sikh immigrants, many of whom had fled war and conflict to bring a sense of security to the next generation, those, in effect, now seen as potential terrorists. The fear affected not only service workers but professionals at all levels. Inder Singh, a Sikh professor of anatomy and dentistry for decades at New York University, was troubled by the uninformed fear of Sikh citizens in the aftermath.[11]

Stories of detention and deportation echoed throughout the narratives of Muslim communities in Queens, in particular. We interviewed a taxi driver whose uncle ultimately died in detention of unknown causes. While we could not directly interview those detained, or those who had been deported, we interviewed lawyers from the American Civil Liberties Union (ACLU), the Center for Constitutional Rights, and diplomats in New York and Washington who recorded human rights and civil liberties violations against those formerly protected. An atmosphere of suspicion, both subtle and direct, affected ordinary people, both citizens and refugees, far more profoundly than we could record at the time, but Ann Cvetkovich's article in this issue describes these effects.

For those who now appeared to be "the enemy" at home, New York City transformed from a site of refuge and belonging into an epicenter of fear. The climate of fear, even trepidation, was palpable and of great concern to many New Yorkers, who felt pride about their city's history of welcoming immigrants and refugees. While we had defined the scope of our outreach in the early days of our work and thus did not record the full impact of the backlash against Muslims or those of Middle Eastern or South Asia descent, these trends bear further investigation in New York City and throughout the country.

The interviews conducted with Latino immigrants and refugees also reflect this profound sense of dislocation, as reflected in reports from Robert Smith, a researcher working in Mexican and Dominican communities. As a first trend he noted in his interviews the simultaneous and conflicting emotions of belonging and alienation experienced by these immigrants. Many of them expressed their sorrow for and sympathy with the victims of the attacks and their families, empathetically expressing that they could have been the unlucky ones. Some went even further and said that they felt more "American" and more "like a New Yorker" in the wake of attacks that had targeted everyone. Yet even in the immediate interviews conducted within two weeks of the attacks, this tremendous sympathy coincided with a more critical stance on the United States and a willingness to find the causes of the attacks not just in the minds of "evil doers who hate America," as many said, but in U.S. foreign policy throughout the world.[12] These interviews, conducted by Mexican researchers trained by Smith, allowed people (from dishwashers to undocumented students) to offer historic interpretations of the September 11 attacks that many others felt too fearful to express.

A second trend Smith and his researchers explored was how the September 11 attacks, the anthrax attacks that followed, and the U.S. government's reaction brought into sharp relief the in-between status of both documented and undocumented immigrants. Undocumented Mexican immigrants, for example, were besieged with calls from their relatives in Mexico to come back and to save themselves from what they believed to be an imminent and massive biological attack on New York. "Don't die for your bad job in the United States" could sum up this sentiment, one reinforced by Spanish-language television in the United States and in Mexico. Some Latino immigrants directly affected by the attacks did not find the responses by U.S. institutions either helpful or appropriate. For example, many of the Federal Emergency Management Agency (FEMA) volunteers came from the Midwest and did not understand New York. One interviewee reported feeling humiliated by a FEMA worker who repeatedly reprimanded the woman for not speaking English after thirty years in the United States but did not really try to find someone to help her. (The woman in fact did understand some English, but she could not speak well.)[13] Finally, the reactions of the city, state, and federal governments to September 11 made many immigrants feel unfairly targeted and insecure. Those interviewed objected both to what they saw (and what was reported on Spanish-language television) as the wholesale roundup of anyone looking Arab and to their being lumped into a suspect category because of their lack of documentation.

In these and other interviews done in the second round of our work, and later in 2004 and 2005, patriotism emerged as the most complex historical theme we investigated, and it begs for an intensive analysis in future readings of the interviews, particularly in relation to the nationalist framing of heroic sacrifice both in New York City and elsewhere.

What Role Does History Play in the Aftermath of Catastrophic Events?

The different ways in which the meaning of the September 11, 2001, events have been written into a national collective consciousness, on the one hand, and revealed in an urban oral memory, on the other, lead to several important questions.

To what degree do we, as scholars and citizens, bear a responsibility to provide a historical accounting of catastrophic political events that acknowledges the life stories and worldviews of those most directly involved? Should we continue to place our faith in those geopolitical experts who have vested interests in maintaining U.S. power at any cost? Can we continue to rely on those government and media sources that first did so much to build a national consensus to go to war in Afghanistan and then uncritically employed manufactured evidence to justify the invasion of Iraq?

This leads us to ask a prominent question in writing the history of an event broadcast more widely than almost any previous event in the world: If official government and media sources were exaggerated or falsified, where do historians turn ten years later — and one hundred years from now — to write the history of September 11, 2001? To whom, other than the lawyer advocates who documented the case histories of illegal attacks on innocent Muslim and Arab Americans, do they turn to in an effort to fully evaluate the aftermath?

In chronicling an event that has been treated as a turning point in U.S. history, one that rationalized two invasions and a wholesale war on terror, the task of historical interpretation that Herodotus would expect lies before us. Meanwhile — as the number of innocent civilian casualties of violence or famine rises and as the terrorizing of citizens and refugees at home continues — the news from New York is that many of the worst fears of those we interviewed have been realized.

Notes

1. The work of Brigitte Nacos, particularly *Mass-Mediated Terrorism: The Central Role of the Media in Terrorism and Counterterrorism* (London: Rowman and Littlefield, 2002), proved extremely helpful in interpreting the complex relationships among the mass media, the government, and policy makers.
2. Peter Bearman and Mary Marshall Clark, "The September 11, 2001, Oral History Narrative and Memory Project," proposal, September 2001.
3. Mary Marshall Clark, "The September 11, 2001, Oral History Narrative and Memory Project: A First Report," *Journal of American History* 89 (2002): 569–79.
4. Our interviewers were also conscious of this goal, and they often began their interviews with statements like "your interviews will be listened to and read forty and fifty years from now." Documenting the present, they asked the narrators they interviewed to imagine themselves as key historic actors in framing the way in which history would ultimately be written, rather than as victims of trauma.
5. In addition to the 450 interviews conducted for the longitudinal project, the Oral History Research Office received funding from the New York Times Foundation to conduct 67 interviews with professionals responsible for the crises that followed the attacks and worked with the School of Public Health to archive 34 interviews with professionals in the field of public health. Additionally, we were funded by the New York Times Foundation to start a public oral history project, called Telling Lives, that was constructed to strengthen vulnerable communities and to teach mainly youth oral history to strengthen their capacity to interpret September 11 and other traumatic events. This program resulted in two after-

school programs and a major initiative in two Chinatown middle schools that encompassed semester-long in-class programs, completed in partnership with the New York University (NYU) Child Study Center. The New York University Child Study Center (CSC) was founded in 1997 to treat children with psychiatric disorders, conduct scientific research, and influence public policy. That work resulted in two exhibits in Chinatown through a partnership with the Museum of Chinese in the Americas (MoCA). We also partnered with MoCA, the CUNY Graduate Center, and NYU to complete an online oral history project interviewing Chinese American leaders about the impact of September 11 in Chinatown. See "Ground One: Voices from Post-911 Chinatown," 911digitalarchive.org/chinatown (accessed March 1, 2011).

6. Reminiscences of Rameen Moshref Javid, the Columbia University September 11, 2001, Oral History Narrative and Memory Project, Oral History Research Office Collection, session 1, 15; interview by Amy Starecheski, November 8, 2001.

7. Reminiscences of James Dobson, the Columbia University September 11, 2001, Oral History Narrative and Memory Project, Oral History Research Office Collection, session 1, 39; interviews by Ed Thompson and Gerry Albarelli, March 6, 2003.

8. These stories only started appearing in the press in the spring of 2002.

9. Reminiscences of Salmaan Jaffrey, the Columbia University September 11, 2001, Oral History Narrative and Memory Project, Oral History Research Office Collection, session 1, 33; interviews by Gerald Albarelli, December 3, 2001, December 4, 2002, and June 21, 2001.

10. Reminiscences of Zaheer Jaffrey, the Columbia University September 11, 2001, Oral History Narrative and Memory Project, Oral History Research Office Collection, session 3, 92; interviews by Gerald Albarelli, November 14, 2001, December 4, 2002, and June 24, 2005.

11. Reminiscences of Inder Jit Singh, the Columbia University September 11, 2001, Oral History Narrative and Memory Project, Oral History Research Office Collection; interviews by Amy Starecheski, January 20, 2002, and March 2, 2003.

12. Robert Smith, portion written in Mary Marshall Clark, director, Oral History Research Office, "Rockefeller Foundation, Final Report on September 11, 2001 Oral History Narrative and Memory Project," 2005.

13. Ibid.

Can the Diaspora Speak?

Afghan Americans and the 9/11 Oral History Archive

Ann Cvetkovich

It's unfortunate that the context and the history doesn't get told until there's some catastrophic event, and the people on the ground in the United States are affected.[1] (Halima Kazem)

Born in Kabul in 1977, freelance journalist Halima Kazem was too young to have any direct memories of her father's arrest when the communist People's Democratic Party of Afghanistan (PDPA) came to power in 1979 or of his subsequent release under Babrak Karmal. But the story has clearly shaped her identity, since these events prompted her family's departure from Afghanistan shortly thereafter. Although Kazem assimilated into U.S. culture because she was very young when her family migrated, she also sustained a strong sense of Afghan identity. After September 11, 2001, she worried that Muslims in general would be blamed for the events and wanted Americans to understand that violence and vulnerability were a constant in Afghanistan. "Welcome to our world," she thought to herself (1:30). Moreover, she was disappointed by what she saw as misguided feminist support for Afghan women: "Let's worry more about the Afghan people's empty stomachs than we should about pulling the chadori off the women" (1:34). But she also felt numb, and despite her professional training as a journalist, she found herself unable to write and explain Afghanistan's history.

     Kazem's interview is one of several with younger Afghan Americans, many of whose families immigrated to the United States in the wake of the 1979 Soviet

Radical History Review
Issue 111 (Fall 2011) DOI 10.1215/01636545-1268722
© 2011 by MARHO: The Radical Historians' Organization, Inc.

invasion, that are included in the September 11, 2001, Oral History Narrative and Memory Project sponsored by Columbia University's Oral History Research Office (see Mary Marshall Clark's article in this issue). Many of the interviewees were eyewitnesses or survivors, including those who worked in the World Trade Center buildings and lived in their immediate vicinity, as well as first responders to the crisis. Yet the project organizers also made a concerted effort to include those who might not have had their experiences documented in more mainstream media. Thus the collection includes interviews with Muslims and Sikhs, Afghan Americans and refugees, for a total of at least eighty immigrants from more than thirty countries (including a large cluster of undocumented Latinos).[2] Casting a wide net to find the stories of those who might have remained on the periphery of the events but who were also affected by them, this oral history project raises important questions about who the survivors of September 11 are.[3]

The interviews with Afghan Americans—alongside those with others from South Asia and the Middle East, some of them practicing Muslims, others secular—reveal a group that experienced the impact not only of the events of September 11 themselves but also that of the racist backlash that followed, which construed them as the enemy. Although this group constitutes a small cluster of interviews, it is an interesting one for considering the broader context of 9/11, especially ten years after the fact.

Gauging the significance of this collection involves evaluating oral history as a form of archive for September 11. At this writing, contests over public memory continue to inform the design of the World Trade Center site and of the museum that will be located there. Because it carries the aura of the attacks' location, this site bears an extreme representational burden (as the outbreak of controversy in 2010 over the downtown Islamic cultural center suggests). September 11 has arguably been the subject of unprecedented documentation in a range of media, including photography and video, books, and performances, a significant amount of which has been informed by personal and informal sources.[4] Alongside public monuments and memorials, 9/11 has prompted many forms of ephemeral commemoration, including street altars, murals, and personal markings such as tattoos. By these means people carry the memory of 9/11 and enact it through ongoing practices.[5]

Oral history lies somewhere between the monumental and the ephemeral and has elements of both. It is not visible or tangible in the way that public memorials and museum exhibitions are (although it can be incorporated into them). Because it is recorded and archived, though, it aims to be more permanent than the stories and memories that circulate in and through ephemeral memorials and performances such as street altars. In the immediate aftermath of 9/11, the appeal of testimony (inspired by Holocaust archives) was strong not just at Columbia University but also elsewhere in the city. It produced populist forums such as the Listening Booth set up at the *Here Is New York* photography exhibition, motivated by

Supporters of the Park 51 Islamic cultural center near the World Trade Center site in New York City during a demonstration against the center, August 22, 2010. Credit: David Shankbone

the desire to gather stories as an authentic voice of public memory and collective democracy.[6] Columbia's September 11, 2001, oral history project is distinctive insofar as it combines these grassroots impulses (as reflected, for example, in the use of nonprofessional interviewers for the quickly arranged initial round of interviews) with the Oral History Research Office's status and resources as a research collection, in which interviews are accumulated slowly and with a view toward long-range historical analysis.

The Columbia oral histories with Afghan Americans on which this essay focuses represent a modest portion of the cumulative archives of 9/11. They constitute a partial and fragmented archive, not a representative sampling or a sociological data set, especially given the small number of interviewees, most of whom come from a relatively elite group of Afghan immigrants. But these oral histories are nonetheless useful for exploring the larger context of the events and their aftermath, the relation between personal or family histories and geopolitical histories, and the connections between everyday life and catastrophe.

Especially important is this archive's deconstructive power in offering counterhistories to the prevailing narratives of 9/11. The value of these interviews lies in their account of the details and nuances of everyday life and of ordinary feelings, rather than in large-scale generalizations about Afghans (which those interviewed often sought to challenge).[7] The interviews are skewed toward a culturally literate group of mostly young people, many of whom are active in producing an Afghan American public culture. Most of them are secular. Most of them have spent the majority, if not all, of their lives in the United States, thus leaving them with only a limited direct experience of Afghanistan. They do not presume to be the most important voices of their community or the kind of spokespeople one might find in the news (although some of them were pressed into service to offer their views in the rush to find the voices of Afghan Americans in the wake of 9/11). The collection is also affected by the interviewers, most of whom were not experts in Afghan culture or history.[8] Yet despite the archive's limits, it nonetheless reveals the experience of 9/11 for a population targeted outside the World Trade Center site, thus raising questions about the location of violence.

The testimony proves especially valuable for connecting 9/11 to a transgenerational legacy of violence in Afghanistan. Most important for my argument in this essay, these oral histories suggest the challenges of cultural politics for those trying to articulate alternative stories; even this culturally privileged group experiences the frustrations and impossibilities of articulating Afghan history and Afghan American experience, and their oral histories thus testify to silences and absences in the archive. They suggest that the public memory of 9/11 must tend to problems of historical representation that continue to affect the popular representation of not just Afghanistan but also the Middle East, Central Asia, and South Asia more generally, the stakes of which remain high.

Trauma in the Diaspora:
September 11, 2001, Afghanistan Histories, and Ordinary Experience

The first building collapses, live in front of my eyes on TV. Then the second one collapses and the word "terrorist" comes up. The second I heard the word terrorist, it threw me into a state of, "Oh god. Here we go. Muslims. Muslims. Muslims. We're going to be blamed." (Halima Kazem 1:29)

I was driving into Manhattan across the Queensboro Bridge. The first and the second building had been hit. And then I knew that America had been had. The very things we had said over the years but hadn't echoed any sort of merit in Washington or credence, America had been had.[9] (Haron Amin)

We were all afraid to really come out. We were all afraid to do anything, really, just for being Muslims. And I think also a sense of guilt that we shared anything with the people who did this. There's a lot of guilt too. Like we're sorry.[10] (Zohra Saed)

Little things that go through your head, like, for example the first time since 9/11 when I was driving over the George Washington Bridge going, "Oh, please don't blow this up," things like that. It just occurs to you when you're in places where you feel vulnerable.[11] (Shekaiba Wakili)

I mean, unfortunately, as Americans, we now feel like we are the target. But I think people have been experiencing this for a very long time. I just feel like we were protected by the two oceans, and now we have joined the rest of the world community. (Shekaiba Wakili, 2:63)

Because the Afghan Americans interviewed for the Columbia oral history project were not immediate eyewitnesses, the interviews do not focus exclusively on their direct experience of the attacks. Yet these are also stories of ordinary New Yorkers headed to work when the planes hit and the towers came down, of people feeling an increasing sense of disbelief or panic as it became clear this was no accident. Like many New Yorkers, these Afghan Americans shared an experience reverberating across the city as people saw the towers collapse from a distance or crossed bridges on foot into Brooklyn or Queens or watched people covered in dust fleeing the area around the World Trade Center. And for this specific group, the realization of a terrorist attack immediately inspired reactions about how Muslims would be blamed.

One of the values of the Columbia archive is thus its documentation of the effect of racism and anti-Muslim sentiment on the everyday lives of Muslim New Yorkers (as well as on the lives of those who *appeared* to be Arab or Muslim, however great the misrecognition, such as male Sikhs, whose turbans made them visible targets). These narratives reframe what it means to be a witness or a survivor of 9/11 by expanding those categories beyond the scope of those who were downtown or in the buildings when the planes hit and the towers fell. Instead, many of those interviewed testified to their experiences of harassment or to those of people they know. In many cases, they described everyday forms of violence, such as being pulled aside at security checkpoints in airports, being called names, or receiving hate mail and calls. These ordinary effects of 9/11 also included a general fear of being visible that sometimes led to subtle changes in behavior. If anything distinctive emerges from these interviews, it is the way that even small actions can produce paranoia and fear: "I remember I had to teach Arab American literature that day [September 11], so someone had said, 'You can't carry around the books, what if someone stops you, and they find it, and then they're going to kill you.' And I was like: 'Oh my God. All right'" (Zohra Saed 2:53, 2005).

Many of these immigrants are not only U.S. citizens but think of themselves as American, even if they have other identities and affiliations as well, and they found it particularly painful to be constructed as the enemy and be denied the right to grieve the losses of 9/11 along with others. Especially important is how the oral history interview captured affective experience, how it *felt* to be Muslim or to be

Afghan in the wake of 9/11. The point is not to equate these feelings with the traumatic effects of death and injury but to register them as part of the widespread and
local effects of the events of 9/11. These interviews construct the damage of 9/11 to
include racism and violations of security and privacy. They connect 9/11 as a catastrophic and sensational event to other ongoing forms of violence that often remain
invisible.

Significantly, this cluster of interviews also registers anguish about Afghanistan and complex reactions to the United States and its foreign policy. Kazem
expresses apprehension because of her double identity: "I knew that the fate of
these people that died are going to be very closely related to the fate of the Afghans
because all of a sudden these two countries that made the two sides of my being are
completely connected now, because of the disaster, because of something horrible"
(1:29–30). In articulating this sense of connection between the United States and
other parts of the world, Kazem suggests that the shared experience of disaster
could open the way to new alliances. But her comments also indicate a profound
ambivalence, and the conflict between the two parts of her national identity also
produces transgressive feelings of anti-American sentiment:

I'm completely devastated and I feel for these families that have lost people, but
it made me—and I'll be completely honest—it made me almost smirk, and say,
"Welcome to a place where there's war. Welcome to a war-torn place. My sisters
and brothers in Afghanistan face this every single day."

So it wasn't almost a gloating, but it was a smirk almost, like we think
we're so immune to it, and yet it's, "Well, welcome to war." It's the first war that
you've had on your ground since the Civil War, and welcome to our world. I
think that's exactly what I said. I said, "Welcome to our world."

It was interesting that I say "Welcome to our world," but who is "our,"
you know? I'm also considered American, but at that time I felt a deeper
attachment to Afghanistan. (1:30)

The media often misrepresents these feelings as unpatriotic or treacherous, and it
is important that the Columbia archive, without the pressure of media sound bites,
allows for the expression of some of these perspectives within a broader context that
situates them emotionally and historically.

Most Afghan immigrants have lived (at least until 9/11) in a state of exile,
with the loss of home and nation as part of their ongoing experience. This more
attenuated effect of trauma is especially vivid in the case of those who left Afghanistan as children or were born in the United States and who thus have only dim memories of their country of origin—or what Marianne Hirsch calls postmemory, the
construction of the past and of places left behind through others' stories or through
photographs and other memorabilia.[12] The Afghan Americans in their twenties have
a strong sense of national identity in part because exile has meant that they must

actively create a sense of cultural citizenship at a distance. Their hybrid identities result from transnational and transgenerational trauma.

These stories, however marked by the privileges of class and its accompanying mobility, form part of the larger narrative of Afghanistan as a nation living with generations of war and severe trauma, and they dramatically recontextualize 9/11 as a moment in this longer history. For example, Fahima Danishgar, who left Afghanistan in 1987 at the age of ten, has memories of traveling north from Kabul as a child and seeing "destroyed parts of tanks, burnt out cars, convoys of Russians that were burnt, missiles, just on the side of the road, you know. And it was normal to us. Now I look back, and I'm just shocked."[13] Her experience of September 11 brought back those memories, but she also tried to resist the connection because "I didn't want to feel scared and I didn't want to feel like I did in Afghanistan, which was you never knew at one point or another you could be attacked, a bomb could hit you or a rocket could hit your house and so on" (2:63).

Can the Diaspora Speak? Cultural Privilege and Subalternity

I felt even to this day, I have a responsibility, whether I like it or not. And that's to really teach people about this region, about this country. It is my responsibility. (Halima Kazem 1:23)

I think my voice, since it's an Afghan American voice, really is for explaining this culture to outsiders. (Halima Kazem 1:23)

Another way it [life after 9/11] has changed is just to always have to explain myself of being an Afghan and being Muslim and being a woman. I have to constantly explain myself. I hear people talking. I hear people saying stupid things. Part of me wants to say, "You're so stupid. You don't understand anything. There are many stories." (Shekaiba Wakili 1:34)

I had a lot of responsibility after that day just because I was Afghan and because it was a little more local, because what happened after September 11th is everyone suddenly remembered I was Afghan and they were interviewing me. Before I had been giving talks and reading my poetry and stuff, and all of a sudden I was so much into the spotlight. It was kind of weird to have that responsibility of speaking for a people. (Zohra Saed 1:6, 2005)

The stories of ordinary Afghan Americans in New York might seem minor compared to the experience of being in the World Trade Center towers at the time of the attack, being a public figure connected to the larger currents of history in Iraq, Pakistan, or Afghanistan, or even being a subaltern not represented in the historical record, such as the many Afghan refugees in Peshawar or in rural areas of Afghanistan. But one of the striking elements of the interviews is the frustrated desire on the part of this literate, intelligent group to be heard about Afghanistan.[14] Having grown up with a sense of their home country as invisible or insignificant, many of these younger citizens of the diaspora with hybrid identities have made it their job to offer more nuanced perspectives. Even if they themselves are not religious, for example, they seek to make Islam more comprehensible. Danishgar says, "I think that my childhood in Afghanistan plays a role in it and my adulthood in the U.S. plays a role in it, and so usually I like to see things in two different lenses and sort of bring those together." (2:77)

One of the notable effects of 9/11 that emerges in these oral histories is that many of the interviewees were pressed into service to speak on behalf of Afghanistan. Yet even when asked to testify, they often saw their efforts to communicate backfire or they felt sensationalized:

It was like this feeding frenzy. Like all of a sudden, everybody wanted to be for Afghan women, help Afghan women, and a lot of it was very superficial. (Shekaiba Wakili 2:66)

It was like being a circus freak show too. Like I met Jane Fonda, and she was like, "Oh, I'm so honored to meet you." And I'm like, "Why? Why? Because I'm Afghan?" It was just weird. (Zohra Saed 2:58–59, 2005)

Especially significant is their ambivalence about American feminist support for Afghan women, including the publicity given to RAWA (Revolutionary Association of the Women of Afghanistan) by groups such as the Feminist Majority. The interviews express significant resistance to the desire to hear Afghan women speak:

And I didn't like the people who wanted to help Afghan women either, because I didn't like them telling me who I was. (Zohra Saed 2:56, 2003)

I came out really disappointed with how ignorant some Western women are about really what happens in Afghanistan. That really became kind of my reason for digging much deeper than what is covered on the surface from Afghanistan's issues. (Halima Kazem 1:26)

The way the U.S. government used the whole notion of the burqa and the enslavement, so-called, of Afghan women, and then the liberation, as a means of this war, really disgusted me. (Fahima Danishgar 1:45)

The interviewees express feminist views but these did not preclude Islamic feminisms or play into liberal feminist condemnations of "traditional" views. Zieba Shorish-Shamley and Danishgar, for example, both used the interviews to offer an extended discussion of women in Islam.[15]

As poets, editors, fiction writers, and journalists, these younger Afghan Americans find themselves engaged in a complex cultural politics to represent a country whose history they hardly know firsthand. But intergenerational differences give them a special role to play: "I didn't just want to be an angry Afghan. I wanted to be an educated Afghan, where I could counter an argument intelligently, as opposed to with anger. That anger was within my parents because they had lost so much. But I didn't feel that sense of loss, and so I was looking at it with a fresh perspective. My father recognized that and realized that my perspective was very important, because I could bring in this really Westernized perspective, but with an internal Afghan upbringing. So he fostered that" (Halima Kazem 1:20–21). Ultimately, these oral histories make a modest yet also significant contribution by gesturing in the direction of the kind of story we might get if the history of 9/11 and Afghanistan's history were fully integrated. They offer testimony to a persistent inability on the part of many interlocutors to hear even the experiences of privileged and assimilated Afghan Americans. Saed, who also served as an interviewer for the Columbia oral history project, speaks about a shared hunger for archives of Afghanistan: "One story that we all said, all the people that I talked to who went to school here, was how every time you went to a library we would go right to see if there's anything on Afghanistan. It became a real library if they had something on Afghanistan" (1:34, 2005). The Afghan Americans interviewed are painfully aware of the lack of information about Afghanistan and eager to see its history documented and to have the ephemerality of the spoken word transferred into the more permanent repository of the transcript in the archives, available from there to be turned into print sources such as this one. Their stories, as well as the longer histories that have given rise to their exile status in the United States, remain only vaguely told in U.S. public culture, and ten years after September 11, 2001, there remains work to be done to represent not only the longer, sad history of Afghanistan under colonization and decolonization but also the experiences of contemporary diasporic citizens who inhabit multiple worlds. In the words of Wakili, "You see, you're healing twenty-five years of war, and that's not one generation. It's two generations of people who have seen nothing but war. You have to deal with that. You have to deal with mental health. All of these take a long time" (2:59).

Notes

1. Reminiscences of Halima Kazem, the Columbia University September 11, 2001, Oral History Narrative and Memory Project, Oral History Research Office Collection, session 1, 27, interview by Zohra Saed, February 10, 2002. Further citations of this interview will be given parenthetically in the running text with reference to session and page number. Other interviews will be cited fully at first mention with subsequent citations included in the running text.

2. The collection includes interviews with twenty-nine Afghan Americans and ten Pakistani Americans. There are an additional eleven interviews with people from the Middle East (all of them immigrants to the United States)—seven from Egypt, two from Saudi Arabia, one from Israel, and one from Palestine. A further twelve interviews were conducted

with people from the South Asian diaspora: nine from India, one from Kashmir, one from Bangladesh, and one from Sri Lanka. These figures are based on either the self-identification of the interviewees in the interviews or an internal analysis of the transcript texts at the Oral History Research Office (for more on the interviewers, see note 8 below).

3. There was a particular emphasis, for example, on interviewing activists and artists, that is, those who might have alternative perspectives or who have a particularly strong relation to downtown New York. For that reason, Chinatown was the focus of one of the follow-up projects, the September 11, 2001, Telling Lives Oral History Project.

4. The bibliography here is potentially vast, encompassing books, films, photography collections, museum exhibitions, and discussions related to the design of the World Trade Center site, especially of the memorial and the museum. Sources of particular importance for my thinking include work in cultural studies and gender studies, such as "Roundtable: September 11 and Gender," in "Gender and Cultural Memory," ed. Marianne Hirsch and Valerie Smith, special issue, *Signs* 28, no. 1 (2002): 431–79; and Judith Greenberg, ed., *Trauma at Home: After 9/11* (New York: Bison Books, 2003). Both of these titles include a version of my brief essay, "9–11 Every Day."

5. Kay Turner, "September 11: The Burden of the Ephemeral," *Western Folklore* 68 (2009): 155–208. See also Marianne Hirsch, "I Took Pictures: September 11 and Beyond," in "Public Sentiments," ed. Ann Cvetkovich and Ann Pellegrini, special issue, *The Scholar and the Feminist Online* 2 (2003), www.barnard.edu/sfonline/ps; and Diana Taylor, *The Archive and the Repertoire: Performing Cultural Memory in the Americas* (Durham. NC: Duke University Press, 2003), especially chap. 9, "Lost in the Field of Vision: Witnessing September 11," 237–65.

6. See Gilles Peress et al., *Here Is New York: A Democracy of Photographs* (New York: Scalo, 2002). I conducted interviews with Pamela Griffiths and Ruth Sergel, who organized the Listening Booth, for Columbia's September 11, 2001, Response and Recovery Oral History Project.

   The September 11 Digital Archive (911digitalarchive.org) includes stories, images, oral history interviews, and other archival materials. It also comprises written stories gathered by the Smithsonian Institute during the *September 11: Bearing Witness to History* exhibition at the National Museum of American History (911digitalarchive.org/galleries.php?collection_id=31).

   Another important collective and populist project was the *New York Times' Portraits of Grief* series, which created profiles of those who died on September 11, 2001. See *Portraits: 9/11/01; The Collected "Portraits of Grief" from the New York Times* (New York: Times Books, 2002), available online at www.nytimes.com/pages/national/portraits/index.html.

7. I am drawing on my collective work with the Public Feelings research group, which includes Lauren Berlant, Kathleen Stewart, and others. See Janet Staiger, Ann Cvetkovich, and Ann Reynolds, eds., *Political Emotions* (New York: Routledge, 2010); and Kathleen Stewart, *Ordinary Affects* (Durham, NC: Duke University Press, 2007).

8. Just three interviewers conducted the bulk of the interviews: Gerry Albarelli and Amy Starecheski, both of whom are experienced oral historians but lack specific expertise on Afghanistan, and Zohra Saed, a young Afghan American writing a PhD dissertation on Afghan culture, who joined the interview team after herself being interviewed (by feminist historian Temma Kaplan) because the project directors realized the usefulness of having an interviewer with specific knowledge of Afghanistan. For Saed's work, see Zohra Saed and Sahar Muradi, *One Story, Thirty Stories: An Anthology of Contemporary Afghan American Literature* (Fayetteville: University of Arkansas Press, 2010).

9. Reminiscences of Haron Amin, the Columbia University September 11, 2001, Oral History Narrative and Memory Project, Oral History Research Office Collection, session 1, 33, September 11, 2011, Telling Lives Project, interview by Gerry Albarelli, February 26, 2002, and March 1, 2002.

10. Reminiscences of Zohra Saed, the Columbia University September 11, 2001, Oral History Narrative and Memory Project, Oral History Research Office Collection, session 1, 15, interview by Temma Kaplan, January 15, 2002, and May 1, 2003, interview by Gerry Albarelli, February 14, 2005, and June 24, 2005. Citations from the 2005 interviews include the year to distinguish them from the earlier interviews.

11. Reminiscences of Shekaiba Wakili, the Columbia University September 11, 2001, Oral History Narrative and Memory Project, Oral History Research Office Collection, session 2, 63, interview by Amy Starecheski, November 6, 2001, and April 2, 2003.

12. Marianne Hirsch, *Family Frames: Photography, Narrative, and Postmemory* (Cambridge, MA: Harvard University Press, 1997).

13. Reminiscences of Fahima Danishgar, the Columbia University September 11, 2001, Oral History Narrative and Memory Project, Oral History Research Office Collection, session 2, 65, interview by Temma Kaplan, January 4, 2002, and June 23, 2003.

14. For a methodologically sophisticated account of the challenges of documenting the experiences of Afghan women, see Anne Cubilie, *Women Witnessing Terror: Testimony and the Cultural Politics of Human Rights* (New York: Fordham, 2005). For a discussion of immigrants affected by 9/11 who are less culturally privileged, see Sunaina Marr Maira's interviews with South Asian Muslim immigrants in *Missing: Youth, Citizenship, and Empire after 9/11* (Durham, NC: Duke University Press, 2009).

15. Reminiscences of Zieba Shorish-Shamley, the Columbia University September 11, 2001, Oral History Narrative and Memory Project, Oral History Research Office Collection, interview by Gerry Albarelli, February 28, 2002.

The September 11 Digital Archive

Saving the Histories of September 11, 2001

Stephen Brier and Joshua Brown

After September 11 everything was different.

This phrase became the mantra employed to justify nearly every action taken by the Bush administration in the aftermath of the attacks in New York, Washington, D.C., and Shanksville, Pennsylvania—whether the circumstances had anything to do with the attacks or not. The repetition of and rationale for misadventure behind the "9/11 made everything different" trope quickly became a cliché, a dismissible simplification that unfortunately obscured some of the events' actual and unique attributes. One of those attributes, one difference demarcating September 11, 2001, from previous epochal historical moments, was its status as the first truly digital event of world historical importance: a significant part of its historical record—from e-mail to photography to audio to video—was expressed, captured, disseminated, or viewed in (or converted to) digital forms and formats. Moreover, the impact of all that digital activity extended beyond downtown Manhattan or northern Virginia, or even beyond the United States, becoming worldwide in scope. And yet, if any form of historical evidence was vulnerable to destruction, whether because of sins of commission or of omission, it was the eminently disposable and ephemeral forms of communication composed of ones and zeroes.

The fate of digital evidence was not the first item on historians' agendas following September 11. While still confronting both the palpable and the psychological effects of the attacks, academic and public historians grappled with the role they should play as they made tentative efforts to identify the historical significance of

Radical History Review

Issue 111 (Fall 2011) DOI 10.1215/01636545-1268731

the event, especially its place among the many disasters that have occurred through-out New York City's history. On the evening of October 4, 2001, for example, about fifty academic and public historians, archivists, librarians, and directors and staff members of museums and historical societies in New York and New Jersey gathered at the Museum of the City of New York and spent an intense few hours pondering appropriate responses to the collection, preservation, and interpretation of materials documenting the attacks and their aftermath. In many ways, the gathering articu-lated more clearly the stunning array of obstacles that confronted all of us in that room than it yielded any kind of coherent program of coordinated preservation or archival action. But the meeting also revealed a striking spirit, a willingness, often at great emotional and physical expense, to act individually and collaboratively, which would result over the course of the next year or two in extensive efforts to collect, preserve, and present significant aspects of September 11.[1]

With that lack of systematic archiving and collecting in mind, in November 2001 staff members at the Alfred P. Sloan Foundation, a major funder of a number of digital media and digital preservation initiatives, invited the Center for History and New Media (CHNM) at George Mason University and the American Social History Project/Center for Media and Learning (ASHP) at the City University of New York Graduate Center to meet at the foundation's Midtown Manhattan offices. Both ASHP and CHNM were located close to one of the attack sites — ASHP in the Tribeca neighborhood of lower Manhattan, CHNM in northern Virginia — but it was our previous digital media work that prompted the meeting. The two organi-zations had worked collaboratively since the mid-1990s on a number of digital his-tory projects — including the second *Who Built America?* (1914–1946) CD-ROM, the History Matters Web site, the *Liberty, Equality, and Fraternity: Exploring the French Revolution* CD-ROM and Web site, and The Lost Museum Web site — that had all been developed, produced, and published by the fall of 2001.[2] ASHP and CHNM throughout their respective histories (thirty years in the case of ASHP; six-teen years in the case of CHNM) had been committed to finding innovative ways to use emerging media and digital technologies to present historical ideas and informa-tion to broad public audiences. Our collaborative efforts helped define the burgeon-ing field of digital history at the turn of the twenty-first century.

At the meeting, the Sloan Foundation staff challenged us to think about what historians fifty years from now would want to know about the September 11 events and what data they would want to have access to in order to construct a full historical narrative of what transpired. The foundation's staff was concerned that without a coherent and deliberate plan to capture, archive, and preserve digital materials related to the September 11 attacks — particularly the stories of individu-als who had personally experienced the events — such materials would be lost to future generations.

With support from the Sloan Foundation, CHNM and ASHP decided to undertake this major project because we believed, as historians, that such digital materials would prove central to any future understanding of September 11 and the larger political, social, and economic meanings of that epochal historical moment. We realized that we could not remain passive because we could not assume that the kinds of diverse information and materials that future researchers needed would still be available in the future, even though September 11 was one of the most well-documented events (in every sense of the term) in human history. In essence, after decades of depending on librarians and archivists to gather, catalog, and make accessible the vital data that we needed to do our work as historians, we decided that we would now have to function in a new role: as archivist-historians.[3]

While we assumed that new role, our previous work as social historians and our commitment to documenting and teaching about working people in U.S. history prompted us to approach the digital record of September 11 with a critical eye. What kinds of information and perspectives, we asked ourselves, were not being fully represented in the huge effusion of documentary evidence that began to emerge in the immediate aftermath of September 11? Mainstream media institutions such as the *New York Times* and CNN had done a good job presenting immediate and often in-depth information about the victims of the attacks. The *Times' Portraits of Grief* series, for example, profiling the nearly twenty-seven hundred people who died in the towers of the World Trade Center, was particularly compelling and will prove especially useful for future historians intent on constructing a picture of the victims of the attacks.[4]

But what about the larger context in which most people experienced these events? What about the attitudes and perspectives of "ordinary" people, here and abroad, especially those deeply affected by the attacks, those who were not necessarily inside or near the towers or in the Pentagon or in Shanksville, but whose lives were nonetheless profoundly affected by what happened on September 11? What about people who did not, a decade ago, have direct access to digital media through which to record their ideas and experiences, let alone preserve them?

The Evolution and Growth of the September 11 Digital Archive

Our initial goal was to quickly get online a free public space for people to contribute their stories and to allow them to deposit the rich array of digital evidence that they had created personally or received electronically, all of which would help future historians document what ordinary people saw and experienced on and immediately after September 11. We mounted the initial version of the September 11 Digital Archive Web site (www.911digitalarchive.org) on January 11, 2002, just two months after our preliminary meeting at the Sloan Foundation. Our first task was to allow individuals to easily and quickly deposit their word-processed "stories" about what had happened to them on the day of the attacks, as well as to submit the e-mails they had received and/or sent to family, friends, and work colleagues in the immediate aftermath of the attacks. We believed that those stories and messages (the full extent of which we could not even begin to comprehend) would contain unique insights

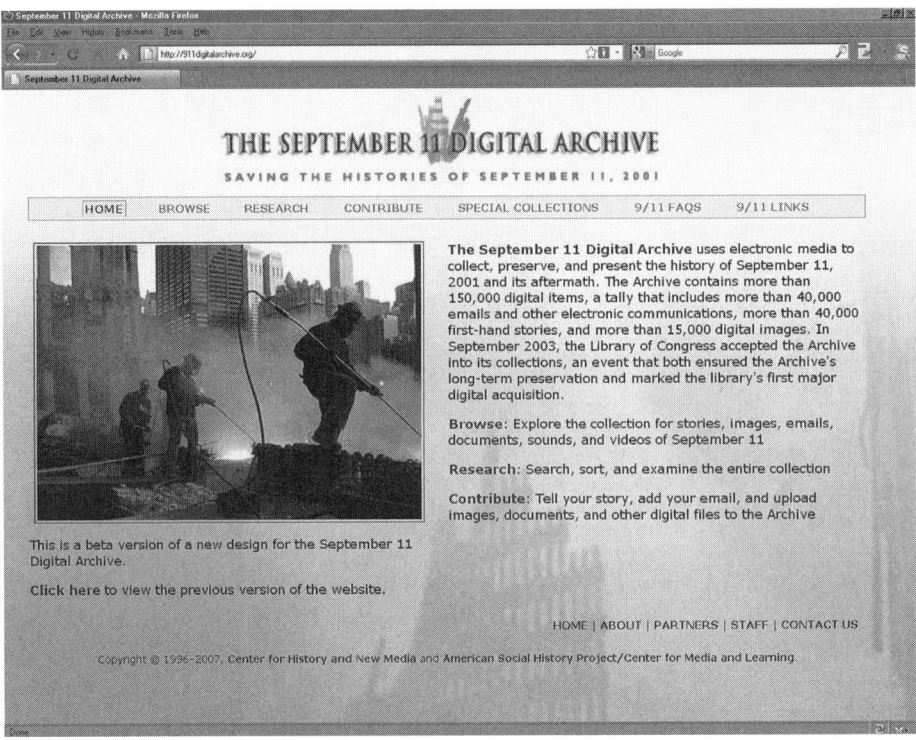

The September 11 Digital Archive home page (911digitalarchive.org) in January 2011

into how people immediately experienced September 11, how it shaped their sub-sequent behavior and beliefs, and how they came to interpret the meaning of those events in their lives. We also decided to seek out and secure for the archive various listservs and Web logs (blogs) that discussed September 11.[5]

We also wanted the September 11 Digital Archive to serve as a space for the general public to deposit what we reasoned would be a large number of digital still and moving images taken or created before, during, and after the attacks, as well as digital sound recordings, including telephone answering machine and voice-mail messages. We were intent, as well, on finding and digitizing as many of the extra-ordinary number of flyers that people pasted all over Manhattan in an effort to find missing loved ones. We also wanted to include myriad political and organizational flyers that appeared around the city after the attacks. While these last two resources were not "born digital" (which had been the Sloan Foundation's primary interest in funding the project), we knew they were an important and perishable historical source that we needed to locate, scan, and deposit in the database of our expanding digital collection. We were fortunate to secure the extensive collection of Michael Ragsdale, a videographer who collected almost a thousand flyers from all over New York City in the days following the attacks. We also saved nearly one hundred Flash files, animated programs posted on the Web that conveyed individual artistic or propagandistic responses to the attacks locally and internationally.[6]

The real burst of online submissions came on the six-month and one-year anniversaries of the attacks. The site went fully public on March 11, 2002, with a series of press releases and media coverage. On the one-year anniversary of the attacks, the existence of the September 11 Digital Archive garnered much media attention on CNN, on MSNBC, in the Associated Press, and in hundreds of newspaper stories. This publicity drove much traffic to our site; more than one hundred thousand visitors accessed the site on the first anniversary, and we received thirteen thousand new personal stories during the next few days.[7]

At this juncture we had to address the inequality of access to digital media. The initial spate of digital submissions tended to be skewed toward particular groups and individuals who were largely white and middle class. Taken as a whole, while indisputably valuable, they did not represent the broad demographic range of submissions that we had hoped would find their way into the archive. That fact indicated that online digital collecting alone would not suffice and that we would need to undertake additional targeted outreach to particular ethnic and national communities if the archive were truly to encompass a wide range of individual and collective responses to the September 11 attacks.

We began that outreach in earnest at the beginning of 2003 by developing a Spanish-language version of the September 11 Digital Archive site to encourage input from the large Latino communities in New York City and Washington, D.C., and we sent project staff to Shanksville, the site of the crash of United Airlines Flight 93, to solicit testimony from that community. We also worked closely with the Middle East and Middle East American Center at the CUNY Graduate Center to reach out to the Arab and Muslim community in New York City and, via the Internet and telephone, to Arab and Muslim Americans across the country. Even though the seventy-two interviews carried out for this project did not represent the full range of opinions of Arab and/or Muslim Americans, the voices of these individuals provide invaluable insights about what members of these communities felt on the day of the attacks and what they have experienced since. Finally, we secured a grant from the Rockefeller Foundation to conduct video interviews in three Chinese dialects (which we also translated into English) with residents, workers and stakeholders in Manhattan's Chinatown community, a neighborhood just ten blocks away from the World Trade Center site.[8]

We also built collaborative ties to other archives and museums, with the goal of having those links help us generate additional submissions. These joint projects included the New York cultural organization City Lore and the New-York Historical Society (where we placed a computer terminal to collect stories from visitors to their 2002 *Missing: Streetscape of a City in Mourning* exhibit); public libraries in Somerset County, Pennsylvania (where Shanksville is located); and public schools in the New York City and Washington, D.C., metropolitan areas. We also collaborated with the National Museum of American History (NMAH), Smithsonian Institution, where thousands of visitors to *Bearing Witness*, an exhibit commemorating the first anniversary of the attacks, had an opportunity to tell their stories and recount their thoughts about September 11 in voice-mail messages on a special telephone instal-lation (which we then captured digitally and transcribed), and also by using old-fashioned pencil and paper (which we scanned in bulk and later imported into our growing database). In the end, we secured thousands of new stories for the archive from visitors to the NMAH exhibition.[9]

Two years after we had conceived and launched the September 11 Digital Archive, we had collected a total of nearly 150,000 individual digital items, including 45,000 personal narratives, 60,000 e-mails and electronic communications (includ-ing blogs and listservs), 14,000 digital images, 6,000 print documents, and 4,500 audio and video files, many of which we streamed on our Web site. The September 11 Digital Archive Web site in the same two-year period received nearly 120 million hits and more than 2 million unique visitors. And to this day it consistently ranks third or fourth among the more than 350 million "September 11" and "9/11" Web pages indexed by Google.

Filling out the Digital Archive Collection and Ensuring Its Permanence

We also worked closely with other September 11 – related archives, several of which asked us to help their collections survive and remain available to the general public on the Web. Two such collaborations are of particular note. The first is the Sonic Memorial Project, which collected hundreds of digital and analog voice-mail mes-sages from inside the World Trade Center towers, concert recordings from the World Trade Center Plaza, works by center artists-in-residence, home movies, tourist vid-eos, rare on-site field recordings, newsreels, and oral histories. These rich audio resources are now preserved in our archive.[10]

The second, and one of our most important collaborations to date, is with Here Is New York: A Democracy of Photographs (HNY). The HNY project, built around a collection of six thousand photographs taken by mostly professional pho-tographers in and around ground zero in the immediate aftermath of the attacks, ranked among the most visible projects internationally about September 11. In addition to the six thousand digitized photographs, several thousand of which were printed and exhibited internationally and published in a widely disseminated book, HNY received hundreds of thousands of e-mail messages on its Web site from individuals around the world. HNY also solicited nearly six hundred digital video interviews with people in New York City, the Pentagon, and Shanksville, to record their feelings and reactions to the events of September 11. After more than a year's negotiations and the formal dissolution of the HNY organization in 2006, the HNY *digital* collection was legally accessioned by the September 11 Digital Archive (the HNY *physical* collection, including its archive of high-quality photographic prints, was given to the New-York Historical Society, which has made some of it avail-able online).[11] HNY's project leaders chose the September 11 Digital Archive as a permanent home for their digital materials because of our commitment to respect and protect the rights and feelings of the people who submitted materials, and also because we had developed a plan for stabilizing and securing our archive and for ensuring an enduring existence for it.[12] Together, the Sonic Memorial and HNY materials comprise an additional one hundred thousand discrete digital items, many of them substantial and important video and sound files that have not yet been fully integrated into the larger structure of the September 11 Digital Archive online database.

By the close of 2003 and the end of funding from the Sloan Foundation, the active collecting phase of the September 11 Digital Archive had been completed. Nonetheless, we continued to incorporate previously acquired materials into the collection and undertook a preliminary redesign of the Web site to better assist online researchers. But now that we had become archivist-historians, we learned that our obligations did not end with collecting. A number of final challenging tasks still lie ahead:

- to stabilize and secure the vast collection of digital resources that currently comprise the September 11 Digital Archive;

- to update the metadata associated with each of the tens of thousands of items in the overall collection to make digital searching easier and more successful;

- to build a robust and open-source database back end to secure materials in the archive and to properly display them on the Web, using Omeka, a leading open-source, collections-based Web publishing platform developed by CHNM (and written for the Linux, Apache, MySQL, and PHP server configurations and released under a GNU General Public License); and

- to make the integrated collection available to the public through a thoroughly redesigned Web site.[13]

In addition to vastly improved searches and browsing, a more standardized digital archive will allow scholars to ask new research questions that can only be answered through the use of powerful data-mining tools. Better structured metadata and the addition of APIs (application programming interfaces, which facilitate the interaction among different software programs) will allow scholars to apply these tools to the archive, uncovering new relationships among digitally created and discovered primary sources.

Finally, we decided that we had to secure a permanent archival home for the September 11 Digital Archive to assure its long-term availability and stability. We have maintained the archive for the past six years without any additional financial support from our original funders. We have recently applied for additional grants to complete the final stages of our work as described above. Neither ASHP nor CHNM, nor our sponsoring universities, have the financial and human resources to sustain this project into the foreseeable future. With that in mind, we approached the Library of Congress (LC) early on in our work to gauge its interest in becoming the ultimate repository for the September 11 Digital Archive. The LC agreed in 2003 to accession the entire archive (the first fully digital collection ever accessioned by the library), which was announced at a major convocation held at the library on September 10, 2003. All of the September 11 Digital Archive servers and our Web site (and those of HNY) will be turned over to the LC, probably sometime in 2013 (on or near the tenth anniversary of the signing of the original agreement). Once that transfer occurs, all the digital data contained in the September 11 Digital Archive will be made available to historical and other researchers at the LC in Washington, D.C. We also hope that the library will continue to make the digital information contained in the archive available to the general public via the Internet.[14]

We hope that members of the public and, particularly, professional historians will in the future use the vast and diverse digital materials contained in the September 11 Digital Archive in sensitive and nuanced ways. To be sure, much of the material submitted to the archive was riddled with jingoistic, racist, xenophobic, and messianic attitudes and opinions. Yet precisely these problematic aspects of the material offer historians a uniquely complex vision of the events that occurred on that clear morning in September 2001. If we might hazard to find one word that succinctly captures what the quarter of a million digital items comprising the archive offer future scholars, it is a sense of the *zeitgeist*: an intricately detailed panoramic view revealing the myriad ways Americans and others throughout the world experienced, understood, deciphered, distorted, and rationalized—*located meaning in*—an epochal traumatic event.

Notes

1. Similar meetings discussing the ways scholars should respond to the attacks (as well as to policies imposed in their aftermath) were held at humanities and social science annual conferences throughout the fall of 2001. See, for example, the special panel titled "September 11, 2001" at the American Studies Association annual meeting, held on November 10, 2001, in Washington, D.C.

2. *Who Built America? From the Great War of 1914 to the Dawn of the Atomic Age* (New York: Worth Publishers/Learn Technologies Interactive, 2000); History Matters: The U.S. Survey Course on the Web (historymatters.gmu.edu); *Liberty, Equality, Fraternity: Exploring the French Revolution* (University Park: Pennsylvania State University Press, 2001); The Lost Museum: Exploring Antebellum Life and Culture (www.lostmuseum.cuny.edu).

3. A large number of people collaborated on the September 11 Digital Archive project, led by Greg "Fritz" Umbach at ASHP and Tom Scheinfeldt at CHNM, who served as codirectors of the archive project. A full list of contributors can be found in two places on the Web; the group that launched the project is detailed at old.911digitalarchive.org/about/staff.html (accessed March 10, 2011), while the group that will be finishing work on the project is detailed at 911digitalarchive.org/about/staff.php (accessed March 10, 2011).

4. The *New York Times' Portraits of Grief* archive is available at topics.nytimes.com/top/news/newyorkandregion/series/portraits_of_grief/index.html (accessed March 10, 2011).

5. Most individuals did not then (and do not now) archive their e-mail messages beyond a few weeks or (at most) a few months. This was especially true in 2001, when digital archiving systems were nonexistent or quite primitive and the cost of digital storage was considerably higher that it has become. Three blogs or listservs of note that are contained on the September 11 Digital Archive site are the Downtown Blackberry group (www.september11digitalarchive.org/email/downtown_blackberry.html); the SEPT11INFO group (911digitalarchive.org/repository_object.php?object_id=83390); and the Hash House Harriers (911digitalarchive.org/repository.php?collection_id=12443). It is important to remember that blogs were still a relatively new and underused digital format in the fall of 2001.

6. For collection of flyers, see 911digitalarchive.org/galleries.php?collection_id=12 and 911digitalarchive.org/galleries.php?collection_id=15 for the Flash files.

7. Our CHNM colleagues Dan Cohen and Roy Rosenzweig describe the early successes of the September 11 Digital Archive in the chapter "Collecting History Online," in their *Digital History: A Guide to Gathering, Preserving, and Presenting the Past on the Web* (Philadelphia: University of Pennsylvania Press, 2005), 185–88.

8. The fruits of the collaboration with the Middle East and Middle Eastern American Center can be found at 911digitalarchive.org/galleries.php?collection_id=14: they include seventy-two anonymous interviews with Arab and Muslim immigrants and Arab Americans. The Chinatown Documentation Project was done in collaboration with the Museum of Chinese in America (MoCA), a Chinatown-based community history museum; New York University's Asian/Pacific/American Institute; and Columbia University's Oral History Research Office. The fruits of the Chinatown project are archived on the MoCA Web site at 911chinatown.mocanyc.org.

9. For the *Missing: Streetscape of a City in Mourning* exhibit, see www.citylore.org/911_exhibit/911_home.html. See www.911digitalarchive.org/smithsoniancards for the results of the more than twenty thousand written recollections gathered from *Bearing Witness* visitors.

10. The Sonic Memorial site is still available on the Web (www.sonicmemorial.org/sonic/public/index.html).

11. For the physical collection, see www.nyhistory.org/web/default.php?section=exhibits_collections&page=exhibit_detail&id=3585525 (accessed March 10, 2011).

12. All rights to materials deposited in the September 11 Digital Archive remain with the individuals who donated them. We refer any publisher or journalist interested in publishing material contained in the archive to the individual donors. The HNY Web site is currently in the process of being accessioned and integrated into the September 11 Digital Archive. HNY's original Web site is no longer available to the public.

13. For details about the Omeka software, see omeka.org.

14. See www.loc.gov/today/pr/2003/03-142.html for the LC's online report on the accessioning of the September 11 Digital Archive. The LC has also made the September 11 Digital Archive part of its ongoing National Digital Information Infrastructure and Preservation Program's Archive and Ingest Handling Test (AIHT), which tests various formats and approaches for absorbing digital materials into the LC's collections.

Introduction to an Index

Chitra Ganesh and Mariam Ghani

Chitra Ganesh and Mariam Ghani have collaborated since 2004 on the project Index of the Disappeared, which is both a physical archive of post-9/11 disappearances and a mobile platform for public dialogue.

As an archive, Index of the Disappeared foregrounds the difficult histories of immigrant, "Other," and dissenting communities in the United States since 9/11. Through official documents, secondary literature, and personal narratives, the Index archive traces the ways in which censorship and data blackouts form part of a discursive shift to secrecy that allows for disappearances, deportations, renditions, and detentions on an unprecedented scale. The Index builds up its collection by collaborating with others actively engaged in political and legal challenges to the policies we track and draws on radical archival, legal, and activist traditions to select, group, and arrange information.

As a platform, the Index presents discussions on ideas and issues related to the materials it archives and draws on materials in the archive to create text-based, site-specific works installed in a range of physical and virtual spaces, including galleries, museums, universities, community centers, libraries, conferences, publications, windows, the street, the Web, and the mail. These visual forms of public dialogue are designed to confront audiences with the human costs of public policies, challenging them to reconsider the abstractions of political debate in specific, individual terms.

An index can be a trace, a signpost, an indicator, or a measurement. Our index begins in the gaps where language ends; that is, in the records of absence and

Radical History Review

Issue 111 (Fall 2011)   DOI 10.1215/01636545-1268740

© 2011 by Chitra Ganesh and Mariam Ghani

in the absence of records where official language fails and new languages must be developed in its place. The Index in its most material form, the archive, preserves and presents the traces of redactions and erasures in the official record, alongside the words of the original actors and witnesses of the histories it explores. For our index, the gaps in those records constitute not flaws in the archive but, rather, the key to its organization. We configure the bits of information remaining in the public domain to make visible the missing links, the submerged body of secret information below the simple surface. The presentation of the Index archive as an artwork in progress, one constantly readapted to the specific sites in which it is installed, encourages visitors to approach it not as researchers seeking facts but rather with the critical awareness that the supposed facts they encounter are in flux, defined and redefined in relationship to time, to their context, and to each other.

At the same time, the Index archive's steadily increasing mass is a visceral measure of the slow and steady creep of the troubling policies it chronicles, through every echelon of our society and through every facet of our culture. In our own research with these materials, we have tried to probe the texts for productive breaks and slippages, for the moments when language escapes from official to unofficial registers, from public to private domains, from political to poetic testimony. These moments become the extracts and fragments of our index, literal signs and visible trails that we circulate in the wider world.

For *Radical History Review*, we have presented a chronology of the project through extracts from, reframings of, and comments on documents that represent both productive ruptures in and particular phases of our research—on "special interest" detention and special registration; on the laws and legal terms that enable and double disappearances in the detention system; on national security letters, libraries, and domestic surveillance; on detainee abuse and deaths in custody; on the individual narratives pieced together from the stray details of tribunal transcripts, interrogation logs, testimony, and trial exhibits; on legal (re)definitions of torture and military codes of conduct; and on the migration of "enhanced" interrogation techniques from the psychological experiments of the SERE program to Guantánamo Bay (GTMO) to Iraq via Afghanistan, where they continue to be practiced today.

INS Specia

Joint Terrorism Task

LIMITED OFFICIAL USE----LA

(b)(7)(A)

(b)(7)(C)

A Number	Name	POB	Arrest Date	Arrest Location
Federal Bureau of Investigation / Other Agencies 29				
███████████	████████	Pakistan	9/22/200█	████████
JTTF Comments: ████████████████████				
Counsel Comments:				
████████████████		Jordan	9/28/2001	████████
JTTF Comments: ████████				
Counsel Comments:				
████████████		India	9/13/200█	████████
JTTF Comments: ████████████████████				
Counsel Comments:				
████████████		Egypt	10/31/2001	████████
JTTF Comments: ████████████				
Counsel Comments: ████				

YOUR NAMES ERASED, AND NOW BLANK SLATES

LIMITED OFFICIAL USE----LAW

Interest List
Force Working Group

W ENFORCEMENT SENSITIVE

Date Charging Document Served	Immigration Charge	Date filed w/EOIR	Custody Location	SIOC FBI Interest	Legally Sufficient
9/22/2001	237(a)(3)(D)	9/25/2001	▮	▮	▮
Bond Info:	(▮)				
DRO Comments	▮▮▮▮▮▮▮▮▮▮▮▮				
9/30/2001	237(a)(1)(B)	10/1/2001	▮	▮	▮
Bond Info:	▮				
DRO Comments:	▮▮▮▮▮▮▮▮▮▮▮▮				
	241(a)(5)		▮	▮	▮
Bond Info.	▮				
DRO Comments:	▮▮▮▮▮▮▮▮▮▮▮▮				
12/6/2001	237(a)(1)(B)		▮)	▮	
Bond Info:					
DRO Comments:	▮▮▮ WHERE ALL FEARS CAN BE WRITTEN ▮▮▮				

28

SECRET

ALL INFORMATION CONTAINED
HEREIN IS UNCLASSIFIED EXCEPT
WHERE SHOWN OTHERWISE

U.S. Department of Justice

Federal Bureau of Investigation

In Reply, Please Refer to
File No

[Drafting] Field Division
[Street Address]
[City, State, Zip]

[Month Date, Year]

[Mr /Mrs.] [COMPANY POINT OF CONTACT]
[TITLE]
[COMPANY]
[STREET ADDRESS]
[CITY, STATE No Zip Code]

Dear [Mr /Mrs] [LAST NAME]:

Under the authority of Executive Order 12333, dated
December 4, 1981, and pursuant to Title 18, United States Code
(U S C), Section 2709 (as amended, October 26, 2001), you are
hereby directed to provide the Federal Bureau of Investigation

b2-2
b7E-1

In accordance with Title 18, U.S.C., Section 2709(b), I
certify that the information sought is relevant to an authorized
investigation to protect against international terrorism or
clandestine intelligence activities, and that such an
investigation of a United States person is not conducted solely
on the basis of activities protected by the first amendment of
the Constitution of the United States

You are further advised that Title 18, U.S C , Section
2709(c), prohibits any officer, employee or agent of yours from
disclosing to any person that the FBI has sought or obtained
access to information or records under these provisions.

b2-2
b7E-1

CLASSIFIED DECISIONS FINALIZED BY
DEPARTMENT REVIEW COMMITTEE (DRC)
DATE: 07-01-2004

CA# 03-2522

CLASSIFIED BY 65179 dml/bce/amw   6/5/2004
REASON: 1/4 (c)
DECLASSIFY ON: X 6/5/2029

Patriot Act II-828

SECRET

DECLASSIFIED BY 65129 dml/bce/Ama

ON 8/3/2004

A LETTER SO SECRET IT COULD NEVER BE SPOKEN OF AGAIN. THE TRICK? RECOGNIZING THE ENVELOPE.

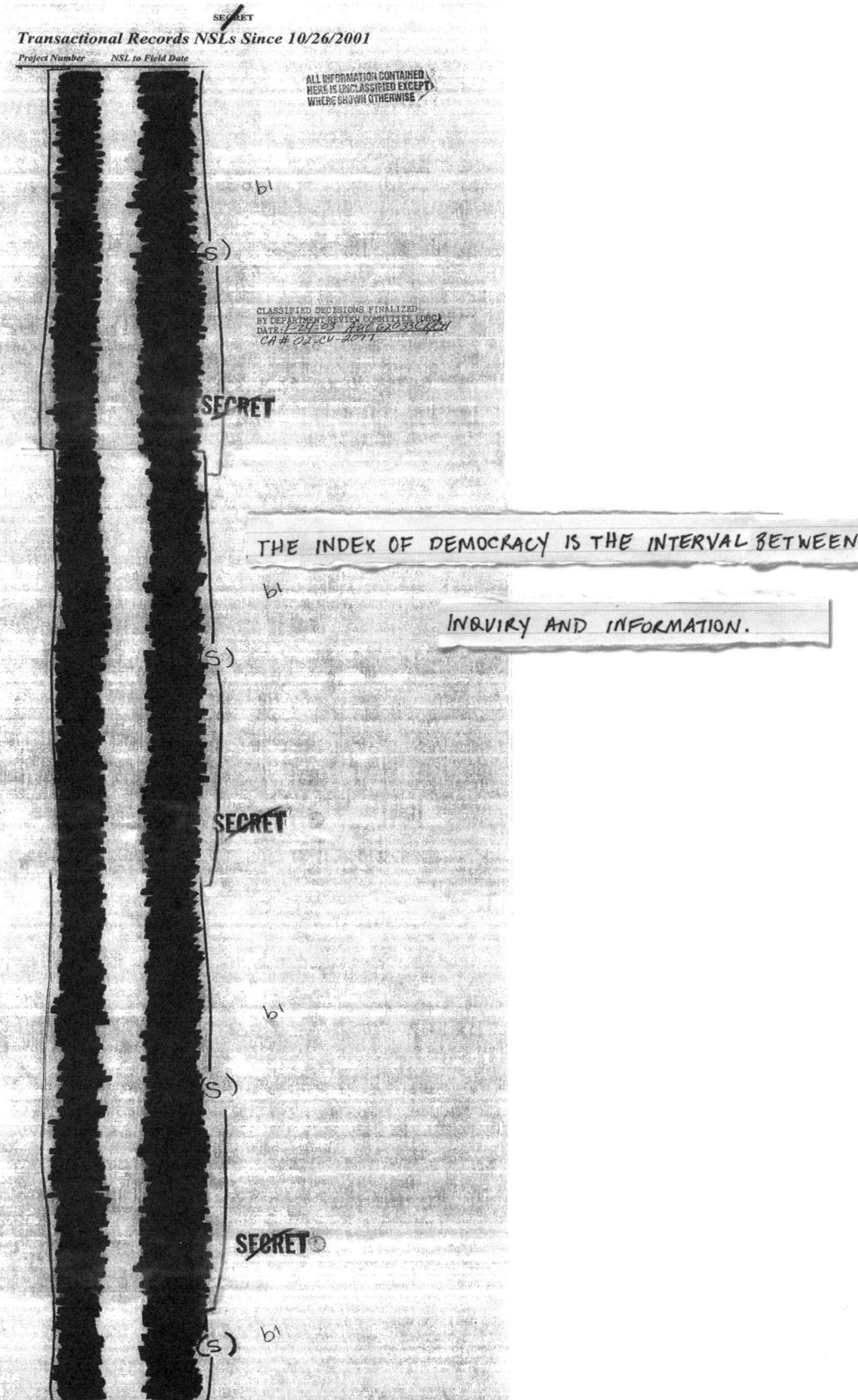

SECRET

Transactional Records NSLs Since 10/26/2001

Project Number   NSL to Field Date

ALL INFORMATION CONTAINED
HERE IS UNCLASSIFIED EXCEPT
WHERE SHOWN OTHERWISE

CLASSIFIED DECISIONS FINALIZED
BY DEPARTMENT REVIEW COMMITTEE (DRC)
DATE:
CA# 02-CV-2077

SECRET

SECRET

SECRET

Grand Total:

THE INDEX OF DEMOCRACY IS THE INTERVAL BETWEEN

INQUIRY AND INFORMATION.

DRAFT

CIA psychologist/interrogators threatened KSM by saying that "if anything else happens in the United States, 'We're going to kill your children.'"

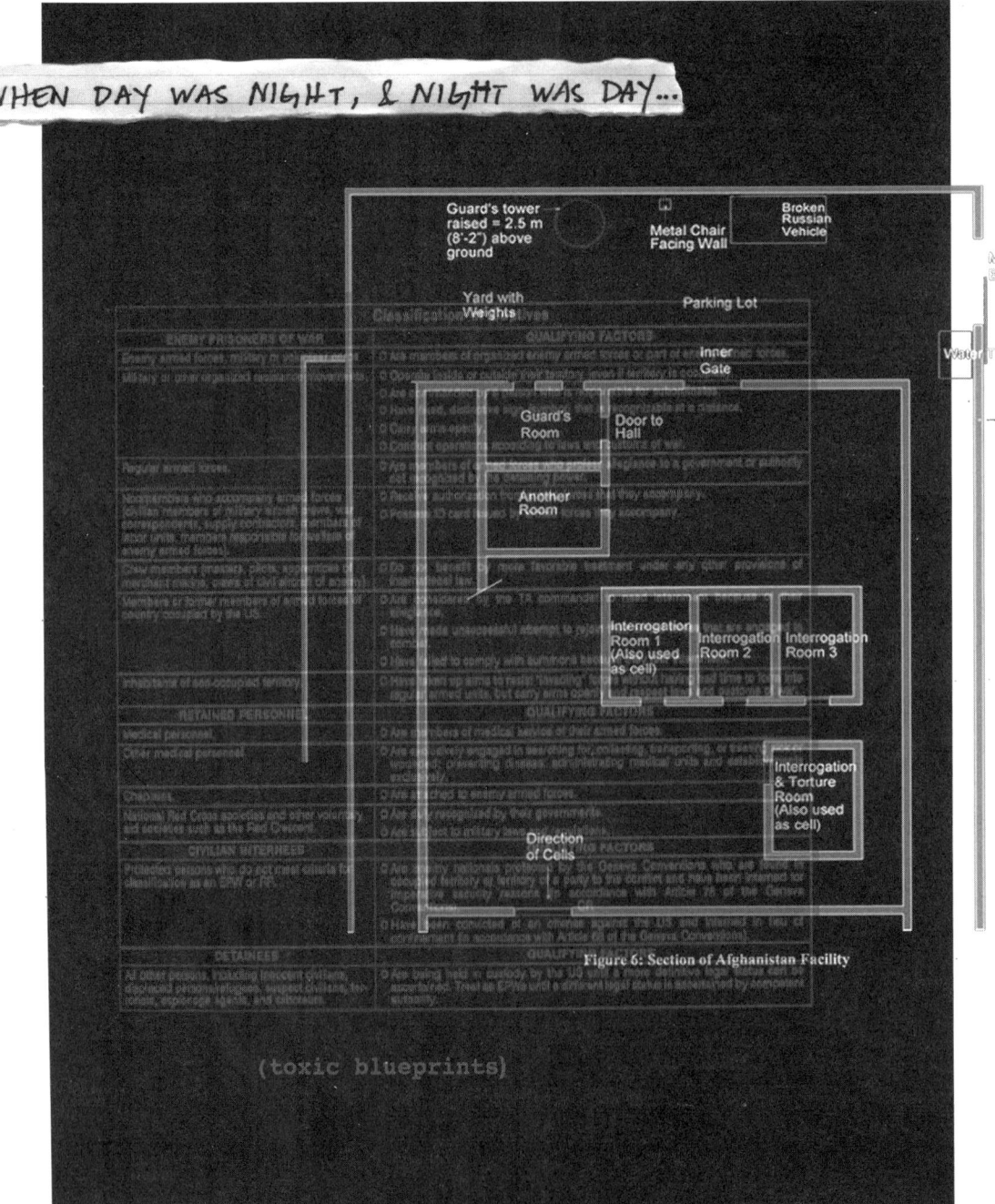

WHEN DAY WAS NIGHT, & NIGHT WAS DAY...

Figure 6: Section of Afghanistan Facility

(toxic blueprints)

UNCLASSIFIED//FOUO

Recorder returned with the materials. Upon the Recorder's return, the Tribunal Member announced that the Detainee indicated he would be more comfortable describing the layout of his compound (for the sketch) to the Tribunal Member. At that time, the Tribunal Member approached the Detainee with the blank paper and pen for the drawing. The Tribunal Member knelt in front of the Detainee and took instructions from him describing his compound. The paper was also placed in front of the Detainee so he could draw directly on it to clarify the layout of the area he was from. This layout included the Detainee's home, surrounding homes, the courtyard, a garden and area roads and rivers.

Detainee: When you go to my house, you will see that it is surrounded by other houses. This is the front of my house (referring to drawing), and you can't see anything because these houses block our view.

Tribunal Member: I am going to place the letter "D" for the Detainee's house in the middle of the circle (on the drawing).

Detainee: This area is a big garden. We have a pomegranate garden.

Tribunal Member: (still knelt in front of Detainee) Then I'll write garden here. When you say garden, what kinds of things are in this area?

Detainee: We have huge garden. There are grapes, plants, and pomegranate trees.

Tribunal Member: Is there a road anywhere near by (referring to the drawing)?

Detainee: The road is all the way up in front of our house.

The Tribunal Member continued to take direction from the Detainee as to the layout of the area, and applied it to the sketch. The Tribunal Member remained directly in front of the Detainee, and referring the Detainee's attention to the sketch, asked the following:

Tribunal Member: When you stepped out into the courtyard, where did you step out to? Put a dot where you stepped out to.

Detainee: Just (place a dot) in the middle of it. We have lots of rooms in our compound. I left the room, I went to the courtyard and I stood in the middle of it.

Tribunal Member: In the middle of this circle, here, that I'm pointing at now?

Detainee: The dot is where I was standing.

Personal Representative: His house has a specific courtyard.

AND THAT GROVE OF POMEGRANATES-- NOT AN ORCHARD AFTER ALL, BUT A RELIQUARY

118

DETAINEE HEALTH AND MEDICAL RECORD OF SCREENING EXAMINATION
(SF600 OVERPRINT, IAW AR 190-8)

detainee was strong and he had no hope of being found innocent. Detainee was
asked what was wanted of him, he replied "If I help you, you will help me".

Detainee appeared to begin to understand his situation and become distressed.

ALLERGY: FOOD, MEDICINES, INSECTS, PLANTS

0500: Head break and 10 minutes exercise. Interrogators continued futility approach.
0700: Head break and taken to x-ray for rest period.

GENERAL INFORMATION: (CHECK ALL THAT APPLY IN THE DETAINEE HEALTH HISTORY)
SURGERIES ( )
CONVULSIONS/SEIZURES ( )
HEMOPHILIA ( )
MALARIA ( )
ASTHMA ( )
DIABETES ( )
HIGH BLOOD PRESSURE ( )
CANCER/LEUKEMIA ( )
HEART TROUBLE ( )
KIDNEY DISEASE ( )
VISUAL IMPAIRMENT ( )
HIV/AIDS ( )
STD ( )

IMMUNIZATION GIVEN AT INTAKE ( )
TB/BLOOD IN SPUTUM/NIGHT SWEATS ( )
LIST ALL MEDICATIONS TAKEN IN THE 10
DAYS PRIOR TO TODAY:

1045: Detainee awoke on his own and urinated through the wire of his cell. When asked why he did this and did not request to go to the bathroom, detainee replied that he woke up and could not hold it and had to go immediately.

1100: Detainee woken up and exercised/ taken to bathroom and moved to booth.
1130: Detainee entered booth and used an emotional love of family approach on

1300: Detainee exercised and taken to the bathroom. Drank water
1315: 2a0761 and 2a0780 entered the booth and questioned the detainees work history.

TOBACCO USE Y/N ___ PER DAY ___ YRS
ETOH USE Y/N

1445: Detainee exercised and taken to the bathroom.
1530: 2a0761 and 2a0780 continued to exploit sources work history.
1700: detainee exercised and taken to the bathroom. Drank water.
1730: 2a0761 and 2a0780 continued to exploit sources work history and began to exploit sources false claims of innocence.
1900: detainee exercised and taken to the bathroom. Drank water
1915: 2a0780 entered booth and went over maps of sources home, Al Kharj, SA.
2000: Detainee ate 1 MRE and drank water.
2100: Detainee exercised and taken to the bathroom.

HT ___ BP ___ PULSE ___ BICEPS CIRC ___
HEIGHT ___ WEIGHT ___ BMI ___

DETAINEE HAS AN OVERALL (GOOD) (FAIR) POOR STATE
OF NUTRITION

VISION: NORMAL ( ) GLASSES ( )
HEARING NORMAL ( ) ABNORMAL EXPLAIN

DENTAL:

OVERALL APPEARANCE

Log reviewed to this point by JTF-GTMO-JMC 7 Jan 02

2115: Interrogation team entered booth, 1ST E, SGT M and a DOD Linguist. Futility

HEENT
HERNIA
SKIN/SCARS/BRUISING

theme began as it was determined that the detainee was holding on to a hope that he would be found innocent. Interrogators explained that this was a false hope.

going on hunger strike.

2230: Head break and 10 minute exercise.
2245: Detainee awoke on his own and urinated through the wire of his cell. When asked why he did this and did not request to go to the bathroom, detainee replied that he woke up and could not hold it and had to go immediately.

MARKED LE ____ DETAILS ON REVERSE SIDE

08 January 2003 Detainee attempts to control the interrogation by complaining about his treatment, his mental illness, and his separation from his brothers

ISN ___ NAME ___
DOB ___ AGE ___ SEX ___

0030: Head break and 10 minute exercise. Detainee drank one bottle of water.
0230: Head break and 10 minute exercise.

PROVIDER

0300: Source HOW DO WE CATCH FATE'S DAGGER-- med the futility approach and centered around why the detainee refuses to tell the truth.

responsibility for his actions. The detainee went as far as to state that certain topics such as the true definition of martyr, and Islamic beliefs. Detainee asked interrogator to tell him about hunting, and interrogator turned the topic back to futility.

Figure G-1. Inprocessing overprint for Standard Form 600

5. MESSAGE
نـص الرسالة

Family and/or private news only
أخبار شخصية أو عائلية فقط

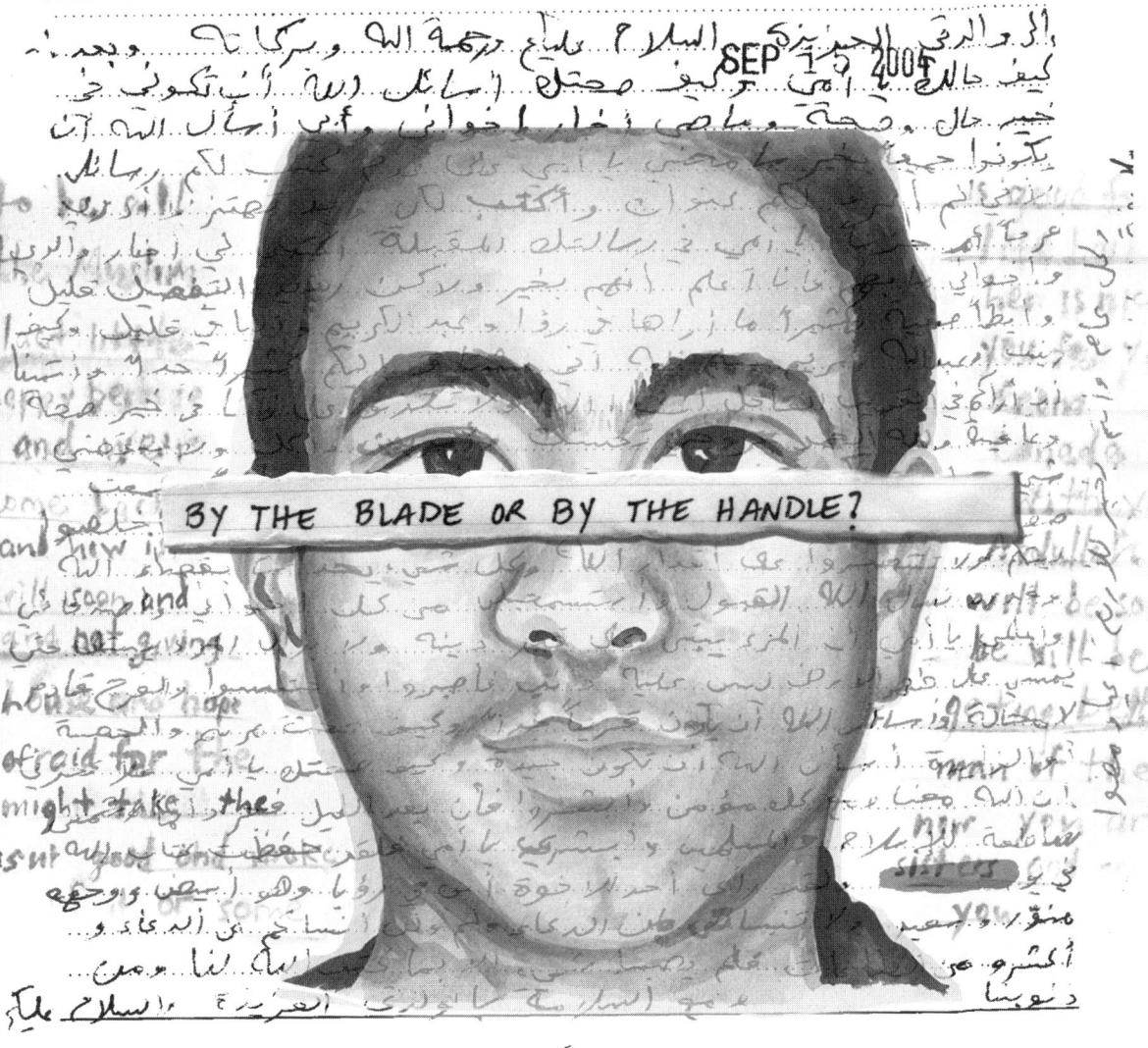

BY THE BLADE OR BY THE HANDLE?

6.

Date 18 / 8 / 2004 التاريخ   Signature Omar. Ahmed. Khdar الإمضاء

The addressee is my Mother .... علاقة الصلة بيني وبين المرسل إليه

-----Original Message-----
From: Migliaccio, Gene A <Gene.Migliaccio@dhs.gov>
To:
CC:
Sent: Mon Mar 21 19:26:30
Subject: FW: SEN Report Notification-32105-1

(WHEN THE BORDERS CROSSED OUR BODIES

Section 635. Visa Waiver Program.
Follow-up to SEN on death of detainee Hassiba Belbachir (A# 97-332-245)

ASSESSMENT AND RECOMMENDATION
With the given information provided, DIHS recommends a medical review of
this facility concentrating on Suicide Standards to determine if
procedures exist and are being enforced. DIHS is concerned that the
detainee committed suicide, in medical pod, after being assessed as a
suicide risk.

*j'ai un collègue. Vous avez important avec un juge puissant avez
tous les jours.

- c'est le bon dieu a qui j'ai des questions a poser.

- tu n'a pas peur du dieu.

BELBACHIR c'est Hass'ba, car il c'est mes intentions et ma façon d'être.

- et comment tu va rencontrer le dieu ? 08/24/1927

- c'est simple, c'est de prendre le chemin le plus logique avec lequel
on a toute la vérité en face.

9097332245

- c'est avoir le chemin donc ?

- c'est bien la mort.

- et tu n'as pas peur de la mort ?

- quelle est la différence entre la prison et la tombe ?

- je ne sais pas

- aucune, dans les deux endroits c'est Sombre, c'est froid et renfermer.

- mais là au moins tu respire

- je respire du CO2 et avoir le cœur engoncé ce n'est pas la peine

- j'ai mal vécu. Je vis mal mais on peux controler le futur pour être mieux

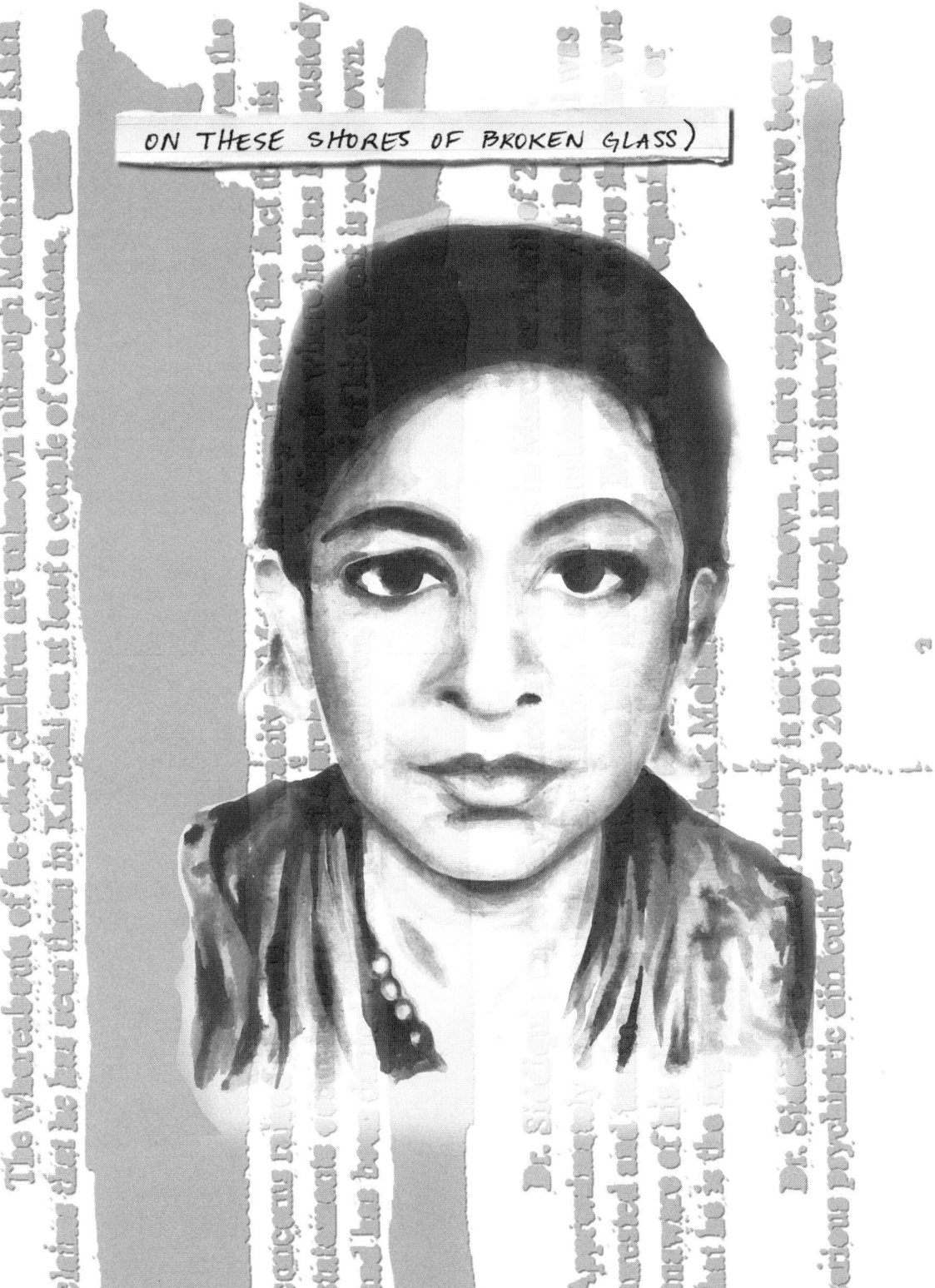

ON THESE SHORES OF BROKEN GLASS)

6. Code of Conduct V.

a. When questioned, should I become a prisoner of war, I am required to give name, rank, service number, and date of birth. I will evade answering further questions to the utmost of my ability. I will make no oral or written statements disloyal to my country and its allies or harmful to their cause.

b. When questioned, a prisoner of war is required by the Geneva Convention and this code to give name, rank, service number (Social Security number) and date of birth. The prisoner should make every effort to avoid giving the captor any additional information. The prisoner may communicate with captors on matters of health and welfare and additionally may write letters home and fill out a Geneva Convention capture card."

c. It is a violation of the Geneva Convention to place a prisoner under physical or mental duress, torture or any other form of coercion in an effort to secure information. If under such intense coercion, a POW discloses unauthorized information, makes an unauthorized statement or performs an unauthorized act, that prisoner's peace of mind and survival require a quick recovery of courage, dedication and motivation to resist anew each subsequent coercion.

d. Actions every POW should resist include making oral or written confessions and apologies, answering question-naires, providing personal histories, creating propaganda recordings, broadcasting appeals to other prisoners of war, providing any other material readily usable for propaganda purposes, appealing for surrender or parole, furnishing self-criticisms and communicating on behalf of the enemy to the detriment of the United States, its allies, its armed forces or other POWs.

e. Every POW should also recognize that any confession signed or any statement made may be used by the enemy as a false evidence that the person is a "war criminal" rather than a POW. Several countries have made reservations to the Geneva Convention in which they assert that a "war criminal" conviction deprives the convicted individual of prisoner-of-war status, removes that person from protection under the Geneva Convention and revokes all rights to repatriation until a prison sentence is served.

f. Recent experiences of American prisoners of war have proved that, although enemy interrogation sessions may be harsh and cruel, one can resist brutal mistreatment when the will to resist remains intact.

g. The best way for a prisoner to keep faith with country, fellow prisoners and self is to provide the enemy with as little information as possible.

YOUR SILENCE WILL NOT PROTECT YOU,

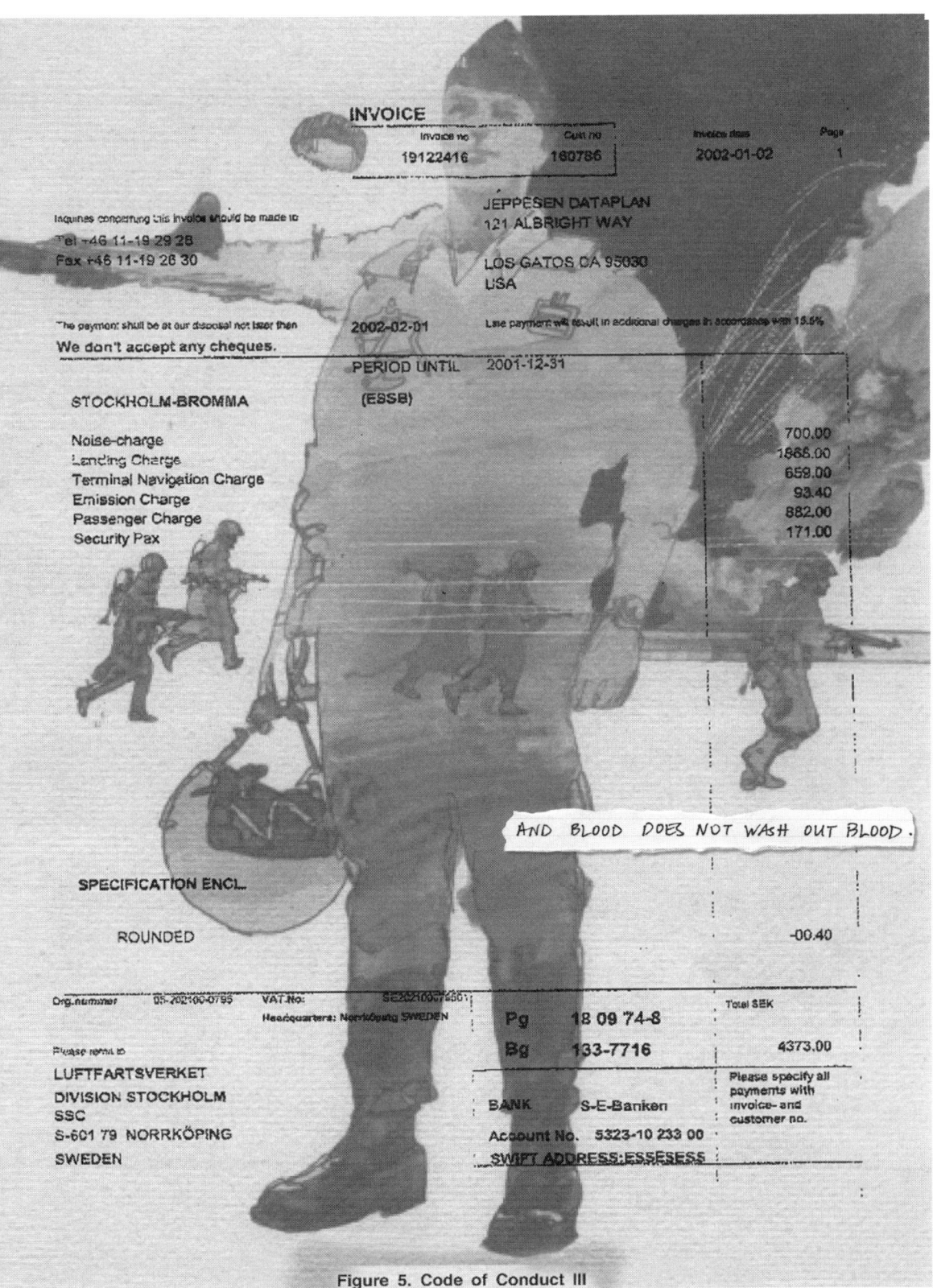

Figure 5. Code of Conduct III

TOP SECRET

Waterboard

...s below 18°C/64°F, detainees should be monitored for the

by far the most traumatic of the enhanced interrogation techniques.

the subject is immobilized on his back, and his forehead and eyes covered with a cloth A stream of water is directed at the upper lip.

This process can continue for several minutes, and involve up to 15 canteen cups of water. Ostensibly the primary desired effect derives from the sense of suffocation

trainers consider it their most effective technique, and deem it virtually irresistible

White noise or loud music

YOUR NAME, YOUR FACE: ONCE HELD AGAINST YOU

LIKE A LOADED GUN,

Shackling

Shackling in non-stressful positions requires only monitoring for the development of pressure sores with appropriate treatment and adjustment of the shackles as required.

TOP SECRET

TOP SECRET ▓▓▓▓

extended periods (up to 72 ▓ours) in a standing position can be approved if the hands are no higher than head level ▓nd weight is borne fully by the lower extremities.

Sleep deprivation

The standard approval for sleep deprivation, per se (without regard to shackling position) is 72 hours. Extension of sleep deprivation beyond 72 continuous hours is considered an enhanced measure. which requires D/CTC prior approval.

A rigid guide to medically approved use of the waterboard in essentially healthy individuals is not possible,

FOR TORTURERS ARE NOT BORN, BUT MADE...

NOTE: Examinations performed during periods of sleep deprivation should include the current number of hours without sleep; and, if only a brief rest preceded this period, the specifics of the previous deprivation also should be recorded.

Cramped confinement (Confinement boxes)

Detainees can he placed in awkward boxes. specifically constructed for this purpose,

confinement in the small box is allowable up to 2 hours. Confinement in the large box is limited to 8 consecutive hours,

TOP SECRET ▓▓▓▓

THEIR IDEA OF AN OPEN SECRET:

BLOOD, WATER, AND INVISIBLE INK...

TRAPPED IN THE PATH OF A SPIDER'S WEB

AS CLOUDS PASS THROUGH THE SKY

Source notes:

Pages 112–113: This was the first document released, after several months of total information blackout, about the 766 men known as the "special interest detainees"—men who were picked up by the U.S. Immigration and Naturalization Service (INS; now U.S. Immigration and Customs Enforcement, ICE) on immigration violations shortly after September 11, 2001, then classified as being of "special interest" in relation to the events of 9/11, and remanded to the custody of the FBI and the Department of Justice. Everything on the list is redacted except the arrest dates and the nationalities of those arrested.

Pages 114–115: A blank "form" National Security Letter (NSL) and a redacted list of all the NSLs served between 2001 and 2005. Both documents were released under the Freedom of Information Act (FOIA) as part of the American Civil Liberties Union's (ACLU) lawsuit on behalf of four Connecticut librarians who refused to release patron records in response to NSL requests.

Page 116: The redacted page comes from the CIA Inspector General report of 2004 (declassified though still very redacted in 2009) about the use of authorized and unauthorized "enhanced" interrogation techniques in CIA detention and interrogation operations. The prisoner classification chart is taken from Army Field Manual 19–4: *Military Police Battlefield & POW Operations*. The prison schematic is taken from a military PowerPoint presentation.

Page 117: Testimony and exhibits from a combatant status review tribunal (CSRT) held at GTMO for an Afghan prisoner named Muhebullah.

Page 118: The sample medical intake form is from U.S. Army Special Text 4–02–46, *Medical Support to Detainee Operations*. The text is extracted from the eighty-three–page-long log detailing the interrogations of and "softening techniques" applied to Mohamed al-Qahtani at GTMO between November 23, 2002 and November 1, 2003. The log was declassified in 2009, and Physicians for Human Rights cited its level of detail in their 2010 report as compelling evidence of human experimentation at GTMO.

Page 119: Watercolor portrait of Omar Khadr by Chitra Ganesh. The letter and the translation of the letter are taken from the exhibits in Khadr's CSRT transcript.

Page 120: Suicide note written by and documents related to the suicide of Hassiba Belbachir, who died in immigration detention. Among other things, her note asks, "What is the difference between prison and the tomb? In both places it is cold, dark and closed."

Page 121: Watercolor portrait of Affia Siddiqui by Chitra Ganesh. The text is taken from a psychiatric evaluation submitted as an exhibit for the prosecution in her 2010 trial.

Page 122: Text and illustration from *Code of the U.S. Fighting Force* (Army Pamphlet 360–512).

Page 123: Illustration from *Code of the U.S. Fighting Force* (Army Pamphlet 360–512). The document is an invoice from Jeppesen Dataplan (a Boeing subsidiary) for charges related to a rendition flight through Stockholm-Bromna airport, obtained via the unsuccessful ACLU lawsuit on behalf of rendition victims, *Bashmilah et al. v. Jeppesen*.

Page 124–125: Extracts from the CIA Inspector General's report cited above.

Page 126–127: Photograph by Mariam Ghani (Kabul, 2010). The text superimposed on the barbed wire is taken from firsthand accounts of experiences in secret prisons in Afghanistan, in particular the "prison of darkness" thought to be located somewhere underneath the grounds of Bagram Air Base.

Texts not linked to a specific source were either composed by the artists, derived from proverbs, or abstracted from fragments of other portions of the same/similar/related documents in the Index of the Disappeared archive.

CURATED SPACES provides a focus on contemporary artists whose work addresses social, historical, or political subject matter.

Arguably the most famous jumper photograph, often referred to as "The Falling Man," taken September 11, 2001. Credit: AP Photo/Richard Drew

"The Most Disturbing Aspects"

Apprehending Public Reaction to Photographs of the 9/11 Jumpers

Jaclyn Kirouac-Fram

I mention these [tragedies] to merely show that New York is peculiarly constructed to absorb almost anything that comes along . . . without inflicting the event on its inhabitants; so that every event is, in a sense, optional, and the inhabitant is in the happy position of being able to choose his spectacle and so conserve his soul.
— E. B. White, *Here Is New York*

On September 12, 2001, dailies across the United States released photographs of people falling from the highest floors of the World Trade Center's twin towers. At least two hundred people jumped from the upper floors of the towers on September 11 in the 102 minutes that elapsed between the first plane's impact and the collapse of the North Tower. Most jumped from the North Tower, fleeing smoke and flames from all four sides of the building.[1] These images show human forms tumbling through the air for a ten-second descent that spanned more than ninety floors. Some are in pairs, holding hands. Some are alone, their silhouettes stark against a bright blue sky, their size obscured by the enormity of the building beside them. Their arms and legs are extended, their clothing is billowing around them, and some have lost their shoes. Although distance and debris obscure their faces, their human form is unmistakable.

Radical History Review
Issue 111 (Fall 2011)   DOI 10.1215/01636545-1268749
© 2011 by MARHO: The Radical Historians' Organization, Inc.

For their decisions to publish these photographs, newspaper editors nation-wide faced harsh charges of exploitation and spectacle from their readers. Charges leveled against the papers implied that publishers had exploited the situation for sensationalistic purposes, stripped the subjects of their dignity, invaded their privacy, and "turned tragedy into leering pornography."[2] Beginning September 13, many newspaper editors openly apologized for their previous lapses and censored photographs of the people who came to be known in popular discourse as "the jumpers," and the latters' images quickly disappeared from the enormous photographic vocabulary henceforth used to describe and understand the attacks. In what was likely the most photographed disaster in history, images of people falling through the air became unanimously taboo in print and video media nationwide.[3] As the journalist Tom Junod wrote in 2003, "In a nation of voyeurs, the desire to face the most disturbing aspects of our most disturbing day was somehow ascribed to voyeurism, as though the jumpers' experience, instead of being central to the horror, was tangential to it, a sideshow best forgotten."[4]

As Benedict Anderson writes, "All profound changes in consciousness, by their very nature, bring with them characteristic amnesias. Out of such oblivions . . . spring narratives."[5] This essay explores public reactions to images of people jumping from the World Trade Center on September 11, 2001, and the narrative implications of critical amnesias resulting from the pictures' subsequent absence. By problematizing both the nature and the severity of public reaction to the photographs, I challenge the perception of these reactions as spontaneous or natural and explore the anxieties that underpin such resounding outcries of abhorrence and accusations of exploitation. It is not my intention to judge whether the media was correct in censoring these images. Rather, I seek to understand public reactions to the photographs and the consequences of their subsequent absence. What are the political implications inherent in the absence or trivialization of these photographs in future archives? What are potential consequences of collective memories and historical narratives that obscure individual, visible deaths on that day in deference to the heroic narratives foregrounded in the subsequent war on terror?

First, however, we must ask why the photographs of people falling from the World Trade Center towers appeared, judging from popular reactions, more disturbing than the often graphic images of war and violence that illustrate the pages of American periodicals on a regular basis. One aspect may be the frustrating anonymity of each body, whose individual identity—race, social class, occupation, and family status—is obscured by soft focus, motion blur, and distance from the photographer. It is impossible to identify the jumpers or, especially for those who lost friends and loved ones in the attack, to rule out potential identification. As Laura Tanner explains, "When the visual signs that we [are] encouraged to read as marks of individuality are stripped away and replaced with signs of impending death . . . photographs document their subjects' collapse into a kind of horrific anonymity."[6]

In the face of this anonymity, viewers cannot offer sympathy or attribute anxiety to a specific individual subject and are instead abandoned to regard a body atomized into any number of possible victims—including the viewers themselves or their loved ones, producing an appallingly intimate moment of self-identification. Furthermore, the awesome size of the towers denies viewers a glimpse of the overall scene; focal lengths that capture a discernable human form inevitably show fewer than fifteen consecutive floors of the buildings. This lack of scale abandons viewers to the terrifying prospect that they are witnessing not an isolated incident but, rather, a bewildering trauma experienced by countless people that day, any of whom could be imagined as a loved one, an acquaintance, or one's self.

Still, the ostensibly pathological appetite for looking at dead and dying bodies is fervent. "There is the satisfaction of being able to look at the image without flinching," Susan Sontag writes in *Regarding the Pain of Others*. "There is the pleasure of flinching."[7] Rather than inspiring revulsion, the single photograph's inherent stillness enhances its potential as a fetish object, existing for the viewer to look at, to put away, to look at again later. The people captured falling from the towers are ceaselessly falling, forever about to die, endlessly indulging this visual appetite. Walter Benjamin describes this power of photographic images as "the dynamite of the tenth of a second": the enhanced ability to view the minute details of movement.[8] To know how a thing falls is one thing; to see the motion of a body falling, broken down into fractions of a second, reveals much more about the mechanics of falling and provides space to study the moment frozen in time. Photographs of the jumpers present viewers with the opportunity to study them for prolonged periods of time, extending an invitation to try to understand how a body falls through space, how it moves through the air, how long it falls, how it must feel. The images compel viewers to imagine the terrifying conditions that would force a person to jump from monumental heights and to visualize how the body will land, to be simultaneously titillated and horrified by its inevitable landing. Again and again, viewers are denied the ability to resolve the imagined yet inevitable deaths. As Sontag writes, "The frustration of not being able to do anything about what the images show may be translated into an accusation of the indecency regarding such images."[9]

Furthermore, the jumpers' inability to demand respect from the photographer on the ground amplifies a sense of their powerlessness: the photographer has caught them unaware, helpless to refuse at the very private moment of their deaths. Looking at photographs of the jumpers forces viewers to reckon with the knowledge that those who jumped willingly took their lives, confronting the durable taboo against discussing suicide as anything other than a sinful, cowardly, and criminal act.[10] They may feel constrained to regard the jumpers as sinners or cowards caught in the act, labels that interfere with the desire to feel sympathy for the jumpers as innocent victims of a vicious attack. Viewers may interpret the publication of these photographs as an act of incrimination implicating the people who jumped, immortalizing them in what some would describe as a highly compromised, shameful position. Junod, when writing his article about the jumpers for *Esquire* in 2003, received the following response from the New York Medical Examiner's Office when he inquired after the number of people who jumped from the towers on September 11: "We don't like to say they jumped. They didn't jump. Nobody jumped. They were forced out, or blown out."[11] As Ellen Borakove, a spokesperson for the Medical Examiner's Office, explained to *USA Today*, "A jumper is somebody who goes to the office in the morning knowing that they will commit suicide."[12] All death certificates issued for victims of the World Trade Center attacks, including those who jumped, list the cause of death as homicide.

If photographs of dying bodies can evoke such critical, intensely personal responses, the question immediately arises: why are photographs of dead and dying victims of previous atrocities some of the most celebrated, honored photographs in history? Consider Eddie Adams's Pulitzer Prize–winning photograph of a Viet Cong fighter executed in the streets of Saigon, taken at the exact moment he is shot in the head, his face twisted in an expression of fear and pain. Consider Robert Capa's famous 1936 photograph of a Spanish Republican soldier, shot and falling backwards, his face blurry but decipherable, his arm extended, flinging his rifle to the left of the frame. Consider the hundreds of photographs that emerged from the Holocaust, of the dead and the dying standing, gaunt and skeletal, in death camp barracks. These photographs display the pain and suffering of dying, but they are commonly regarded as acceptable for view and for study, shaping our collective memories of the wars from which they emerged. We can celebrate these images, I argue, because they contain specificity and scale, the two elements that enable viewers to identify the victims and place sympathy on a single body or a knowable number of bodies on whom knowable perpetrators are enacting a violence beyond the victims' control, in a time safely ensconced in the past, often in a foreign land.

In addition to their anonymity, their startling intimacy, and their palpable invasiveness, the photographs of the 9/11 jumpers provide a rationale for abandonment that sets them apart from acclaimed and revered images of death and dying. First, one might argue that they are too painful and specific in their focus on individual bodies, superfluous in an already expansive field of traumatic images that emerged immediately following the attacks on September 11. Unlike images of death set in foreign lands, these images were created in the most iconic American city. To focus on the deaths of individual Americans in such a particularly American city is perhaps not only morbid when considering the abundance of sufficiently traumatic wider-angle images, but may also strike viewers as unpatriotic. Furthermore, these images are incongruous with the narrative of heroics and triumph that emerged immediately following the attacks. Because the photographic archive of historical events emerges after the rhetorical tone of remembrance has been set, photographic archives construct and shape the historical record according to accepted ideologies. The collection and reception of representative imagery, therefore, is tied to the specific context in which the images emerge and through which we judge them as appropriate or inappropriate representations.[13] We do not build an archive from every possible image, but rather make selections based on narratives we hope to illustrate.

So while news media and media consumers agreed that the World Trade Center attacks were unprecedented, many Americans searched for historical antecedents as a way to direct their understanding of the events and frame the emerging narrative. In press accounts that appeared in the days following the attacks, interviewees, pundits, commentators, President George W. Bush, and members of his administration repeatedly mentioned the attacks on Pearl Harbor as a reference point, a suggestion that performed significant cultural work. Collective memories and cultural knowledge of what unfolded in the weeks following the attacks on Pearl Harbor, of the triumph of the United States in World War II, legitimized the subsequent declaration of war on Afghanistan, garnered national support for that war and the administration's subsequent declaration of war with Iraq, and positioned the 9/11 attacks as the opening salvo for an extended war in the Middle East. Heroism in the indomitable spirit of the opening days of World War II became the overriding sentiment, buttressed by the highly publicized sufferings of victims' families.[14] Wartime public morale necessitates images of nationalism and strength; in this context, the media's implicit censorship of these images was illegible and relatively invulnerable. Implications of suffering or weakness, most notably present in images of people jumping from the towers, were not greatly missed. They became what Shawn Michelle Smith describes as "signifying absences" in the larger image archive of that day, their conspicuous silences marking the boundaries of a controlling narrative of heroism, nationalism, and revenge.[15]

Although readers chastised media outlets for their initial publication of such discomfiting imagery, the lack of visible bodies in the dominant narratives of the World Trade Center attacks created an equally distressing cognitive gap for many grieving Americans. As Donna Bassin writes, "Mourning requires a confrontation with the emptiness occasioned by loss. It requires a body and a place."[16] Newspaper articles in the days following the attacks focused almost obsessively on the distressing lack of bodies recovered from the wreckage, and on the consequential lack of closure for grieving families. People who did not personally suffer the death of anyone in the attacks experienced a similarly profound and perplexing sense of what Tanner describes as phantom grief, the struggle "to apprehend as lived experience a loss that both is and is not virtual."[17] Iconic images of the crumbling twin towers left viewers without an anchor for their grief or understanding; the dying bodies inside were invisible, an abstracted number, vanished. Despite numerous obituaries, memorials, and printed biographies of the dead that emerged following the attacks, Americans wrestled with their inability to reckon with actual people's deaths, to embody their imaginings of death, "to access the object of a deeply felt but anonymous loss."[18] Photographs of the people who jumped from the towers may have provided one opportunity to assuage that sense of disorientation by allowing both for a more personal connection to the events and for a deeper understanding of the tragic magnitude of each individual death.

Photographs outline what elements our society has chosen to contemplate, what our society has chosen to know about past events. To this end, the uncollected photographs and videos of people who jumped from the top floors of the World Trade Center can serve as a powerful counterarchive, offering an alternative understanding of the events of September 11, 2001. In a survey of photo editors who decided to publish one or more of these images, one editor states, "Something like this, I think it's our duty to bring out the exclamation points and the visual sledgehammers so that we can tell this in the enormity of the story, as best as we possibly can."[19] Another editor concurs: "The horror of the event and the magnitude just demanded that you get that across in a very forceful and powerful way, [and] when you have the image before you, it just helps convey what was really going on that day. You can't *not* run a picture like that."[20] Although photographs of lynching victims taken in the late nineteenth century and the early twentieth differ in significant ways from those of the jumpers, I suggest a similar argument in favor of viewing both sets of controversial, traumatic images: to recognize the events and the systems that supported them as real, to ensure that they are not forgotten. Looking at these photographs, viewers participate in what Dora Apel describes as "the responsibility of historical witnessing."[21]

That the images described throughout this essay carry evidence of anguish possibly traumatizing to viewers constitutes no reason to ban them. While I am neither prescribing the repeated viewing of the photographs nor advocating their wider circulation, I do suggest that their free circulation may have enabled a shift in their meaning away from personal attack and toward something resembling reflection.[22] In this shift, photographs that prick our awareness of atrocity and enlarge our sense of injustice may not rouse a sense of helplessness as much as they may arouse a sense of reality, better equipping us to take steps toward halting violence now and in the future. It is difficult to review and revisit violence, to strive for reflection rather than spectacle, but it constitutes urgent and important work. As Sontag reminds us, "Heartlessness and amnesia seem to go together."[23]

Notes

1.   Dennis Cauchon and Martha T. Moore, "Desperation Forced a Horrific Decision," *USA Today*, September 3, 2002.
2.   Tom Junod, "The Falling Man," *Esquire* 140, no. 3 (September 2003): 179.
3.   For a discussion of the photographic documentation of 9/11 and its aftermath, see Barbara Kirshenblatt-Gimblett, "Kodak Moments, Flashbulb Memories: Reflections on 9/11," *Drama Review* 47 (2003): 11–48.

4. Junod, "Falling Man," 180. Junod explains that between 7 and 8 percent of those who died in New York City that day jumped from a building; if we take into account only the North Tower, which suffered impact first but stood for much longer than the South Tower, and from which most people jumped, that percentage rises to just under 20 percent. Most claims of exploitation and sensationalism rely on the argument that only few people jumped.

5. Benedict Anderson, Imagined Communities: Reflections on the Origin and Spread of Nationalism (New York: Verso, 1991): 208.

6. Laura E. Tanner, *Lost Bodies: Inhabiting the Borders of Life and Death* (Ithaca, NY: Cornell University Press, 2006), 55.

7. Susan Sontag, *Regarding the Pain of Others* (New York: Picador, 2003), 41.

8. Walter Benjamin, *Illuminations*, ed. Hannah Arendt, trans. Harry Zohn (New York: Harcourt, Brace and World, 1955): 238–39.

9. Sontag, *Regarding the Pain of Others*, 117.

10. Thomas Szasz, *Fatal Freedom: The Ethics and Politics of Suicide* (Westport, CT: Praeger, 1999), 9; Margaret Pabst Battin, *Ethical Issues in Suicide* (Englewood Cliffs, NJ: Prentice Hall, 1995), 53–54.

11. Junod, "The Falling Man," 180.

12. Cauchon and Moore, ""Desperation Forced a Horrific Decision."

13. Susan Sontag, *On Photography* (New York: Picador, 1977), 19.

14. Elaine Tyler May, "Echoes of the Cold War: The Aftermath of September 11 at Home," in *September 11 in History: A Watershed Moment?*, ed. Mary L. Dudziak (Durham, NC: Duke University Press, 2003), 35–36.

15. Shawn Michelle Smith, *Photography on the Color Line: W. E. B. Du Bois, Race, and Visual Culture* (Durham, NC: Duke University Press, 2004), 7.

16. Donna Bassin, "A Not So Temporary Occupation Inside Ground Zero," quoted in Tanner, *Lost Bodies*, 230.

17. Ibid, 226.

18. Ibid.

19. Renee Martin Kratzer and Brian Kratzer, "How Newspapers Decided to Run Disturbing 9/11 Photos," in *Media in an American Crisis: Studies of September 11, 2001*, ed. Elinor Kelley Grusin and Sandra H. Utt (New York: University Press of America, 2005), 32–33.

20. Ibid., 30.

21. Dora Apel, "On Looking: Lynching Photographs and Legacies of Lynching after 9/11 (Exhibition Review)," *American Quarterly* 55 (2003): 459.

22. This suggestion owes much to Judith Butler's position on the implications of banning hate speech in Judith Butler, *Excitable Speech: A Politics of the Performative* (New York: Routledge, 1997), 127–64.

23. Sontag, *Regarding the Pain of Others*, 114–15. In this section, Sontag describes the positive implications of a shift from helplessness to reality, one provoked by images of violence.

Jeff Danziger's wordless single-panel cartoon appeared in the *Washington Post* on September 12, 2001.
Credit: Jeff Danziger, distributed by the New York Times Syndicate

New York City, 9/11, and Comics

Kent Worcester

New York City enjoys a special relationship to the cartoon arts. Numerous illustrators and cartoonists live and work in the city, which has served as a magnet for commercial and fine artists since the nineteenth century. According to William B. Scott and Peter M. Rutkoff, "New York became the center of American art" in the "aftermath of the Civil War," when it "eclipsed its earlier rivals, like Boston and Philadelphia."[1] A profusion of publishers, distributors, print shops, advertising agencies, corporate headquarters, syndication outfits, and graphic design firms, many of them located in Lower Manhattan, helped ensure the city's preeminence in the commercial arts as well. The emergence of superhero, mystery, adventure, and other comic-book genres in the late 1930s and 1940s was itself a by-product of the informal circuits that linked the city's printers, illustrators, pulp writers, low-rent publishers, and bottom-feeding entrepreneurs—"geeks and gangsters," as Gerard Jones has affectionately described them.[2]

More recently, the shock of 9/11 generated a long wave of graphic commentary, memoir, and thinly disguised fiction from cartoonists and graphic artists who in many cases watched the towers burn with their own eyes. While individual filmmakers, poets, playwrights, and novelists have addressed 9/11–related themes, 9/11 and its aftermath resonated in a singular way within an industry and subculture that remains anchored in the five boroughs. The destruction and horror of the attack on downtown Manhattan affected many cartoonists personally, and in a few cases inspired their best work. The events produced some cartoon kitsch as well. The outpouring of 9/11 comics speaks to the reassuring intimacy of the handcrafted

Radical History Review
Issue 111 (Fall 2011)   DOI 10.1215/01636545-1268758
© 2011 by MARHO: The Radical Historians' Organization, Inc.

text-image, the undiminished role of cultural geography, and the long-standing connection between the city and visual narrative.

All Kinds of Formats

Comics and cartoons come in many shapes and sizes, from editorial cartoons, magazine cartoons, and comic strips to comic books, *manga* (Japanese comic art), and graphic novels. The responses to 9/11 also assumed a variety of forms, from single-panel graphics and references in daily comic strips to visits to ground zero in the pages of superhero titles. Many of these pieces appeared within hours or days of the events themselves.[3] Syndicated cartoonists for weekly alternative newspapers weighed in, as did newspaper editorial cartoonists and mini-comic self-publishers. Hand-drawn images provided a means of mourning the dead, conveying anxiety, reaffirming civic values, and, for some cartoonists, of sounding the alarm.

While many of the resulting cartoons were single-panel, single-tier pieces, or ones otherwise limited in scale, the events of 9/11 also led to the publication of a number of longer-format works. For example, two industry veterans, Sid Jacobson and Ernie Colón, produced a full-length graphic adaptation of *The 9/11 Commission Report* that became a national best seller. Their book, the first full-scale effort to use comics to narrate the 9/11 attacks as history, soon turned up on high school reading lists and in airport bookshops. It was one of several nonfiction graphic titles that made an impression on book retailers and trade publishers in the first decade of the twenty-first century.[4] In addition to depicting the plot of using passenger planes to attack targets in the United States, as well as its immediate aftermath, the book symbolized the medium's newfound respectability as a purveyor of public policy–minded historiography.

Deploying an array of comic book devices, from silhouettes and cinematic close-ups to splash pages, timelines, and a restrained use of color, the creators transformed the report of the 9/11 Commission (National Commission on Terrorist Attacks upon the United States) into a visually appealing text. His goal as an artist, Colón later remembered, was to "make everything look as neutral as possible . . . you have to make the image work on the page but you also have to be true to the historical record."[5] In this context, the "historical record" was the report itself, and the graphic adaptation was accordingly boxed in by the self-imposed limitations of the commission's own research agenda. But Jacobson and Colón kept their partnership going. Their subsequent collaboration, a work of "graphic journalism" on the war on terror, did not find as many buyers, but it offered a carefully researched, factually grounded, and relentless critique of U.S. foreign policy under the Bush administration.[6]

The category of "9/11 comics" is sufficiently well established to merit its own Wikipedia page. As the entry points out, the big comics companies published anthologies that brought together dozens of pencillers, writers, inkers, and colorists.

While DC Comics came out with the modestly titled *9/11: September 11, 2001 (The World's Finest Comic Book Writers and Artists Tell Stories to Remember)*, Marvel published no fewer than three 9/11–related charity projects, including *Heroes: The World's Greatest Superhero Creators Honor the World's Greatest Heroes*, a book of sixty-four full-color illustrations that paid tribute to the city's police officers, firefighters, and emergency workers, and *A Moment of Silence*, which featured a quartet of wordless stories based on actual events.[7]

Three mid-sized companies, Dark Horse, Chaos! Comics, and Image Comics, collaborated on *9/11: September 11, 2001 (Artists Respond)*, which was issued in tandem with the DC volume. A smaller publisher, Alternative Comics, rounded up nearly a hundred artists and writers to contribute "personal non-fiction accounts of their experiences related to the tragedy" to *9/11: Emergency Relief*.[8] The beneficiaries of these fund-raising efforts were the United Way, the Red Cross, the Survivors Fund, the World Trade Center Relief Fund, and the Twin Towers Fund. As Wikipedia intones, "9–11 comics emerged following the terrorist attacks in New York City, Washington, DC, and Pennsylvania," when "cartoonists turned to art to express their grief and support."[9]

The category "9/11 comics" potentially encompasses a far greater range of material than the Wikipedia entry allows, of course. Almost any comic book or graphic novel published in the past decade that touches on foreign policy, for example, is likely to reference 9/11, either explicitly or by implication. Two obvious examples are Ted Rall's *To Afghanistan and Back*, published in 2002, and David Axe's *War Fix*, published in 2006.[10] Rall is probably the better known of the two. His thick-lined, argumentative cartoons are widely syndicated, and he has authored or edited more than a dozen graphic memoirs, graphic novels, and cartoon collections. He was a regular guest on Bill Maher's *Politically Incorrect* when he published a tart, six-panel cartoon in early 2002, "Terror Widows," which depicted some of the spouses of 9/11 victims as "greedy publicity hounds who turned personal tragedies into lucrative book deals."[11] Once the controversy broke, the *New York Times* pulled the strip from its Web site, and Bill O'Reilly brought Rall onto his prime-time cable show so he could call him a jerk. The conservative commentator Alan Keyes went so far as to suggest that supposedly anti-American cartoons by Rall and others of his ilk should be banned: "Assaults on the decent judgment of American citizens regarding the just and noble character of a national struggle are, literally, attempts to poison the sovereign. And we should not tolerate those who seek to debase our judgment and destroy our unity and resolve."[12] As pundits debated the merits of Rall's stick-in-your-eye approach, the cartoon provocateur was making his way to Central Asia as a nonembedded journalist who used text and images to "separate propaganda from reality; in other words, to eliminate some of our puzzlement." "America must have its vengeance," he ironically suggested in the opening chapter of *To Afghanistan and Back*. "We're not the kind of people to sit around and mourn a few thousand dead office workers when there's some serious ass to kick. So we'll bomb or invade or something. It won't matter, but that doesn't matter. It's what we do."[13] Rall's follow-up project, *Silk Road to Ruin: Is Central Asia the New Middle East?*, similarly combined cartoons, photographs, and short essays to give readers a taste of how the post-9/11 war on terror was playing out in Afghanistan and in neighboring countries. In the summer of 2010, Rall returned to Central Asia, where he filed "cartoon blogs" via satellite for the *Los Angeles Times*.[14]

While Rall is a cartoonist turned journalist, Axe is a journalist turned graphic memoirist. In the mid-2000s he joined with the illustrator Steven Olexa to produce a memoir of his stint as an embedded journalist in Iraq. Like Rall, Axe had long been interested in war and foreign policy. The ramped-up war on terror provided him with the opportunity to witness the consequences of post-9/11 decision making up close. Not surprisingly, it also placed him in dangerous situations. As the concluding pages reveal, he nearly lost his life as a result of a roadside IED (improvised explosive device), yet found himself making plans to return to Iraq even as he attempted in vain to reconnect with his girlfriend. Like Rall, Axe has become a "war junkie."[15] Both creators remain critical of U.S. foreign policy even as they relish the chance to observe the world's mightiest engine of chaos in action.

The impact of 9/11 and its aftermath also manifested in comics that had little or nothing to do with U.S. foreign policy. The collapse of the towers served as a dramatic backdrop for all sorts of stories. *The Alcoholic* (2008), a DC/Vertigo graphic novel written by Jonathan Ames and illustrated by Dean Haspiel, features as a main character a writer with a drinking problem. After spending the evening of September 10, 2001 in an alcohol- and drug-fueled daze, Jonathan A. wakes to discover the towers on fire. Like many thousands of city residents, he witnesses the event firsthand. "After the second tower collapsed, I went to the roof of my building and I could see the smoke in the distance." He tries to donate blood at a local hospital, but is turned away because "they couldn't take any more blood." "All you could hear was sirens. That's one of the things I remember most from those days—the constant wail of sirens." He thinks about the sirens as he looks out with others on the smoke pouring out of Lower Manhattan.[16]

In this kind of story, 9/11 serves as a reminder that catastrophe can jolt even the most self-involved characters out of their slumbers. In *The Alcoholic*, Haspiel's stark depictions of the burning towers carry undeniable metaphorical resonance. For one, they serve as a wake-up call. In the aftermath of 9/11, Jonathan A. starts to reach out to his neighbors and pays closer attention to his surroundings. In short, he learns to care again. At the same time, he is fearful and parties hard. Only belatedly does he realize that "you don't get everything you want in life." The final page, a lovely single-panel illustration, shows Mr. A. pausing wistfully in front of a neighborhood bar. Even the shock of 9/11 did not suffice to fix his condition.

The metaphorical quality of 9/11 can be invoked by stories that may not specifically refer to the day's events. An example is arguably provided by one of the best-reviewed graphic novels of the past ten years, David Mazzucchelli's *Asterios Polyp* (2009). The improbably named Polyp is a tenured professor of architecture with strong opinions about art, design, and urban living. For most of the story he struggles to impose his mechanistic and binary view of the world on students, colleagues, and lovers. He learns to regret his dogmatism when he falls in love with a more intuitive colleague, whom he marries and subsequently pushes away. From the standpoint of 9/11 and comics, what is noteworthy is the way the novel both begins and ends with violence that comes as a bolt from the blue. The underlying message, which practically screams "9/11," both as a shared experience and as a powerful cultural narrative, is that the protagonist—and by implication the reader—needs to get his act together *right now*, before the world falls to pieces.[17]

Editorial Cartoons

That sense of urgency also emerged in the dozens of editorial cartoons that appeared in daily papers in the days and weeks following 9/11. Every editorial cartoonist in the country would have felt obligated to come up with material related to the events, if only a grim-faced Uncle Sam accompanied by a quote by Franklin D. Roosevelt ("a day that shall live in infamy" etc.). While this example is hypothetical, two researchers, Donna Hoffman and Alison Howard, in a 2007 study titled "Representations of 9–11 in Editorial Cartoons," found that "of the memorializing cartoon type, there were three dominant themes: WWII references, patriotism, and remembrances of heroes and victims."[18] Only rarely did cartoonists use 9/11 iconography to make unambiguously political statements. "Have the images of the 9–11 attacks become a constricted symbol?" the researchers asked. "The answer appears to be a qualified yes. Few cartoonists have relied on these images for social and political commentary, but yet these images are an important visual representation of a pivotal event in American social and political history."[19]

A useful resource for tracking U.S. (and Canadian) editorial cartooning is the *Best Editorial Cartoons of the Year* series, which has been edited by Charles Brooks since the early 1970s. Brooks is a past president of the Association of American Editorial Cartoonists, and as an editor he often seems more attuned to center-right opinion than to liberal and left views. His annual volumes make it plain that progressives do not dominate the profession. Indifferent to the efforts of so-called alternative cartoonists, whose work appears in weekly urban newspapers and nowadays online, Brooks tends to stick with reliably mainstream figures whose work appears in daily newspapers that serve large and mid-sized cities. Some of his favorite cartoonists lean in a liberal direction, while others are conservative, but he plainly disfavors the work of cartoonists who regularly publish in the left-wing press such as Tom Tomorrow, Jen Sorensen, Keith Knight, Matt Wuerker, Ruben Bolling, Ward Sutton, Terry LaBan, and so on.

The 2002 edition of the volume, which covers the period from the summer of 2001 to the summer of 2002, largely consists of oversized, single-panel pen-and-ink drawings with word balloons and the occasional caption. The volume reproduces 427 cartoons by roughly two hundred creators, of which nearly two hundred refer to 9/11 and/or to the war on terror in some way. Without the 9/11 material the 2002 edition would appear a little flimsy. True to its documentary mission, the book offers a snapshot of how newspaper cartoonists responded to one of the decade's biggest news stories.

The book's cover features a drawing by Mike Luckovich of a wide-eyed, tear-stained Statue of Liberty, while the back-cover illustration, by Joe Heller, shows a police officer and a firefighter standing together amid Lower Manhattan's smoldering wreckage ("The Twin Towers of New York"). The volume includes a cartoon by Rall, but it constitutes one of his tamer efforts.[20] The covers and the inside pages suggest that editorial cartoonists tended to respond to the attacks with somber imagery that often relied on familiar national symbols and tropes. Hoffman and Howard argue that "images of 9–11 were primarily used in non-political ways. They were used to memorialize the event. . . . In no way did these cartoons attempt to provoke any feelings other than sorrow, rage, dismay and patriotism."[21] Yet their argument does not convince entirely. Inciting feelings of, say, rage and patriotism may be "non-political" in the sense of not calling on the reader to support a particular political party or a proposed public policy, but it most certainly is "political" if we take the idea of cultural politics seriously. Only a small percentage of the cartoons in the Brooks book celebrate Bush's presidency, but a much larger percentage articulate the kinds of concerns and anxieties that helped him win the 2004 election.

Many of the best editorial cartoons of 2001–2 as selected by the volume are somewhat predictable — Lady Liberty weeps, Old Glory waves, bald eagles soar, firefighters march through heaven's gates, and Osama bin Laden burns in hell. While many of the cartoons incorporate terms like *terrorists* and *Bin Laden*, the words *Muslim* and *Islam* remain conspicuously absent. Still, for every image that strikes a note of mourning, another adopts a more belligerent stance. While some illustrations express open-faced wonder — *How could this have happened?* — others treat the attacks as declarations of war. In the days and weeks that followed 9/11, many editorial cartoonists called for military action against al-Qaeda in general and Bin Laden in particular. In many instances, these calls came from papers published in the southern or western parts of the United States. From the examples provided by Brooks's volume, there seems to have been an inverse correlation between proximity to the attacks and blanket support for military action.

Quite a few of the reprinted cartoons are aimed at the Taliban — "Say, didn't we have mountains here before?" asks one Taliban soldier as he looks out onto smoldering ruins and a smoke-filled sky. Several depict Bin Laden running from U.S. planes, fighting with his supporters or cowering in a cave. "Oh Osama . . . it's time for *you* to come out and be a martyr," smirks a turban-wearing warrior. More than a few works express unqualified confidence in the country's armed forces. In a two-panel cartoon by Dick Locher, an aircraft pilot shouts "Mayday" into his headphones as a bearded man threatens him with a knife. In the next panel, we see a stream of bombs pouring out of a U.S. fighter plane. "Payday," reads the caption. Some newspaper cartoonists seemed captivated by the possibility that a spirit of raw vengeance could motivate the country's foreign policy.[22]

A few of the cartoons strike a didactic note. In one, by Richard Crowson of the *Wichita Eagle*, a neighbor asks, "Heard you were doing some major re-prioritizing. . . . What's got into you?" "September 11," the father replies, while standing with his son. On the windowsill we see three oversized objects—an American flag, labeled "patriotism," a framed picture ("family"), and a religious text ("spirituality"). Some of the featured cartoons now seem ironic rather than sentimental, however. A single-panel graphic by John Branch shows two men talking amid the rubble of the towers. "Some are concerned that our airstrikes could end up making things worse . . . ," one of the men says. "It's hard for me to think in terms of 'worse' right now . . . ," says the other. In view of the meager results and extraordinary toll of the wars in Afghanistan and Iraq, this failure to think in terms of worst-case scenarios seems more than a little complacent.

A number of editorial cartoonists could not contain their admiration for the forty-third president. "Isn't Bush doing a great job?" asks a woman as she watches the news. "Shut up, Tipper," Al Gore bristles, in a wry cartoon by Mike Peters. In a cluster of cartoons, George and Barbara Bush express unabashed pride in the accomplishments of their younger son. "My . . . how you've grown since we last saw you, son!" they exclaim, as they look up at a massive pair of cowboy boots. In general, the period immediately following 9/11 presented a bonanza of patriotic iconography. Robert Ariail's no-nonsense rendering of a muscular Uncle Sam rolling up his sleeves as if preparing for battle is probably as representative of the reanimated nationalism on display in these pages as any of Brooks's selections.[23]

Superheroes

Only a couple of the cartoonists represented in *Best Editorial Cartoons of the Year* were based in New York. The opposite was the case for the DC and Marvel charity projects, which heavily relied on local talent. Marvel even recruited Rudy Giuliani to write a foreword to *A Moment of Silence*, in which "America's mayor" praised comic book publishers for making "their home in our City. I think we all now realize that we do not have to read fiction to find examples of heroism." In turn, Marvel's president, Bill Jemas, thanked the mayor for "helping to lead a nation in one of its most trying moments." The anthology's wordless stories were suitably respectful, with numerous panels showing rescue workers pulling rubble from the site. Some of the artwork had a sedate, painterly quality in keeping with the solemnity of the moment.

A couple of the stories favored the slick, almost greasy look that has become Marvel's house style in recent years. A greater range of visual styles was on display in the *Heroes* collection, which featured lush spreads by big guns like George Perez, Paul Dini, Frank Miller, Richard Corben, Jim Lee, and Frank Quitely.[24]

Produced in a matter of weeks, the benefit volumes published by DC and Image/Chaos!/Dark Horse "undoubtedly enjoyed the smoothest ride in the marketplace," reported Michael Dean in a 9/11–themed issue of the *Comics Journal*. "Due to DC's considerable clout and because it was perceived as a definitive joint comics-industry effort," the two books were "put together with the cost-free cooperation of every participant, including printer Quebecor World Montreal and suppliers Sun Chemical Inc., UPM-Kymmene, and Kruger." According to Dean, the Dark Horse volume raised roughly $230,000 out of a print run of forty thousand copies. He does not provide figures for the DC book.[25]

The two volumes resemble each other so much, complains the critic Robert Fiore in the same *Comics Journal* issue, that "it seems pointless to differentiate between them, and between them they define the parameters of their short-lived genre" (the 9/11 comics fund-raiser).[26] While he praises Sergio Aragones for producing "some truly beautiful work in service of an unfortunately pedestrian script," he lambastes Stan Lee for "really taking the fruitcake" by coming up with an "undiscovered Aesop's fable" that pits good mice against bad mice and bad mice against a "benevolent elephant." He also pours scorn on a story by Alex Simmons and Angelo Torres, titled "Spirit," in which Abraham Lincoln, Winston Churchill, Martin Luther King, Golda Meir, and other historical figures deliver sermons from beyond on the value of peace. "It looks like the statesman's version of the stateroom scene in *A Night at the Opera*," Fiore quipped.[27]

Fiore had a point about "Spirit," but he overstates the similarity between the two volumes—for one thing, the visuals in the Dark Horse collection are more eclectic, with half rendered in black and white and half in color (the DC volume is full color, which in this context implies a mainstream aesthetic). Several of its contributors, such as Sam Henderson, Michael Kupperman, Eric Drooker, Mitch O'Connell, and Jim Mahfood, would have proved a little too experimental or noncommercial for a company like DC at the turn of the century. The tonal contrast between Drooker's melancholic cover, which places a lonely artist perched on top of one of Manhattan's skyscrapers, and Alex Ross's gleaming image of an awe-struck Superman gazing up at 9/11 heroes, is striking. At the same time, both books intentionally steer clear of the kind of belligerent fist shaking that characterizes many of the contributions to *Best Editorial Cartoons of the Year*. "We had stories to tell and images to share," Paul Levitz, DC's president, wrote. "We needed to lift our pens, measure them against the swords of vengeance and the crumpled steel of anger."[28]

While the DC and Dark Horse volumes are filled with competent and in some cases stunning artwork, the implausible scale of the day's events inspired mostly timid scripts in which characters talk on the phone, stare at the television screen, and struggle to find something meaningful to say. "My thoughts immediately go to friends in New York," writes Stan Sakai in one of the volumes' innumerable monologues. "Man, what a beautiful day," Mark Crilley says to himself, as he strolls his safe suburban streets. "What a beautiful . . . *horrible* day . . . ," he then corrects himself, as he pictures a passenger jet crashing into a World Trade Center skyscraper.[29]

Even Superman indulges in a little solipsism as he reflects on how he can "defy the laws of gravity . . . ignore the principles of physics," and "breathe in the vacuum of space." "The one thing I can not do," he reluctantly admits, "is break free from the fictional pages where I live and breathe."[30] Most of the contributions simply emphasized the storyteller's shaken state at 9/11 and his or her gratitude for the bravery of the emergency workers. One exception, Darwyn Cooke's one-page story "Human Values," drew a vivid contrast between how the labor market rewards nurses and firefighters, on the one hand, and pop stars and movie actors, on the other.[31] Cooke's piece aside, few contributions to these fund-raising efforts embraced a skeptical view of our own moral certainties. On the other hand, these high-profile mainstream projects embraced liberal humanism and eschewed anti-Muslim rhetoric. The last thing they sought was to place the nation on a war footing.

Alternative Comics

Compared to the DC and Dark Horse projects, the Alternative Comics fund-raising volume showed some teeth. The opening one-page story, by Harvey Pekar and Tony Millionaire, in which Pekar listens to the radio and says to himself, "I bet it don't get any easier from here on . . . ," sets the tone.[32] Rather than encouraging platitudes, the publisher gave contributors to the volume permission to confront difficult questions of foreign policy and political leadership.[33] While the volume included nuanced reminiscences, such as Jessica Abel's formally inventive untitled story in which a conversation between two couples dissolves into a white light of nothingness, it also left room for Fly's astringent reflections on the attack from her vantage point as a squatter on the Lower East Side.[34]

"Now we are 'encouraged' to give up our democratic rights in order to preserve democracy," she mused. "Our 'leaders' panic and declare war on terrorism to wipe evil off the face of the earth—it sounds like a bad stupor hero comic . . . "[35] Or, as Tom Hart's surrogate antihero Hutch Owen grouched, "now we'll roll over more countries, drill in Alaska, deny every treaty left standing and re-elect those oil baron bastards in four years."[36] For my money, the burned-out pessimism expressed by Fly and Hart holds up better than, say, Joe Kubert's pious liberalism: "The efforts of people with conscience will result in a better and stronger nation, and a world that must eventually live in peace. There is no alternative, after all."[37]

Critical perspectives could also be found in the 9/11 special issue of *World*

War 3 Illustrated that came out at the end of 2001. An irregularly published anthology of political comics, *World War 3 Illustrated* was launched at the dawn of the
Reagan era and occupies a unique position in the comics subculture. Overseen by
an all-volunteer collective, the magazine offers a forum for cartoonists who want
to express fiercely held points of view without having to censor themselves. As the
editor Kevin Pyle recalled, "There were a lot of artists who contributed to that issue
[no. 32] who have said, '9/11 has me thinking about these issues but I don't have
anywhere to put this stuff, because everyone is holding back.'" "There was definitely
a chill in the air," agreed the *World War 3 Illustrated* cofounder Peter Kuper, in
the same interview. "One of my first coherent thoughts after 9/11 was, 'Hmm, this
would be a good time to be working on an issue of WW3.'"[38] Along with strips and
stories by established leftist cartoonists, including Kuper, Tom Tomorrow, Ward Sutton, and Seth Tobocman, the special issue included a sequence of eerie sketches by
Mac McGill and a memorable full-page drawing by Sue Coe. There were not a lot of
superheroes, or even unqualified heroism, in the collection, but there were plenty of
references to loyalty oaths, the Middle East, and the oil companies.[39]

    World War 3 Illustrated was already known for its commitment to grim-
faced, reality-based cartooning. For the magazine's artist-editors, the events of 9/11
could be understood and represented within preexisting visual and narrative frame-
works. For visual humorists and satirists, however, 9/11 posed a special set of problems. The syndicated humor cartoonist Ruben Bolling, for example, initially found
it difficult to put pen to paper:

> One of the reasons was that I didn't really care that much about comics right
> after September 11th. The other thing is that every aspect of what happened
> and the implications of it translate so poorly to what I do as a satirist and
> ironist. It's light-hearted stuff. I didn't know what I was going to do. I was at a
> loss for how this was going to affect my comic that week, in the weeks to come,
> and, really, my career. So the first one I did was a *Super-Fun-Pak Comix* . . .
> which is a form I use when I do a fake newspaper comics page. I would use
> a normal set-up, but every single time the punch line would be "Terrorists
> destroyed the World Trade Center killing thousands." It was much more
> heartfelt than a lot of my work.[40]

The result was one of the more powerful responses to 9/11 to emerge out of the comics subculture. Rather than adopting a sedate, generic, or painterly approach, and
switching off his instincts as a humorist, Bolling found a way to mash together silly
comics conventions with a New Yorker's characteristic bluntness. A follow-up strip
dropped a Tintin-like figure named "Billy Dare, Boy Adventurer" into the comic
strip universe of his nemesis, "Dr. Mordu." This strip was equally deft in integrating
contemporary history and comic book norms. "I'm the good guy in this strip," Billy
Dare insists. "No, you're the bad guy," replies one of Dr. Mordu's followers. "When
did I get in that insane strip?" Billy asks his faithful parrot, Quentin, in the final

Peter Kuper's parody of Harvey Comics cover art of the 1960s places President Bush at the center of a cast of lovable characters. Credit: Peter Kuper

panel. "They think you've *always* been in it," replies the wise bird.[41] Asked about the reaction that his post-9/11 strips provoked, Bolling said that "every cartoonist I've talked to said they got the weirdest emails after 9/11 . . . I got many emails that were extremely positive. But then there were a few people who were clearly misinformed. The venom that they put forth in their emails was unbelievable. They really personally attacked me for what they thought was trivializing the tragedy."[42]

Long Shadow

Art Spiegelman's *In The Shadow of No Towers* (2004) addressed both the phenomenology and the political metaphysics of 9/11. The book consists of ten poster-sized cartoon essays that trace the author's evolving relationship to the World Trade Center attack, followed by seven equally massive reprints of early twentieth-century newspaper strips. Along with thousands of others, Spiegelman and his family experienced 9/11 firsthand. He depicts the actual attack in the second page, where he reports that his "daughter had just started high school at the foot of the towers three days before." He shows himself carrying a bald eagle around his neck like an albatross. "Everything's changed! Awk! Go out and shop! Awk!" screeches the bird. Off to one side, Bin Laden and Bush face each other as cardboard cutouts, one hoisting a flag and a gun, the other a bloody sword.[43]

Yet the page is dominated by the event itself, not by the Bush–bin Laden standoff. In a key panel, Spiegelman and his wife walk away from the towers, having dropped their daughter at school. They look like themselves, like New Yorkers, rendered in two-dimensional form. In the following panels, which take place in the moments after the first plane crashes into the South Tower, the towers themselves morph into frantic characters from the classic comic strip *The Katzenjammer Kids*. The shift from everyday life to cartoon imagery is deliberate, of course. As in *Maus*, the use of familiar visual icons simultaneously domesticates and amplifies the horror. Rather than being arranged in a standard format, with rows of neat rectangular panels, each cartoon essay constitutes a complex assemblage of strips, caricatures, digressions, and free-floating illustrations. Each plays with the idea that the boundary between nightmares and normality is more fluid than we imagine. And all of them feature an anguished, cartoonified Spiegelman, who says things like "The sky is falling!" and "I can no longer distinguish my own neurotic depression from well-founded despair!"[44]

While Spiegelman's response to 9/11 was stubbornly autobiographical, it was also inextricably political. He is as afraid of "the gang in power" as he is of the "new, improved Jihad." "Why did those provincial American flags have to sprout out of the embers of Ground Zero?" he asks. "Why not a globe?" Elsewhere he describes himself as "equally terrorized by Al-Qaeda and by his own government," a formulation almost unsayable in many contexts. His third-camp perspective lands him in

Billy Dare, Ruben Bolling's Tintin-style "boy adventurer," discovers he's in someone else's comic strip.

Credit: Ruben Bolling, distributed by Universal Uclick Syndicate

trouble when he is recruited to take part in an NBC broadcast featuring "a collage of interviews with typical New Yorkers." Rendering himself as Happy Hooligan, a hapless comic strip character from the early twentieth century, he answers every question with precisely the wrong answer. When asked where he feels "most American," he exclaims, "Paris, France!" When invited to identify "the greatest thing about America," Spiegelman attests that "as long as you're not an Arab you're allowed to think America's not always so great!" As he's kicked out of the studio, Happy (Art) comically thinks to himself, "Rats! I shoulda said 'American tobacco.'"[45]

Spiegelman finds solace in the whimsy of decades-old newspaper strips. "The only cultural artifacts that could get past my defenses," he explains, "were old comic strips: vital, unpretentious ephemera from the optimistic dawn of the twentieth century. That they were made with so much skill and verve but never indeed to last past the day they appeared in the newspaper gave them poignancy; they were just right for an end-of-the-world moment."[46] He shares several of these forgotten treasures with the reader, including a revealingly jingoistic *Yellow Kid*, a sweet *Krazy Kat* page, and a jaw-dropper from Winsor McKay's *Little Nemo in Slumberland*, where a sleepwalking Nemo climbs Manhattan's steel-and-glass canyons. Each of the selections touches in some way on the contemporary anxieties that permeate *In The Shadow of No Towers*.

. . . . .

Cartoonists responded to 9/11 in a myriad of ways, from austere drawings of a grief-struck Statue of Liberty to complex short stories and full-length histories. While some cartoonists treated it as an inexplicable tragedy, others sought to explore the day's roots in history, geography, and foreign policy. To some extent, cartoonists played their assigned parts. Liberal creators used the moment to call for dialogue, while conservative ones shook their symbolic fists. Some radical illustrators used the occasion to flag larger questions about foreign policy, the national interest, and the rhetoric of consensus. A few cartoonists even found ways to incorporate humor into their post-9/11 comics. Yet for all of the creativity unleashed by the day's violence, comics probably played a modest role in fixing people's memories of 9/11, or in framing it as a historical event. How comic artists reacted to 9/11 no doubt mattered much more inside the comics subculture than beyond.

Notes

1. William B. Scott and Peter M. Rutkoff, *New York Modern: The Arts and the City* (Baltimore: Johns Hopkins University Press, 2001), xviii.
2. See Gerard Jones, *Men of Tomorrow: Geeks, Gangsters, and the Birth of the Comic Book* (New York: Basic Books, 2004).
3. Writing about 9/11 comics, Joseph Witek noted "how unusual it is for American comics to respond so immediately to particular real-life events. While topicality is the lifeblood of editorial cartooning . . . mainstream comic books and syndicated comic strips in the United

States rarely respond to unexpected events, mostly because of the long lead times required." For the comics subculture, 9/11 became an exception not only because of the scale of the suffering but because it landed on the industry's front lawn. See Joseph Witek, "Long Form/ Short Form: Narrative Strategies of Some 9/11 Comics" *International Journal of Comic Art* 5 (2003): 281.

4. Additional examples include Jonathan Hennessey and Aaron McConnell, *The U.S. Constitution: A Graphic Adaptation* (New York: Hill and Wang, 2008); Joe Sacco, *Palestine* (Seattle: Fantagraphics, 2002); Marjane Satrapi, *Persepolis* (New York: Pantheon, 2007); and Howard Zinn, Mike Konopacki, and Paul Buhle, *A People's History of American Empire* (New York: Metropolitan Books, 2008).

5. Kent Worcester, "The Ernie Colón Interview," *Comics Journal*, no. 285 (2007): 84–85.

6. See Sid Jacobson and Ernie Colón, *The 9/11 Report: A Graphic Adaptation* (New York: Hill and Wang, 2006); and Sid Jacobson and Ernie Colón, *After 9/11: America's War on Terror (2001–)* (New York: Hill and Wang, 2008).

7. See *9/11: September 11, 2001 (The World's Finest Comic Book Writers and Artists Tell Stories to Remember)* (New York: DC Comics, 2002); *Heroes: The World's Greatest Superhero Creators Honor the World's Greatest Heroes* (New York: Marvel Comics, 2002); and *A Moment of Silence: Saluting the Heroes of 9/11* (New York: Marvel Comics, 2002).

8. *9/11: Emergency Relief* (Gainesville, FL: Alternative Comics, 2002), back-cover blurb.

9. See "9–11 (Comics)," Wikipedia, en.wikipedia.org/wiki/9–11_(comics) (accessed February 17, 2011).

10. See Ted Rall, *To Afghanistan and Back: A Graphic Travelogue* (New York: Nantier, Beall, Minoustchine, 2002); and David Axe, *War-Fix* (New York: Nantier, Beall, Minoustchine, 2006).

11. Chris Lamb, *Drawn to Extremes: The Use and Abuse of Editorial Cartoons* (New York: Columbia University Press, 2004), 17.

12. Quoted ibid., 18.

13. Ted Rall, *To Afghanistan and Back*, 9, 13.

14. See Ted Rall, *Silk Road to Ruin: Is Central Asia the New Middle East?* (New York: NBM, 2006); and "Opinion L.A.," *Los Angeles Times*, opinion.latimes.com/opinionla/2010/09/ ted-rall-cartooning-live-from-afghanistan-day-14.html (accessed February 17, 2011).

15. See Joe Sacco, *War Junkie: Illustrated Tales of Combat, Depression, and Rock 'n' Roll* (Seattle: Fantagraphics, 1995). Axe's latest book, with illustrations by Matt Bors, is *War Is Boring: Bored Stiff, Scared to Death in the World's Worst War Zones* (New York: NAL), 2010.

16. Jonathan Ames and Dean Haspiel, *The Alcoholic* (New York: DC/Vertigo, 2008), 92–95. Haspiel also wrote and illustrated an intense, somewhat feverish autobiographical story for the Alternative Comics fund-raising volume; see Dean Haspiel, "91101," in *9/11: Emergency Relief*, 92–97.

17. See David Mazzucchelli, *Asterios Polyp* (New York: Pantheon, 2009).

18. See Donna R. Hoffman and Alison D. Howard, "Representations of 9–11 in Editorial Cartoons," *PS: Political Science and Politics* 40 (2007): 271.

19. Ibid., 273.

20. Published during the anthrax scare, the cartoon shows a couple at home, watching TV. The TV announcer says, "This is the election broadcast network. Had this been an actual election, you would have been told who won and why you should care. Please stay tuned." The cartoon is a little bleak but unlikely to offend nonleftist sensibilities. See Charles

Brooks, ed., *Best Editorial Cartoons of the Year: 2002 Edition* (Gretna, LA: Pelican, 2002), 109.

21. Hoffman and Howard, "Representations," 272.

22. Brooks, *Best Editorial Cartoons of the Year: 2002 Edition*, 66, 62, 61.

23. Ibid., 53, 66, 85, 75, 47.

24. See *A Moment of Silence: Saluting the Heroes of September 11th* (New York: Marvel Comics, 2002); and *Heroes: The World's Greatest Superhero Creators Honor the World's Greatest Heroes* (New York: Marvel Comics, 2001).

25. See Michael Dean, "9/11, Benefit Comics, and the Dog-Eat-Dog World of Good Samaritanism," *Comics Journal*, no. 247 (2002): 10.

26. R. Fiore, "A Moment of Noise," *Comics Journal*, no. 247 (2002): 46.

27. Ibid., 48.

28. Paul Levitz, introduction to *9/11: September 11, 2001 (The World's Finest Comic Book Writers and Artists Tell Stories to Remember)* (New York: DC Comics, 2002), 10.

29. See Stan Sakai, "The Last Time I Was in New York City . . ." and Mark Crilley, "That Day," in *9/11: September 11, 2001 (Artists Respond)* (Milwaukee, OR: Dark Horse, 2002), 178–79 and 180–81.

30. Steven T. Seagle, Duncan Rouleau, and Aaron Sowd, "Unreal," in *9/11: September 11, 2001*, 15–16.

31. Darwyn Cooke, "Human Values," in *9/11: September 11, 2001*, 69.

32. Harvey Pekar and Tony Millionaire, "News," in *9/11: Emergency Relief* (Gainesville, FL: Alternative Comics, 2002), 1.

33. In a post-9/11 e-mail to potential contributors, Jeff Mason, Alternative Comics' publisher, said he was "really shocked and dismayed by some of the rhetoric and behavior I've seen from some in the guise of patriotism and I think that a book that promotes an alternative to xenophobia and antagonism would be a good thing." See Dean, "9/11, Benefit Comics, and the Dog-Eat-Dog World of Good Samaritanism," 12.

34. See Jessica Abel, untitled contribution, in *9/11: Emergency Relief*, 13–14; and Fly, "9–11–01," in *9/11: Emergency Relief*, 98–99.

35. Fly, "9/11/01," in *9/11: Emergency Relief*, 98–99.

36. Tom Hart, "Attacking, Attacked, Attacking," in *9/11: Emergency Relief*, 130–33.

37. Joe Kubert, "What of Tomorrow?" in *9/11: September 11*, 215.

38. Kent Worcester, "The *World War 3 Illustrated* Interview," *Comics Journal*, no. 276 (2006): 162.

39. Peter Kuper, Seth Tobocman, and Jordan Worley, eds., *World War 3 Illustrated*, no. 32 (December 2001).

40. Kent Worcester, "The Ruben Bolling Interview," *Comics Journal*, no. 247 (2002): 68.

41. See Ruben Bolling, *Thrilling Tom the Dancing Bug Stories* (Kansas City: Andrew McMeel, 2004), 147.

42. Worcester, "Ruben Bolling Interview," 68.

43. Art Spiegelman, *In The Shadow of No Towers* (New York: Pantheon, 2004), 2.

44. Ibid., 8.

45. Ibid., 10.

46. Ibid., 11.

9/11 on the Screen

Giving Memory and Meaning to All That "Howling Space" at Ground Zero

Thomas Riegler

Historicizing is commonly understood as the transformation of current affairs into a subject of historical interest through a gradual process of shifting perception and interpretation over time. In this context cinema is often overlooked, despite its power in shaping historical memory through the power of visual media. Filmmakers play a key role in the creation of "history" as the past is imagined, imitated, and envisioned on screen. The written work of history also attempts to transpose us into the worlds of the past, but as the historian Robert Rosenstone has argued, "our presence in a past created by words never seems as immediate as our presence in a past created on the screen."[1]

Cinematic narratives of history exercise unique powers of representation. Especially in complex and ambivalent times of crisis, whether due to economic hardships, internal dispute, or war, these visual texts simplify historical events for their audience—often explaining them in Manichaean black-and-white terms and thereby offering orientation, understanding, and guidance. There is also an element of mobilization and moral uplift: the narratives channel emotions and aggressions against an "enemy other," give meaning to suffering and sacrifice, or edify catastrophe. Overall, visual historicizing frames past events—presenting them as synchronized, closed, completed, and ultimately as a sort of cognitive tool to engage and deal with present realities.

Radical History Review

Issue 111 (Fall 2011)   DOI 10.1215/01636545-1268767

© 2011 by MARHO: The Radical Historians' Organization, Inc.

The present article explores the general theme of historization in regard to the visual representation of 9/11 in U.S. popular culture. I hold that Hollywood and television constituted the foremost cultural apparatuses for coping with 9/11, which had left Americans struggling in the "desert of the real."[2] After some initial probing (*25th Hour*, *The Guys*), a direct exploration of 9/11 emerged in 2005–6: two major feature films (*United 93* and *World Trade Center*) and a string of TV dramas (*DC 9/11: Time of Crisis*, *The Flight That Fought Back*, *Flight 93*, *The Path to 9/11*) addressed the event, its background, and its aftermath from the perspectives of politicians and decision makers, victims, and relatives.[3] While most of these films and TV dramas took a supposedly apolitical and distanced stance, a variety of documentary films offered alternative and intimate insights (*Answering the Call: Ground Zero's Volunteers*, *Class of 83*, *Beyond Belief*, *Seven Days in September*).[4] In the years since, the focus has shifted further—to the war in Iraq, the progress of the global war on terror, and the role of the United States in international affairs. Yet 9/11 remains a reference, mainly on an emotional level, as in *The Great New Wonderful*, *Reign over Me*, *Remember Me*, and *Dear John*.[5]

Narratives of Loss

Right from the start cinematic images and metaphors were adapted to contextualize, frame, and interpret the "unspeakable" horrors of 9/11. Some commentators even blamed Hollywood for the events, because its movies had prefigured, even "inspired" the terrorist perpetrators. Thus, in the period after 9/11, Hollywood steered clear of the subject of terrorism and focused instead on fantastical escapism, nostalgia, and family entertainment. Famously, the twin towers were digitally removed from most movies in the production line, no matter whether or not they dealt with terrorism, wholly or partly. According to the *Observer*, the overriding executive mantra was: "No more movies of mass destruction."[6]

The direct confrontation of 9/11 constituted a taboo at this stage, and it extended to all sorts of themes dealing with American ambivalence. For example, Miramax declined to release *The Quiet American* (dir. Phillip Noyce, 2002), an exploration of the destabilizing U.S. role in Southeast Asia prior to the Vietnam War. "You cannot release this film now. It is unpatriotic. America has to be cohesive and band together," the studio executive Harvey Weinstein declared.[7] Thus the first films relating to 9/11 did so in a consciously distanced way, aiming not to attract controversy. *The Guys* (dir. Jim Simpson, 2002), based on a play by Anne Nelson, featured a journalist helping a FDNY (New York City Fire Department) captain who had lost nine men in the twin towers compose eulogies. More detached is Spike Lee's *25th Hour* (2002), released fifteen months after the terrorist attacks. The story follows a convicted New York drug dealer on his last day of freedom before beginning a seven-year prison sentence. While other productions at this point had either ignored or deleted any reference to the terrorist attacks, this film integrated 9/11, but merely as an atmospheric and emotional background setting. The characters mainly respond to uncertainties, sadness, and fear, capturing the post-9/11 climate of a "wounded" New York City.[8]

With Hollywood largely avoiding the topic, it was left to documentary filmmakers to explore the 9/11 tragedy in great variety. These mostly independent productions included themes subject to a sort of informal censorship in the immediate aftermath of 9/11: horror, death, trauma, grief—often at the personal level and through the use of "unofficial" images and footage. Later, in the wake of the box-office success of *Fahrenheit 9/11* (dir. Michael Moore, 2004), another wave of documentaries investigated the political responsibilities of the Bush administration and the structural failures of government agencies—thereby forming counternarratives to the more streamlined and often unquestioning output of the mainstream.

The Narrative of the Citizen Soldier

It took more than four years for the entertainment industry to finally tackle 9/11 in earnest. The specific angle chosen for the approach reveals much about the functionality and mechanisms of historization. On September 11, 2001, one of the hijacked planes—United Airlines 93—did not reach its intended target because its thirty-seven passengers and seven crew members mounted an assault against the terrorists. As a result, the plane crashed into a Pennsylvania field at Shanksville, only twenty minutes by air from Washington, D.C. In the immediate aftermath, the story of Flight 93 was overpowered by the sheer magnitude of the other 9/11 events, but by 2002 and following the proclamation of the global war on terror, this flight had achieved a special status in the culture remembering 9/11. This held especially true after exponents of the Bush administration mythologized the "sacrifice" of passengers and crew as the first act of resistance, an act that prevented the hijackers from crashing the plane into the U.S. Congress, or possibly into the White House. In this manner, the story of United Airlines 93 was remembered and presented in a militarized fashion, offering a heroic counternarrative to the deeply traumatizing experience of 9/11, which exposed the United States as vulnerable, victimized, and ultimately humiliated. The heroism on board Flight 93 differed from the "seeming passivity" on the other hijacked planes, which "is reminiscent of the Holocaust," Charles Krauthammer wrote in *Time*.[9] In a "ferocious assault," *Newsweek* reported, a "band of patriots came together to defy death and save a symbol of freedom."[10] Susan Faludi has described the functionality of this sort of hero worship in the wake of 9/11: "The suddenness of the attacks and the finality of the tower's collapse left us little in the way of ongoing chronicle or ennobling narrative. So a narrative was created and populated with pasteboard protagonists whose exploits would exist almost entirely in the realm of American archetype and American fantasy."[11]

Exactly because the story of United Airlines 93 offered that kind of reasserting narrative, it was dramatized three times in a row, first on TV. *The Flight That*

Fought Back (2005), a Discovery Channel production, mixed the reenactment of events on board the flight with interview sequences with relatives and friends of the victims, while Kiefer Sutherland acted as the narrator. A&E Network's *Flight 93* (2006) was a simple feature film. "It's the real thing, and all the more chilling for depicting how real, ordinary people lived their final moments and prepared for their deaths," the *New York Times* commented.[12] The *National Review* praised it as a metaphor for the war on terror: "The bad guys wield box cutters, invoke the name of Allah, and kill people; the Americans vote, say the Lord's prayer, and fight back."[13] The program achieved the highest ratings in the history of A&E and seemed to demonstrate that the audience was ready for a cinematic version of 9/11. The release of *United 93* in 2006 marked the first attempt. In this 15 million–dollar production the British director Paul Greengrass stuck to the cinema verité style that characterized his earlier works. Nervous handheld camera movements, improvised dialogue, parallel montage, and natural light combined to establish a "plausible truth."[14] The decision for a no-name cast was also deliberate to establish the passengers as a collective—this is most evident in the closing scene, when the camera shows many different arms struggling with the remaining terrorist for the control of the cockpit.[15]

Through these stylistic elements *United 93* claims to tell its story as it happened and without overt political undertones. Much of what actually happened onboard United Airlines 93 is indeed known through black box recordings and mobile phone calls by passengers. But Greengrass also took some artistic license. For example, there is no evidence that a European passenger panicked ("I am a German. I don't want to die.") and even went so far as to warn the hijackers of the coming onslaught. A German businessman, Christian Adam, was indeed onboard United Airlines 93 on September 11, 2001, but it was the actor assigned his part who suggested his supposedly defeatist attitude. Undoubtedly, the behavior of this "capitulation weasel" reinforced stereotypes about European willingness to compromise in the face of suicide terrorism.[16] There is also no proof for the final claim that the passengers indeed managed to break into the cockpit. The 9/11 Commission investigating the terrorist attacks stated in its report: "The hijackers remained at the controls but must have judged that the passengers were only seconds from overcoming them."[17]

The last seconds of *United 93* show total chaos in the cockpit, while the ground is rapidly coming closer and closer during the dive, until suddenly the frame turns black—making clear that nobody survived. Despite this fact, *Time* called *United 93* "in 9/11 terms, a feel good movie," because it depicts an old American myth: of average citizens rising to the challenge, while political and military command centers fail to grasp the situation and the rest of the public passively watches the spectacle unfolding on TV.[18]

World Trade Center: The Narrative of the Heroic Rescue Workers

The second major picture addressing 9/11 was Oliver Stone's *World Trade Center* (2006). Contrary to what the title suggests, the movie does not show the planes hitting the towers, but instead concentrates on a "true" human-interest story of the miraculous rescue of two survivors from ground zero: John McLoughlin (Nicolas Cage) and Will Jimeno (Michael Peña) of the Port Authority Police Department (PAPD). Responding to the initial emergency, they were buried under the rubble of the collapsing twin towers. The two men were eventually recovered from ground zero, alongside only eighteen other survivors. Like Greengrass in *United 93*, Stone strives for a semidocumentarian quality, given weight by the presence of the real protagonists as consultants on the set, the supposedly faithful retelling of their story, and the active participation of colleagues and coworkers (more than fifty played themselves).[19] The action takes place on different levels: there is the claustrophobic predicament of those buried alive ("pain is your friend"), the superhuman efforts of the rescue workers, and the painful waiting of the (passive) wives at home, who hover constantly between desperation and hope. A familiar theme is the initial chaos and disorganization of the rescue effort, which leaves room for American individuals to take matters into their own hands.

Two volunteers eventually locate McLoughlin and Jimeno, basically because they follow their own instincts. One of them, Dave Karnes (Michael Shannon), a businessman and an ex-staff sergeant from Connecticut, is of particular interest to the story. He is seen first at home, where he gets the news about the terrorist attacks and comments, "This country is at war." He slips into his old uniform and makes his way into the disaster zone. Karnes's repeated cries of "United States Marines" and "We don't leave you; you are our mission" finally alert the trapped Jimeno, and he answers with signs of life. With this rescue mission done, Karnes proclaims the start of a new phase: "They are gonna need some good men out there—to revenge this."[20] The postscript reveals what is meant with "out there": the real-life Karnes reenlisted after 9/11 and completed a seventeen-month tour in Iraq. Interestingly, he did not cooperate with the filmmakers, and his intentions were blurred: "In the movie, many of Karnes's lines are cryptic religious references that make him seem like a robotic soldier of Christ—a little wacky and simplistic. This may be why test audiences didn't believe he existed, according to a report in *Newsweek*." The other marine, who aided Karnes in locating the two survivors, revealed his identity only after the completion of filming: he was an African American, cast as a white man in the movie.[21]

Stone stressed that *World Trade Center* was not meant as a political film, but it nevertheless carries a deeply ideological subtext. Even more than *United 93*, the film provides an uplifting tale by depicting the courage of the rescue workers, the hope of the relatives, and the will to survive. No matter how desperate the situation, the buried men never lose faith in the outside world, and in a general sense in the

United States itself. As a result they live to see their rescue, and their country in turn is redeemed through their successful recovery.[22] While *United 93* ended with a black screen making it clear that nobody survived, *World Trade Center* culminates in a sort of happy end and the triumph of the "American Spirit" over the murderous malice of the terrorists. After attending the premiere, the real-life Jimeno drew a revealing comparison: "The main thing is that when you leave the theatre, you leave with a sense of hope and love. I went to see *United 93* the night it came out. When I walked out, I walked out empty."[23]

Conservative Narratives: *DC 9/11* and *Path to 9/11*

In the aftermath of 9/11 there was widespread speculation about a "Hollywood-Washington pact." A meeting between high-ranking officials of both sides in December 2001 was interpreted as a sign that Hollywood was enlisting itself in the war effort, much like after the Japanese attack on Pearl Harbor in 1942, to promote patriotism. The concrete output mainly amounted to distributing pro-U.S. films to troops overseas and to their families, and a revival of the USO (United Service Organisations) shows.[24] Yet in the following years some productions offered indeed a particularly affirmative view of the Bush administration's counterterrorism actions. On September 7, 2003, *DC 9/11: Time of Crisis* aired on Showtime. It was written by Lionel Chetwynd, a well-known conservative involved in the various Hollywood – White House "conclaves" and serving on the President's Committee on the Arts and Humanities.[25] The film featured a portrayal of the inner workings of the White House in the time from the initial attacks until September 20, when George W. Bush addressed a joint session of Congress to proclaim the war on terror. The film presents the president in the most favorable light — as a compassionate, bold, and decisive leader firmly in charge. Ironically, the president is impersonated by Timothy Bottoms, who had earlier satirized him in the comedy *That's My Bush!*[26] Critics mostly lamented the production; one journalist complained at the "primitive propaganda that portrays Bush as the noblest hero since Mighty Mouse."[27]

More controversial was the TV miniseries *The Path to 9/11*. The five-hour docudrama aired on ABC on September 10 and 11, 2006. Filmed in twenty countries with a budget of $30 million, it retold the prelude of the terrorist attacks — mainly from the perspective of the FBI agent John O'Niell (Harvey Keitel), who had warned repeatedly about an al-Qaeda threat during the 1990s but whose admonitions only fell on deaf ears. In recounting the events leading up to the catastrophe, *The Path to 9/11* draws a bleak picture of the actions of the U.S. government, which in hindsight appears inefficient, deeply flawed, and characterized by bureaucratic turf wars.[28]

Even before the program aired, *The Path to 9/11* inspired controversy. The former president Bill Clinton and members of his administration saw their counterterrorism policies tarnished by the film's political bias. One scene depicting an event in 1998 drew particular ire: there, a team of U.S. Special Forces led by the CIA agent "Kirk" (Donnie Wahlberg) accompanies the Afghan warlord Ahmed Massoud on a mission to kill Osama bin Laden in a nighttime strike at his camp. "The package is ready," Kirk reports back to Washington via satellite phone. But Clinton's national security advisor, Sandy Berger (Kevin Dunn), is not prepared to give the "go" order and hangs up. "Are there any men left in Washington, or are they all cowards?" Massoud (Mido Hamada) asks.[29] The former U.S. counterterrorism czar Richard Clarke insisted that this version of events was completely invented, as the CIA had no boots on the ground in Afghanistan at this stage nor was any operation underway: "It didn't happen. There were no troops in Afghanistan about to snatch bin Laden. There were no CIA personnel about to snatch bin Laden. It's utterly invented."[30]

In striking contrast, *The Path to 9/11* shows the Bush White House in a favorable light. For example, when Condoleezza Rice, the national security advisor, is briefed on the al-Qaeda threat, she replies, "We're on it."[31] *The Path to 9/11* shows "an incompetent Clinton administration and a resolute Bush-Cheney administration committed to fighting terrorism," Douglas Kellner argued.[32] Some critics worried that the docudrama was likely to shape the perspective of millions of Americans on 9/11: "The ABC dramatization, of course, is intended to reach millions of viewers who don't read books, let alone government reports, and don't watch documentaries. The danger is that this false version will be seen by millions and accepted by them as truthful."[33] Approximately 13.1 and 12.3 million people, respectively, watched the two episodes,[34] but the program became so discredited in the process that no DVD edition has yet been released.

Return to Themes of Grief and Loss

The most recent productions retreated to the apolitical formula, offering emotional human-interest stories about coping with trauma and loss. *The Great New Wonderful* (2005) presents vignettes of incidents taking place concurrently around Manhattan. The *Los Angeles Times* commented, "What links the stories is that they occur simultaneously at a moment that seems at once meaningless and portentous: September 2002, a year after the terrorist attacks. Not that Sept. 11 itself is ever mentioned in the movie — that would be too obvious, too literal, and thus contrary to the filmmakers' apparent intention to tease and mystify."[35] 9/11 underwent further domestication in the buddy movie *Reign over Me* (dir. Mike Binder, 2007), in which two former college roommates accidentally meet up again on a Manhattan street corner. Charlie (Adam Sandler) lost his family on 9/11 — they were on "one of the planes that crashed" — and is unable to cope with the tragedy. Alan (Don Cheadle) reconnects with him, to their mutual benefit: Charlie resumes his path toward social reintegration, and his friend starts mending a broken marriage.[36] 9/11 features as the emotional climax in the teenage love drama *Remember Me* (dir. Allen Coulter, 2010): Tyler (Robert Pattinson) is last seen in his father's office on the eighty-eighth floor of the World Trade Center, and the date is later revealed as September 11,

2001. The event also radically affects a soldier's romance with a college student in *Dear John* (dir. Lasse Hallström, 2010): following 9/11 John Tyree (Channing Tatum) is torn between his sense of duty and returning home.[37]

The most blatant and exploitative adaptation of 9/11 imaginary belonged to a completely different genre. *Cloverfield* (dir. J. J. Abrams, 2008) reimagined September 11 as a monster movie—it featured a sudden devastating attack by a giant monster that topples skyscrapers and major landmarks. The action replicates iconic 9/11 images like people fleeing from Manhattan across the Brooklyn Bridge and clouds of dust and debris. By placing the story firmly in the pulp universe, the filmmakers cleverly navigated mined territory and did not attract the same level of controversy as if they had devised a more realistic story. The box-office results demonstrated the success of this both escapist and safely immersing take on 9/11.[38]

Conclusion

This article has explored the cultural representation and historicizing of 9/11 in Hollywood films and on TV. It identifies several key narratives: general themes of loss and trauma, a rousing tribute to both United Airlines 93's citizen soldiers and to rescue workers, but also the affirmation of the political leadership in times of crisis. Historical narratives, like popular myths and legends, fulfill a key function in the legitimization and stabilization of the current order. A shared "history," centered on key dates and events, unites an otherwise disparate collective, providing a common identity and easy orientation in a complex global environment. The case of 9/11 and its historization may serve as a prime example of this process.

All different kinds of 9/11 narratives share the same standpoints on humanization, depoliticization, and reconciliation among a deeply divided American public. With the exception of some documentaries, films and TV dramas spare the viewer of any political context: there is no reflection on the political background of the terrorist attacks, there is no "aftermath." While most productions do not constitute overt propaganda, they do tend to avoid any problematic or ambivalent aspects of the war on terror—the invasions of Afghanistan and Iraq, Guantánamo, and the torture images of Abu Ghraib. Instead, they put the wheel of history into reverse—back to September 11, 2001, a sort of "zero hour" of shattered American innocence and of a brutal awakening to new dangers. This perspective symbolically returns 9/11 to the victims of monstrous terrorist aggression and remains uncompromised by subsequent U.S. actions. Thus we see on the screens mainly images of a victimized yet unbroken United States rising to the challenge.[39] In this process, the country's founding myth is reenacted and the invincibility of the United States becomes reinforced, eradicating the temporary humiliation at the hands of the nineteen hijackers.[40] The films discussed here have further placed emphasis on therapy and healing: mainly first-person narratives function to mediate and formulate experiences that many Americans shared on September 11, 2001, and its aftermath. These pictures have no political content but are suffused with a "deep, enduring sense of grief born in the tragedy's wake."[41] Finally, productions like *DC 9/11* and *The Path to 9/11* offer a simplified and selective interpretation of events to serve a partisan agenda.

Compared to other historical myths, ones essentially carved by Hollywood—like the Wild West or aspects of World War II, or of the Vietnam War—9/11 still stands apart. For a large segment of the public, the traumatic event still proves too raw, too hard to grasp in its entirety, and is thus considered an unsuitable theme for mere entertainment. Box-office sales suggest as much: *United 93* and *World Trade Center* only covered their production costs.[42] The even more disappointing numbers for films on the war in Iraq demonstrate that the public has little appetite for such cinematic fare right now. We might also take into consideration that both September 11 and the Iraq war belong to the most reported news, which may have discouraged filmmakers from pursuing the topic.[43]

Problematically, the terrorist attacks were perceived from the outset through the lenses of a Hollywood scenario: scenes of urban destruction, whether it be from *King Kong*, *Towering Inferno*, *Godzilla*, or *Armageddon*, immediately leapt to mind when watching the destruction of the World Trade Centre. This understanding of 9/11 as a movielike event still presents a major challenge, as Karen Randell highlights: "The difficulty for Hollywood filmmakers in representing the World Trade Center catastrophe is that the notion of consensus of memory of 9/11 seems to render the image beyond the conventional models of representation. How do you make a movie of a day that already played out like a movie."[44]

Another explanation often given for the relatively low output of 9/11 themes is that the war effort and the struggle against terrorism continue, meaning that contemporary movies can offer neither real catharsis nor a "pleasant," enjoyable narrative. Instead they tend to remind audiences that the present conflicts go on with little chance of resolution yet with the likelihood of more casualties. Thus viewers cannot extricate themselves from what they are watching on the screen.[45]

Overall, the cultural mirror of 9/11 tells of a society deeply affected by fear, uncertainty, and aggression, while struggling to find new meaning and purpose in a radically changed environment—since the terrorists effectively shattered the symbolic coordinates of prevailing American reality. The films and TV shows discussed here constitute a major effort to frame and interpret the unspeakable event in the familiar terms of American popular culture. It is likely that 9/11 will be addressed more frequently and in-depth with the passing of more time. "Tolstoy wrote 'War and Peace' some 60 years after Napoleon's invasion of Russia. Benjamin Britten's 'War Requiem,' memorializing World War II, was not heard until 1961," noted Michiko Kakutani. She added: "Novelists, filmmakers, and other artists are still trying, in Don DeLillo's words, to 'understand what this day has done to us,' and to give 'memory, tenderness and meaning to all that howling space' at ground zero."[46]

Notes

1. Robert A. Rosenstone, *Visions of the Past: The Challenge to Our Idea of History* (Cambridge, MA: Harvard University Press, 1995), 55.

2. Slavoj Žižek, *Die Revolution steht bevor: Dreizehn Versuche über Lenin*, trans. Nikolaus G. Schneider (Frankfurt am Main: Suhrkamp, 2002), 147–58.

3. *25th Hour* (dir. Spike Lee, 2002); *The Guys* (dir. Jim Simpson, 2002); *United 93* (dir. Paul Greengrass, 2006); *World Trade Center* (dir. Oliver Stone, 2006); *DC 9/11: Time of Crisis* (dir. Brian Trenchard-Smith, 2003); *The Flight That Fought Back* (dir. Bruce Goodison, 2005); *Flight 93* (dir. Peter Markle, 2006); *The Path to 9/11* (dir. David L. Cunningham, 2006).

4. *Answering the Call: Ground Zero's Volunteers* (dir. Lou Angeli, 2005); *Class of 83* (dir. Curt E. Soderling, 2004); *Beyond Belief* (dir. Beth Murphy, 2007); *Seven Days in September* (dir. Steve Rosenbau, 2002).

5. *The Great New Wonderful* (dir. Danny Leiner, 2005); *Reign over Me* (dir. Mike Binder, 2007); *Remember Me* (dir. Allen Coulter, 2010); and *Dear John* (dir. Lasse Hallström, 2010).

6. Kevin Maher, "Back with a Bang," *Observer* (London), June 30, 2002.

7. Jon Wiener, "Quiet in Hollywood," *Nation*, November 26, 2002, www.thenation.com/article/quiet-hollywood.

8. Mick LaSalle, "9/11: Five Years Later—Spike Lee's '25th Hour,'" *San Francisco Chronicle*, September 10, 2006.

9. Charles Krauthammer, "The Greater the Evil, the More It Disarms," *Time*, September 24, 2001, www.time.com/time/covers/1101010924/escharles.html.

10. Karen Breslau, Eleanor Clift, and Evan Thomas, "The Real Story of Flight 93," *Newsweek*, December 3, 2001, 54–67.

11. Susan Faludi, *The Terror Dream: Fear and Fantasy in Post-9/11 America* (New York: Metropolitan Books, 2007), 61–64.

12. Alessandra Stanley, "On a Doomed 9/11 Flight, Heroes Are Humans, Too," *New York Times*, January 30, 2006.

13. John J. Miller, "9/11: The Movie," National Review Online, January 30, 2006, www.national review.com/articles/print/216647.

14. Clayton Neuman and Rebecca Winters, "Let's Roll! Inside the Making of *United 93*," *Time*, April 9, 2006, www.time.com/time/magazine/article/0,9171,1181589,00.html.

15. Jere Longman and Paul Greengrass, "Filming of Flight 93's Story, Trying to Define Heroics," *New York Times*, April 24, 2006.

16. Xan Brooks, "United 93 'Surrender Monkey' Defends His Role in Film," *Guardian*, June 7, 2006.

17. *The 9/11 Commission Report: Final Report of the National Commission on Terrorist Attacks upon the United States* (New York: Norton, 2004), 13–14.

18. Longman and Greengrass, "Filming of Flight 93's Story."

19. Peter Brinkemper, "Nationales Filmdenkmal oder internationaler Kassenschlager," *telepolis*, August 13, 2006, www.heise.de/tp/r4/artikel/23/23314/1.html.

20. Rüdiger Suchsland, "Jesus mit Wasserflasche," *telepolis*, September 28, 2006, www.heise.de/tp/r4/artikel/23/23637/1.html.

21. Rebecca Liss, "Oliver Stone's World Trade Center Fiction," *Slate*, August 9, 2006, www.slate.com/id/2147350/.

22. Georg Seeßlen, "Menschen unter Trümmern," *epd Film*, no. 10 (2006): 28–31.

23. Brinkemper, "Nationales Filmdenkmal."

24. Dana Calvo and Robert Welkos, "Hollywood Shakes Off Fear of Terror Images," *Los Angeles Times*, May 20, 2002.

25. Jim Hoberman, "Lights, Camera, Exploitation," *Village Voice*, August 26, 2003.

26. Paul Farhi, "'D.C. 9/11' Spins Tale of President on Tragic Day," *Washington Post*, June 19, 2003.

27. Tom Shales, "Dull Paean," *Washington Post*, September 6, 2003.

28. Edward Wyatt, "A Show That Trumpeted History But Led to Confusion," *New York Times*, September 18, 2006.

29. Stephen Prince, *Firestorm: American Film in the Age of Terrorism* (New York: Columbia University Press, 2009), 266–67.

30. Jesse McKinley, "9/11 Miniseries Is Criticized as Inaccurate and Biased," *New York Times*, September 6, 2006.

31. Joe Conason, "The Sept. 11 That Never Was," *Salon*, September 8, 2006, www.salon.com/news/opinion/joe_conason/2006/09/08/path_to_9_11.

32. Douglas Kellner, *Cinema Wars: Hollywood Film and Politics in the Bush-Cheney Era* (Malden, MA: Wiley-Blackwell, 2010), 115.

33. Conason, "The Sept. 11 That Never Was."

34. Hal Boedeker, "9–11 Programs Draw Plenty of Viewers—But No Ratings," *Orlando Sentinel*, September 13, 2006.

35. Rachel Abramowitz and John Horn, "Post-9/11 Anxieties Influence Spate of Films," *Los Angeles Times*, January 29, 2005.

36. Prince, *Firestorm*, 120.

37. Neil Smith, "Is Hollywood Finally over 9/11?" *Guardian*, March 30, 2010.

38. Rebecca Winters, "*Cloverfield:* Godzilla Goes 9/11," *Time*, January 16, 2008, www.time.com/time/arts/article/0,8599,1704356,00.html.

39. Robert Misik, "Der Stoff unserer Zeit," *Falter*, no. 36 (2006): 8–9.

40. Seeßlen, "Menschen unter Trümmern."

41. Stephen Faber, "9/11 Is Sneaking onto a Screen near You," *New York Times*, March 13, 2005.

42. Smith, "Is Hollywood Finally Over 9/11?"

43. Patrick Goldstein, "Hollywood's 9/11 Story," *Los Angeles Times*, September 12, 2002.

44. Karen Randell, "'It Was Like a Movie': The Impossibility of Representation in Oliver Stone's *World Trade Center,*" in *Reframing 9/11: Film, Popular Culture, and the "War on Terror,"* ed. Jeff Birkenstein, Anna Froula, and Karen Randell (New York: Continuum, 2010), 141–52.

45. Johanna Schneller, "One Casualty of War: The Box-Office Bomb," *Globe and Mail* (Toronto), March 19, 2010.

46. Michiko Kakutani, "And Now, Back to Our Regularly Scheduled Programming," *New York Times*, September 11, 2002.

A nation in love with images of its own destruction. Courtesy of Paramount Pictures

Enjoying 9/11

The Pleasures of *Cloverfield*

James Stone

Did you see that? Oh, my god! Oh, my god!" The words are delivered in a breathless, fearful, but undeniably exhilarated fashion. They are the typical utterances of Hudson "Hud" Platt (T. J. Miller), one of a group of youthful New Yorkers trying to survive an attack on Manhattan by a giant, reptilian monster. With the metropolis in flames and loved ones dying around him, Hud holds fast to a camcorder, doing his best to document the cataclysmic event. This stalwart videographer is a character in *Cloverfield* (dir. Matt Reeves, 2008), a highly successful Hollywood movie. Hud's reaction to the assault on his city—shocked but energized—is the very response that *Cloverfield* attempts to elicit from its viewers. When Hud screams, "Are you seeing this? Are you seeing this?" we sense that he is addressing us, as well as his companions. We are being asked to share his adrenaline-fueled fascination with massive destruction. This request startles, since the images we see through the lens of Hud's camera look very much like the iconic video footage captured on September 11, 2001. *Cloverfield* reimagines 9/11 as a monster movie and eagerly invites us to gaze upon the carnage.

As skyscrapers explode, the air fills with myriad pieces of drifting paper. Bloodied and bewildered New Yorkers stagger though the streets. The film's main characters take shelter in a convenience store as a rapidly advancing cloud of dust envelops the street outside. Panicky hordes flee across the Brooklyn Bridge. One of the twin towers of the Time Warner Center collapses against the other, rescuers racing up the building's stairwell in an attempt to save a trapped survivor. Each of these

Radical History Review
Issue 111 (Fall 2011)   DOI 10.1215/01636545-1268776

moments, like everything else in *Cloverfield*, comes to us via the kind of raw, shaky video that we associate with coverage of 9/11. Many viewers see it as a convincing recreation of events. Jessica Wakeman, who was in New York during the attacks, writes, "*Cloverfield* nails what that morning felt like: the confusion at first and then fear overwhelms and all you can think about is the possibility of dying and needing to escape by getting out-out-out."[1]

With so many of the movie's scenes echoing the well-known images of that day, we might expect it to adopt a somber, reflective tone. Nothing could be further from the truth. This is moviemaking that grabs us by the scruff of the neck, whisking us from one exciting, 9/11–inspired display to the next. By so blatantly enlisting the terrorist attacks in the service of entertainment, *Cloverfield* suggests that we have reached the point where they can be treated with a little less reverence. More importantly, it unearths a notion, partially buried since 2001, that while 9/11 was undeniably traumatic, it was always, on some level, a thrilling spectacle.

Many will undoubtedly find the idea that any pleasure might be derived from 9/11 an obscene suggestion. If people lost loved ones or colleagues in the disaster, they almost certainly have no place for such a reaction. But for those who witnessed the attacks from a distance, via a television screen, the feelings of dread and sadness may have been accompanied by the kind of awestruck *frisson* that *Cloverfield* asks of its viewers. The vast plume of smoke rising from the shattered World Trade Center and the swift, rumbling collapse of the towers possess the same kind of dreadful splendor that many have found in images of mushroom clouds. And yet, in 2010, while a Web site as conventional as Life.com points out the "terrible beauty" of atomic explosions,[2] there is no real place in Western culture for an open discussion of 9/11's dark aesthetic appeal.

This taboo is all the more notable in the United States, a nation in love with images of its own destruction. For a hundred years before 9/11, the U.S. film industry presented ever more spectacular images of blasted buildings and fleeing crowds. The skyscrapers of New York came under threat from a multitude of perils—from King Kong to wayward meteorites—images of their collapse suggesting the transitory nature of wealth and power. Minutes after American Airlines Flight 11 collided with the North Tower of the World Trade Center, television news began to offer astounding images that "looked like a movie" to many viewers. Since Americans had so often thrilled to similar footage, can it be possible that they felt not a scintilla of pleasure at the "real" thing? Put bluntly, 9/11 was the most spectacular action movie ever made. As Slavoj Žižek stated, the "oft-repeated shot of frightened people running towards the camera ahead of the giant cloud of dust" is "a special effect which outdid all others."[3] But surely the knowledge that the shocking footage from New York was drawn from real life ensured the absence of any sense of gratification.

A brief flip through cable TV channels would suggest otherwise. Documentary footage of violence and destruction constitutes a staple of the entertainment landscape. The History Channel feeds not only our desire to be more informed about the past but also our wish to see bombing raids, gun-camera footage, and any number of brutal human interactions from Pol Pot's Cambodia to gangland Los Angeles. The vogue for prison documentaries, appearing even on reputable news channels such as MSNBC, means that we can witness security-camera footage of exercise-yard stabbings while better understanding the rarefied world of maximum security. Documentary violence arguably proves more compelling when presented to us live, since it thereby becomes charged with suspense. TV news networks regularly drop scheduled programming to bring us helicopter shots of police pursuits, teasing us with the possibility of a spectacular crash. Live footage of the bombardment of Baghdad—the so-called shock-and-awe campaign—was a staple of rolling news bulletins in 2003. We were able to scan the cityscape in real time, certain that we would witness explosions, but never quite sure when they would occur. In short, we do not halt our enjoyment of violent imagery because it is real.

This does not necessarily make us monstrous. Feelings of excitement do not preclude emotions like sorrow or sympathy. We are quite capable of experiencing sadness at the human cost of a tragedy while simultaneously appreciating its spectacular qualities. But to express such a combination of responses, especially with regard to 9/11, will ensure one's vilification. In September 2002, the British conceptual artist Damien Hirst told the BBC News Online that 9/11 was "visually stunning" and "an artwork in its own right."[4] While he made sure to note that the event was "wicked," his words instigated such a furor that he was forced to issue a follow-up statement in which he apologized "unreservedly for any upset I have caused, particularly to the families of the victims of the events on that terrible day."[5] A similar chain of events followed the German composer Karl-Heinz Stockhausen's claim, just five days after 9/11, that "what happened there is, of course—now all of you must adjust your brains—the biggest work of art there has ever been."[6] Despite Stockhausen's assertion that "it is a crime, you know, of course, because the people did not agree to it," his words were characterized by a German broadsheet newspaper as the "the monstrous result of radical artistic egocentrism."[7]

While Hirst and Stockhausen may deserve criticism for the insensitivity of their remarks, they should be celebrated for their honesty. They candidly expressed an attraction to the aesthetics of violence that many of us feel but are unwilling to admit. Quite possibly they were pilloried, at least in part, for exposing the hidden truth, ably expressed by the scholar Emmanouil Aretoulakis: "We are too deeply immersed in the culture of visual violence *not* to appreciate aesthetically, or take secret pleasure in, real violence when it occurs."[8]

Following 9/11, far from admitting our attraction to violent imagery, we went to great lengths to hide from it. For weeks after the attacks, U.S. TV networks and movie studios were loath to screen any film that reveled in flames and high-speed impact. The release of the Arnold Schwarzenegger action movie *Collateral Dam-*

age (dir. Andrew Davis, 2002) was postponed until February 2002. Even the first TV airing of the anime *Full Metal Panic!* (dir. Koichi Chigira, 2002) was delayed because it involved a terrorist hijacking a plane. The vacuum left by the absence of such imagery was filled by a single spectacle of destruction: the footage of the attacks. On September 11 and for many days afterward, news anchors discussed the latest developments while sitting before a looped video backdrop of the burning towers. New camera angles of the event regularly surfaced and were quickly rushed into our living rooms. Perhaps the footage was screened so often because it beggared belief and therefore required multiple viewings to fully comprehend. The scholar Kathy Smith supports this theory, suggesting that repetition of the images of 9/11 signified "a global attempt to admit its possibility and to come to terms with the act."[9] Patricia Mellencamp, in her classic study of "catastrophe coverage," argues that repeated viewings of traumatic events such as the assassination of President Kennedy or the Challenger disaster allow us to "acknowledge, then alleviate fear and pain."[10] She draws on Sigmund Freud's essay "Beyond the Pleasure Principle" to argue that the compulsion to repeat can result in mastery over loss.

Maybe we did watch the footage so obsessively for therapeutic reasons. And yet we did not just watch it. We lovingly manipulated it to form an ever-shifting and hypnotic montage of jet fuel igniting, pedestrians fleeing, and towers falling. Many news reports and documentaries on 9/11 were edited to replicate the aesthetic qualities of the action movie. Geoff King discusses the HBO production *In Memorium: New York City* (2002), specifically the sequencing of two shots of the second plane hitting the South Tower. He notes that "each shot of the fireball starts just before the stage of its development reached in the previous shot . . . , the overall effect of which is to heighten the impact."[11] Such careful reshaping suggests that we wanted stimulation as well as healing from our compulsive rewatching of the footage.

TV channels could bring us the excitement of 9/11 by calling it news. Hollywood, on the other hand, an institution associated primarily with entertainment, could not easily revisit the famous images of destruction without facing accusations of exploitation. Therefore, *United 93* (dir. Paul Greengrass, 2006) confined us largely to the interior of a hijacked plane and *World Trade Center* (dir. Oliver Stone, 2006) trapped us, for the majority of its running time, in the rubble of the destroyed towers. *Cloverfield* is the first Hollywood movie not only to dwell on the destruction in Manhattan but also to revel in it. It manages this feat by removing us just far enough from reality that we do not have to confront our fascination with the death and destruction wrought on 9/11. By reconfiguring the event as a science-fiction monster movie, it allows us to experience the terrorist attacks as an exciting spectacle without any attendant feelings of guilt.

A group of friends is gathered for a going-away party when a series of explosions rocks the city. "Think it's another terrorist attack?" asks a frightened guest as the revelers spill into the street. From here on, it is chaos. Characters run, scream,

Hiding under a bridge in Central Park as violence explodes all around: *Cloverfield* **reminds us of our dependence on cameras and our compulsion to record. Courtesy of Paramount Pictures**

and try to rescue a stranded compatriot as a behemoth wreaks havoc all around them. And we go along for the ride, revisiting many of the familiar 9/11 sights, goaded into ever more dizzying levels of amazement by Hud's breathless commentary.

The experience is made yet more involving by the fact that every image in the film is a shaky, swishing point-of-view shot. The subjective camera is designed to give us a sense that we are part of the on-screen world, living through *Cloverfield*'s version of 9/11. In what might be considered an act of exuberant communion with those who endured the real-life attacks, we get to run through dust-shrouded streets and up the stairs of a collapsing building. At movie's end we even get to die, the final reward offered by a movie that has studiously pursued every aspect of the September 11 experience. In a climactic scene, the monster's huge jaws bear down on the camera, devouring Hud—and us, too, it would seem.

Cloverfield offers an intensified version of the real thing, providing a greater degree of destruction and violence than even the famous video images of the attacks. Instead of confining the devastation to a relatively small area of New York City, the film makes sure to level vast tracts of densely inhabited urban space. Multiple skyscrapers explode and numerous vehicles are engulfed in flames. By the climax, as stealth bombers attempt to dispatch the creature, most of Manhattan is ablaze and Central Park is wiped from the map.

Cloverfield gives us a stunningly violent 9/11. In discussing broadcast images of the real attacks, Žižek notes that "it is surprising how little of the actual carnage we see—no dismembered bodies, no blood, no desperate faces of dying people . . . in clear contrast to reporting on Third World catastrophes."[12] *Cloverfield* gleefully fills in the blanks. We are offered an eviscerated corpse on a stretcher, horrific wounds in close-up, and a character that explodes in a shower of blood.

The film engages in various strategies to keep us focused on the excitement of destruction lest we begin to contemplate the more troubling aspects of a widespread slaughter. For instance, by offering us no character with whom to empathize, the film studiously discourages feelings of loss or grief. Ross Douthat of *National Review* notes that we are presented with "the blandest, most vacuous group of pretty faces."[13] And while the shallowness of the film's characters makes it difficult for us to care about them, their elite social status means that we may even enjoy their suffering. Many a critic has displayed a pronounced animus for the rich, beautiful loft-dwellers who populate the movie. The *Village Voice* pillories the film's "neo-yuppies" and applauds the film for doing the same, arguing that "*Cloverfield* enacts its deft simulation of that infamous September morning to brutalize the society that flourished from its ruin like some tacky, tenacious, condo-dwelling fungus."[14] Like a horror movie in which an obnoxious band of bourgeois youth are chased by a chainsaw-wielding proletarian, *Cloverfield* gives us every opportunity to side with the monster as it metes out punishment to the privileged.

The film was released in January 2008, just as the full magnitude of the previous year's financial collapse began to hit home. It was certainly a timely work, allowing audiences to vent their frustration at the social class that had, arguably, been the chief cause of so much misery. Is it also possible that by mobilizing resentment against New York's upper class, *Cloverfield* taps into a very dark, but entirely plausible, response to 9/11: a sense of satisfaction at witnessing the demise of so many of the nation's wealthy elite. Ward Churchill saw the ruination of his academic career after he suggested that the attacks constituted a legitimate revenge on the "little Eichmanns inhabiting the sterile sanctuary of the twin towers."[15] Without openly endorsing such a theory, *Cloverfield* proffers the suffering and death of banal, beautiful office workers during an attack on New York as an entirely palatable and pleasurable spectacle.

The presentation of any sympathetic characters in *Cloverfield* would threaten our enjoyment of the violent spectacle. If the film dwelled on the ideological complexities of 9/11, our experience might be completely ruined. And so, instead of al-Qaeda, we are offered a monster. Unlike terrorists, monsters are not driven by ideology. We do not have to think about why the monster wreaks destruction, it just does. Its violence is "senseless," a term favored by many a media pundit unwilling to confront the root causes of the attacks. Certain politicians and political commentators flourished by portraying 9/11 as a straightforward "us-and-them" scenario, thereby allowing Americans to support the notion of "payback" in the war zones of Afghanistan and Iraq. *Cloverfield* presents us with an "us-and-it" scenario, the enemy reduced to an individual monster that is an easily definable, visible, and therefore killable threat.

The movie presents further revisions of the 9/11 narrative, downplaying the more disquieting aspects of the attacks. On September 11, the emergency services proved well-nigh helpless. Communication devices malfunctioned and confusion reigned. But *Cloverfield* presents no confused firefighters or harried rescue personnel. Instead, we can thrill to gruffly efficient soldiery. Here is the story not of a chaotic rescue operation but of a clear-cut war in which the authorities are already on the offensive. On September 11, the military arrived late and American Airlines Flight 11 and United Airlines Flight 175 got through to their targets because Air Force jets were not scrambled in time. *Cloverfield* offers us military personnel quickly on the scene, fighting the enemy at close quarters. And in this version of 9/11, victims of the disaster can be rescued. After the collapse of the twin towers, as Mikita Brottman notes, "there were no miraculous rescues for us to applaud, no half-dead bodies to be pulled proudly out of the rubble."[16] A lengthy sequence in *Cloverfield* is devoted to a successful rescue in the half-destroyed Time Warner Towers. Rather than the dispiriting sight of ground zero workers collecting pieces of charred flesh, we can gaze upon a knight in shining armor rescuing a damsel in distress.

And so a multifaceted and harrowing event is transformed into a simple adventure. *Cloverfield* drains 9/11 of any significance other than its potential to yield exciting images of destruction. Anything that could distract us from wallowing in the carnage—be it sympathetic characterization or the complexities of a terrorist attack—is kept from intruding on our pleasure.

All *Cloverfield* wants to do is look. As if to underscore the film's interest in the act of looking, it reminds us constantly of our dependence on cameras. They are a ubiquitous and constant presence, turning up in the bedroom of two lovers, at Coney Island for a day trip, at the going-away party, and then, of course, during the monster's rampage. While the decapitated head of the Statue of Liberty lies in the street, bystanders pull out their cell phones to capture the image. Everywhere there is a compulsion to record. As Hud says, "People need to see this, you know? This is gonna be important. People are gonna watch this."

While *Cloverfield*'s characters are quite able to see and record, they have far more trouble expressing their emotions. Speaking of a bereaved friend, Hud laments, "I don't know what to say to him. Like, I feel I should say something, but I don't know what to say." That line, "I don't know what to say," becomes a motif in the movie, characters feeling tongue-tied as they try to express their feelings about the attack on New York. Perhaps we should, after all, feel some empathy for these people. When contemplating 9/11, it is hard to know what to say. Perhaps "Did you see that?" is the best most of us can do.

Notes

1. Jessica Wakeman, "On *Cloverfield* and 9/11," *Huffington Post*, January 21, 2008, www .huffingtonpost.com/jessica-wakeman/on-cloverfield-and-911_b_82518.html.
2. "Terrible Beauty: A-Bomb Tests," *Life*, www.life.com/image/first/in-gallery/33842/terrible -beauty-a-bomb-tests (accessed March 7, 2011).
3. Slavoj Žižek, *Welcome to the Desert of the Real: Five Essays on September 11 and Related Dates* (London: Verso, 2002), 11.
4. Rebecca Allison, "9/11 Wicked but a Work of Art, says Damien Hirst," *Guardian* September 11, 2002.
5. Ibid.
6. William Osborne, "Documentation of Stockhausen's Comments re: 9/11," www.osborne -conant.org/documentation_stockhausen.htm (accessed March 7, 2011).
7. Julia Spinola, "Monstrous Art," *Frankfurter Allgemeine Zeitung*, September 25, 2001.
8. Emmanouil Aretoulakis, "Aesthetic Appreciation, Ethics, and 9/11," *Contemporary Aesthetics*, March 31, 2008, www.contempaesthetics.org/newvolume/pages/article .php?articleID=510.
9. Kathy Smith, "Reframing Fantasy: September 11 and the Global Audience," in *Spectacle of the Real: From Hollywood to Reality TV and Beyond*, ed. Geoff King (Bristol: Intellect Books, 2005), 67.
10. Patricia Mellencamp, "TV Time and Catastrophe; or, *Beyond the Pleasure Principle* of Television," in *Logics of Television: Essays in Cultural Criticism*, ed. Mellencamp (Bloomington: Indiana University Press, 1990), 258.
11. Geoff King, "'Just Like a Movie?' 9/11 and Hollywood Spectacle," in King, *Spectacle of the Real*, 52.
12. Žižek, *Welcome*, 13.
13. Ross Douthat, "Less Than Monstrous," *National Review*, February 11, 2008, 55.
14. Nathan Lee, "Cloverfield Is One Giant, Incredibly Entertaining 'Screw You' to Yuppie New York," *Village Voice*, January 15 2008, www.villagevoice.com/2008–01–15/film/cloverfield -is-one-giant-incredibly-entertaining-screw-you-to-yuppie-new-york/.
15. Ward Churchill, "'Some People Push Back': On the Justice of Roosting Chickens," Ward Churchill, www.kersplebedeb.com/mystuff/s11/churchill.html (accessed March 7, 2011).
16. Mikita Brottman, "The Fascination of Abomination: The Censored Images of 9/11," in *Film and Television after 9/11*, ed. Wheeler Winston Dixon (Carbondale: Southern Illinois Press, 2004), 166–67.

Literary Lions Tackle 9/11

Updike and DeLillo Depicting History through the Novel

Bob Batchelor

Here is an argument for serendipity: John Updike, who normally spends his mornings writing in seclusion at his home in Beverly Farms, Massachusetts, happens to be less than a mile away from the World Trade Center on September 11, 2001. He might otherwise have watched from home via repeated news clips, but fate intervened, resulting in the author viewing the twin towers fall from a tenth-floor vantage point, on what he deemed an otherwise mundane trip "visiting some kin" in Brooklyn Heights.[1] Consequently, one of America's foremost writers witnesses firsthand the defining moment of the early twenty-first century. The *New Yorker* published Updike's account in its September 24, 2001, issue, the first to appear after 9/11.

Given Updike's prolific work as a journalist and critic, one presumes that his thoughts on the terrorist attacks would have seen print whether or not he actually saw the destruction, but his on-the-scene reporting gave his words added consequence. Updike's description of the horror and of his personal response provided readers with an additional tool to process the events. He captured the heartache Americans felt, explaining, "We knew we had just witnessed many deaths; we clung to each other as if we ourselves were falling."[2] Updike also summarized the post–September 11 fear that gripped the nation, saying, "The nightmare is still on. The bodies are beneath the rubble, the last-minute phone calls—remarkably calm and long, many of them—are still being reported, the sound of an airplane overhead still bears an unfamiliar menace, the thought of boarding an airplane with our old blasé blitheness keeps receding into the past."[3]

Radical History Review
Issue 111 (Fall 2011)   DOI 10.1215/01636545-1268785
© 2011 by MARHO: The Radical Historians' Organization, Inc.

Shortly thereafter, in the December 2001 issue of *Harper's*, the novelist Don DeLillo offered his analysis of the tragic day and its repercussions. In contrast to Updike's intimate account, DeLillo's piece focused on broader subjects: globalization, technological hegemony, and the consequences of hypercapitalism. DeLillo envisaged a vicious cycle: "America" penetrating the rest of the world through "the thrust of our technology" and "blunt force of our foreign policy," which then compelled terrorist response.[4] As a result of the attacks, he foresaw a new order: "The future has yielded, for now, to medieval expedience, to the old slow furies of cut-throat religion. Kill the enemy and pluck out his heart."[5]

After addressing the attacks' consequences in these high-profile essays, both authors turned to fictional accounts. In *Terrorist* (2006) and *Falling Man* (2007), Updike and DeLillo present two contrasting yet compelling visions of the 9/11 United States. There is much to be learned from analyzing these novels, produced by two of the world's leading literary figures, particularly in understanding how fiction is used to depict history.

Updike's novel, which landed him on the *New York Times* best seller list for the first time in decades, is set in a recognizable near future and portrays a nation that narrowly escaped an apocalyptic moment, consequently increasing its vigilance against further attacks. His central character is an eighteen-year-old recent high school graduate, Ahmad Mulloy, whose intense Muslim faith carries him toward homegrown-terrorist status.

The setting in the near future enables Updike to use the events of that day and its implications as a framework for harshly critiquing American society and culture. Updike's worldview in *Terrorist* offers a near-complete reversal from his reputation as the nation's foremost suburban and pro-American chronicler. Instead, Updike paints a picture of a new nation that emerges as not more innocent, but rather simultaneously more suspicious and solemn, yet filled with citizens willingly self-deluded and distracted by popular culture and consumption.

In contrast, DeLillo's novel begins as the World Trade Center towers fall. The corporate attorney Keith Neudecker emerges from the North Tower in a daze, covered in ash and blood. In the ensuing days and months, he attempts to find meaning in this new world—one that literally came crashing down all around him. DeLillo's viewpoint speaks to disconnectedness, with many characters almost ghost-like after the attacks, appearing and disappearing in a wash of futility.

The terrorists, including the leader Mohamed Atta, are depicted as well, providing a contrasting view as they prepare to die for their beliefs. However, against stereotype, DeLillo portrays Hammad (an Atta underling) not as a hell-bent murderer, but as an individual filled with doubt as the mission looms.

Updike and DeLillo stand as two of the foremost literary lions in the United States—respected, critically acclaimed, and widely read. As a result, their 9/11 novels drew a broad audience and much critical commentary. Their fictional renderings of a watershed moment in history helped readers as they attempted to make sense of the world after the attacks. Despite all the media coverage, analysis, and public discussion of 9/11, Updike and DeLillo provided the public with an additional avenue inside the day and its aftermath through the highly personal act of reading.

Updike's Homegrown Terrorist

The question at the heart of Updike's novel is how a potential homegrown terrorist— of whatever persuasion—might develop. At publication in 2006, this plot seemed far fetched, yet as more information regarding homegrown terrorism is uncovered, Updike seems prophetic. For example, an October 2010 study by researchers from the Institute for Homeland Security Solutions and the RAND Corporation examined eighty-six potential terrorist plots in the United States from 1999 to 2009, using a broad definition of terrorism that includes white supremacist groups as well as plots resembling those of al-Qaeda. While the study focused on how these plans were thwarted (primarily through observations made by the general public and/or law enforcement personnel, not the Jack Bauer–like counterterrorism efforts that dominate popular culture), the number and variety of potential plots listed in the report make *Terrorist* much more realistic. Updike's use of real-life events to fuel his storytelling exemplifies the complicated links that exist between self, topics, and experiences for both authors and readers.[6]

Terrorism itself is a subject defined according to cultural understandings (and possibly prior to 9/11, misunderstandings) of the concept, yet as a writer, Updike also interprets the idea based on his own lived experiences and his social interaction with others. Making matters more complex, the author's perceptions of terrorism and its consequences are filled with a lifetime of cultural representations, drawn from film, television, books, and journalistic accounts of terroristic acts. Interestingly, the characters in the novel confront the same issues. Although *Terrorist*'s fictional world of New Prospect, New Jersey, is imaginary, characters in the novel face the quasi-realistic framework in which 9/11 occurred and presents ramifications.

For example, Ahmad's Lebanese American boss, Charlie Chehab, discusses parallels between modern jihadists and the revolutionary forces led by George Washington. Charlie's underlying assumptions about both groups are drawn primarily from cultural representations, though he does in fact have firsthand experience with would-be terrorists. The idea of Washington as the hero of the Revolutionary War also presents its own meaning, since in American lore Washington is the leader of a revolution against an unjust power. The sociologist C. Wright Mills explains how the cultural machine is used to create the self, calling it "the lens of mankind though which men see; the medium through which they interpret and report what they see. It is the semiorganized source of their very identities and of their aspirations."[7] Charlie's heroic stance — tying jihadists and anti-American Muslims to the nation's preeminent founding father — enables him to manipulate Ahmad based on their shared cultural representation of Washington. Concurrently, the reader must also interact and digest the information.

Terrorist is a product not only of the events Updike witnessed that day in Brooklyn Heights but is also derived from what pundits deemed "the post-9/11 world," a new cultural environment fundamentally different from what had existed before. In an interview, Updike discussed his rationale, saying: "I'm interested in Islam as a more fiery and absolutist and, some would say, fanatical brand of theistic faith. So it was not just my happening to have been there but my sensation that I was qualified to speak about why young men are willing to become suicide bombers. I can kind of understand it, and I'm not sure too many Americans can."[8] Immediately after September 11, the nation turned more patriotic, lauding the heroic efforts of firefighters and police officers in New York City and around the country. President George W. Bush also garnered nearly universal support for military efforts, including the military invasion of Afghanistan and other efforts to destroy Osama bin Laden's al-Qaeda terrorist network.

The Bush administration also launched a series of domestic security programs to counter potential future terrorist threats. Bush authorized the creation of the Department of Homeland Security to coordinate efforts at home, naming the former Pennsylvania governor Tom Ridge as its first director. Homeland Security initiated a national alert system indicating the threat level at any given time, ranging from red (severe risk) to green (low risk). The president also worked with members of Congress to pass the USA PATRIOT Act (2001), which granted federal authorities broad powers to sniff out and counter possible security threats.

On the cultural front, commentators argued that 9/11 would fundamentally change the nation's viewing, reading, and media habits. In response, many radio stations dropped songs with lyrics that might be considered offensive. Movie and television studios censored themselves. For example, executives delayed the release of the Michael Caine film *The Quiet American* (dir. Phillip Noyce, 2002), based on the Graham Greene novel and set in 1950s Vietnam, because of sensitivities to potential anti-American sentiments in the movie. Although Updike's work is noted for the role nostalgia plays in it, *Terrorist* focuses on what remained in the wake of September 11.

In a prepublication interview with Charles McGrath in the *New York Times*, Updike discussed writing *Terrorist*, explaining that he thought he had "something to say from the standpoint of a terrorist": "I think I felt I could understand the animosity and hatred which an Islamic believer would have for our system. Nobody's trying to see it from that point of view. I guess I have stuck my neck out here in a number of ways, but that's what writers are for, maybe." He added that detractors could not have asked for a "more sympathetic and, in a way, more loving portrait of a terrorist."[9] This belief in himself as an interpreter of or interloper into the mind of an eighteen-year-old religious zealot and would-be jihadist speaks to Updike's confidence as a novelist. The qualifier *maybe* in the quote above adds a smidgeon of modesty, but it also accentuates how Updike feels about the role of the writer: attempting to understand the inner workings of characters, taking chances that may or may not be popular, and confronting potential critics.

For an author labeled resolutely pro-establishment and pro–suburban America, Updike has little use for authority figures or institutions in *Terrorist*. From the teachers who traverse the halls at dreary, cracked New Prospect High School to the police officers patrolling the Lincoln Tunnel, no one who holds a position of power remains unscathed. While an air of once-held power emanates from the second main character, Jack Levy, Updike undermines that aura by revealing Jack's fear of old age and his sense that he no longer matters. Even God comes under fire, sometimes from Levy's soliloquies against the Jewish religion and sometimes from Ahmad's temptations and doubts, although he proclaims he feels "God standing beside him — so close as to make a single, unique holy identity, *closer to him than his neck-vein*."[10] Updike consistently undermines those holding power, showing that the brave facades, whether propped up in public or questioned in silent contemplation, are illusory. Authority that lacks true belief or faith reveals the absurdity of power in the post-9/11 United States.

DeLillo's Near History

DeLillo's portrait of 9/11 asks readers to question broad societal issues, such as U.S. hegemony, but it also demands the examination of more intimate details, such as personal relationships, fate, and identity. In comparison to Updike's overt scolding, DeLillo only subtly critiques American culture, focusing more attention on the way 9/11 fractured individuals and how they comprehend the world altered by terrorism.

The most striking feature of *Falling Man* is the way DeLillo replicates the chaos of 9/11 and its aftermath through literary techniques. Starting the novel as the main character emerges from the rubble, for example, immediately demands that the reader reexamine deep-rooted feelings about the day from a historical perspective, given the novel's publication in 2007. In other words, the reader confronts the visceral action on the page — "falling ash and near night" — while simultaneously drawing on his or her own mental images from the day, a personal inventory including imagery gathered from newscasts, photographs, and Web-based sources.[11]

As the novel progresses, DeLillo keeps the reader alert by starting sections of text and chapters with pronouns, rather than with character names, thus asking the reader to shuffle through competing characters and story lines to uncover the current speaker or person described. A representative, jarring segment begins, "She was awake, middle of the night, eyes closed, mind running and she felt time pressing in, and threat, a kind of beat in her head."[12]

DeLillo also uses the notion of time to amplify the turmoil. The resulting ambiguity symbolizes the disjointed nature of the post-9/11 United States. For example, Keith more or less devolves from corporate attorney to professional poker player in a series of set routines that enable him to avoid facing up to more important issues, such as his family and post-traumatic stress from living through the terrorist attack on the World Trade Center. The narration blurs between an omniscient view-point and Keith's, explaining, "He was also going home periodically, three or four days, love, sex, fatherhood, home-cooked food, but was lost at times for something to say."[13]

As Keith jets from one poker tournament to the next, he revels in the habits this lifestyle dictates. Essentially, he relies on the routine, and wonders "if he was becoming a self-operating mechanism, like a humanoid robot . . . but totally, rig-idly controllable."[14] At the same time, however, Keith cannot completely escape the post-9/11 realities, admitting "every time he boarded a flight he glanced at faces on both sides of the aisle, trying to spot the man or men who might be a danger to them all."[15] From DeLillo's perspective, the terrorist attacks eliminate the kind of day-to-day certainties that provided people with meaning or mileposts. Afterward, even seemingly ordinary events take on a mystical aura when the threat of terrorism is ever present.

For the characters in *Falling Man*, an indissoluble distinction exists between pre- and post-9/11. At one point, after making love to Florence, a fellow North Tower survivor, Keith contemplates time since the attack, calling it the "after-days." He explains, "These are the days after. Everything now is measured by after."[16] Later, when he finally opens up a little to his wife, Lianne, about his new state of being, including the rigidity and devotion to habit, Keith makes the distinction clearer, explaining, "That was before, this is after."[17]

For DeLillo, then, American society revolves around before and after. The literary critic John Leonard sees the power of *Falling Man* in the author's ability to portray the eras of before and after the attacks: "How we really felt before we were bushwhacked; of our fugue state on that election day, in the endless night-mare feedback loop of jet plane, firebomb, towers falling, another in a long line of cheesy Hollywood films in which the crystal palace of Manhattan is destroyed by comets, plagues, apes, aliens, insects, androids, hydrogen bombs, tidal waves or toxic waste."[18] In this before/after transformation, DeLillo creates characters that stand in for the wash of emotion the nation felt following the terrorist attacks. Keith, the survivor, represents victimization. He copes but is out of sync with those around him, basically falling into a monotonous trance. The routines he develops give him a mechanism to survive, but he is too emotionally wired to manage. Lianne symbol-izes the fear that gripped the nation. She sees terror all around her and searches for answers in the deaths and destruction, but she cannot look away, even as 9/11 tightens its hold on her.

Literature as History

One might reasonably ask what role novels might play in depicting the terrorist attacks, or how they could help readers grasp the topic given the multiple channels accessible to people for information on 9/11. Updike once famously remarked, "My fiction about the daily doings of ordinary people has more history in it than history books."[19] *Terrorist* and *Falling Man* test this hypothesis by illustrating 9/11 and its consequences based on a mixture of "real-world" fact, impressions, memories, and even misperceptions and the fictional framework the authors create. The mixture of authorial creation (itself a merging of intent with input from numerous editors, proofreaders, and others) with reader response proves particularly profound with a global event as powerful as 9/11.

Tackling the issue of the enduring power of novels in the technology age, the writer Tom Wolfe noted that movies, for instance, fail to get "inside the minds of the characters" and cannot explain complication without sacrificing the medium's desire for constant motion and imagery. As a result, people often complain that movies made from novels rarely live up to expectations.[20] A similar idea speaks to the popularity of 9/11–themed novels. In chaotic times people often desire a window into the minds of others. *Terrorist* and *Falling Man* provide those portals, from authors whom readers trust to provide a penetrating analysis.

Readers approach the work of famed authors like DeLillo and Updike with preconceived expectations. According to James Phelan, "The lines between author, reader, and text become blurred. . . . Rhetoric is the synergy occurring between authorial agency, textual phenomena, and reader response."[21] As such, the reading public carves out of its collective consciousness what to expect from their work. One imagines in this sense that the actual Updike or DeLillo dissolves or disappears as the reader interacts with what they produce, understanding, however, that it is an "Updike" or "DeLillo" work.

In each author's fiction, readers anticipate (or possibly require) an identifiable voice, and they feel part of each subsequent novel because they sense in it something to which they can relate consciously or subconsciously. "Most readers," Janice Radway explains, "willfully engage texts from their own ground, wandering about within them sometimes aimlessly, sometimes hell-bent on a purpose. They raid them, remake them, perform them . . . they write them anew."[22] In other words, readers return to authors who provide them with a setting, situation, or characters they can adapt in their own minds. The old adage "diving into a book" takes on new meaning here—the reader also dives into the author.

Interestingly, both novels use 9/11 as a vehicle for critiquing American culture. For Updike, the United States that gets back on its feet after 9/11 retains its hyperfocus on popular culture and its addiction to consumerism, and it has grown increasingly fat and apathetic. But the nation is also capable of greatness, particularly when its people hold on to their beliefs.

Given modern American society's obsession with consumerism, popular culture, and the self, one perceives that in Updike's new world, those who do the opposite—focus on societal advancement and preservation—will become the new heroes. Perhaps the larger issue at stake is whether or not Updike thinks it matters. While blips of hope dot the landscape, blind, fat, and stupid America lurches toward the apocalypse, sidetracked by media-generated distractions as the end draws near.

Updike's vision of the post-9/11 United States centers on the idea of faith and lack of faith in the modern world. For Updike, consumerism and its consequences replaced religion and people's belief in the U.S. political and social system, ultimately debasing the foundational ideas that built the nation. Instead of a fervent belief in the American way or the American dream, Jack, a high school guidance counselor, laments the impulse to purchase "tawdry junk" that fills people's daily lives.[23] The lack of faith, passion, or commitment to "the right path" leads to a world "full of nuzzling," according to Ahmad's mentor, Sheik Rashid, "blind animals in a herd bumping against one another, looking for a scent that will comfort them."[24]

In *Falling Man*, Keith represents a version of the United States that still lurches forward, despite the blow of the attacks. He relies on routine to get him through each day, just as Americans in the real world fought through "after-days" fixated on endless images of the attacks and the aftermath via television and the Web. He explains to his wife, who yearns for answers, "Nothing is next. There is no next. This was next. . . . The time to be afraid is when there's no reason to be afraid. Too late now."[25] The people around Keith want to understand his survival, even as he repels the notion that stories matter anymore.

What we take from these depictions of real events in novels, then, is a way into the topic that other media channels struggle to provide. Even the severe video of the planes hurtling into buildings and the towers falling cannot compare to fiction. DeLillo discussed this notion in an interview, saying that novels in many respects constitute posthistory, because they allow us to "enter unknown territory . . . [into] interior lives, what a character sees, feels, thinks, hears, even what a character even dreams." In this respect, fiction enables probing into "elements ordinarily beyond the grasp of historians, or social theorists, or journalists."[26]

Fiction writers assume real risk in taking on events as emotionally charged as 9/11, including potential backlash from readers and criticism from professional commentators. Yet the interior viewpoint one obtains from fiction, combined with the deeply personal act of reading itself, enables novelists to create works that interpret historical events in new and meaningful ways. Whether or not fiction can be more historical than history or journalism (or even posthistory) is a subject open for debate. Many audiences, however, expect novelists to investigate and unravel society and culture. In turn, we grant fiction writers much trust in confronting and depicting history.

Notes

1. John Updike, *Due Considerations: Essays and Criticism* (New York: Ballantine, 2007), 117.
2. Ibid.
3. Ibid., 117–18.
4. Don DeLillo, "In the Ruins of the Future," *Harper's Magazine*, December 2001, 33.
5. Ibid., 37.
6. Kevin Strom et al., *Building on Clues: Examining Successes and Failures in Detecting U.S. Terrorist Plots, 1999–2009* (Research Triangle Park, NC: Institute for Homeland Security Solutions, 2010).
7. C. Wright Mills, *Power, Politics, and People: The Collected Essays of C. Wright Mills*, ed. Irving Louis Horowitz (New York: Ballantine, 1963), 406.
8. Alden Mudge, "Holy Terror: Updike Goes inside the Mind of a Muslim Teen," BookPage, www.bookpage.com/0606bp/john_updike.html (accessed March 10, 2011).
9. Charles McGrath, "John Updike's Latest, a 'Loving Portrait of a Terrorist,'" *New York Times*, May 31, 2006.
10. John Updike, *Terrorist* (New York: Knopf, 2006), 144–45.
11. Don DeLillo, *Falling Man* (New York: Scribner, 2007), 3.
12. Ibid., 67.
13. Ibid., 197.
14. Ibid., 226.
15. Ibid., 198.
16. Ibid., 137.
17. Ibid., 215.
18. John Leonard, "The Dread Zone," *Nation*, May 28, 2007, 21.
19. John Updike, *Picked-up Pieces* (New York: Fawcett, 1975), 482.
20. Tom Wolfe, *Hooking Up* (New York: Farrar, Straus and Giroux, 2000), 169.
21. James Phelan, *Narrative as Rhetoric: Technique, Audiences, Ethics, Ideology* (Columbus: Ohio State University Press, 1996), xii.
22. Janice Radway, "What's the Matter with Reception Study? Some Thoughts on the Disciplinary Origins, Conceptual Constraints, and Persistent Viability of a Paradigm," in *New Directions in American Reception Study*, ed. Philip Goldstein and James L. Machor (New York: Oxford University Press, 2008), 339.
23. Updike, *Terrorist*, 20.
24. Ibid., 10.
25. DeLillo, *Falling Man*, 10.
26. National Public Radio, "Interview: Don DeLillo," June 20, 2007, www.npr.org/templates/story/story.php?storyId=11223451&ps=rs.

The Depiction of 9/11 in Literature

The Role of Images and Intermedial References

Sonia Baelo-Allué

The 9/11 terrorist attack on the United States can be considered a cultural trauma and an intermedial phenomenon. The attack has become one of the most represented disasters in history since it produced an unprecedented visual impact on those around the world who watched the second plane crash into the South Tower live on television. That 9/11 was a media event is inextricably linked to the way we remember the attacks and the way we coped with them when they took place. Many spectators watched the same loop of video footage and images over and over during the days following the attacks and used the TV screen as a protective shield against the reality they perceived. In an attempt to make sense of the unfolding trauma, and due to the ubiquity of similar disasters in U.S. cinema, many people compared the events with a Hollywood disaster movie;[1] the suicide attackers were likened to actors in a global superproduction.[2] Such views underlined the seemingly unreal nature of the events and the way they shattered our sense of reality.

Maybe because the attacks seemed unreal, media reports on them used some of the conventions of fiction. Andrew O'Hagan in the *New York Review of Books* even claimed that September 11 offered "a few hours when American novelists could only sit at home while journalism taught them fierce lessons in multivocality, point of view, the structure of plot, interior monologue, the pressure of history, the force of silence, and the uncanny. Actuality showed its own naked art that day."[3] For O'Hagan it seems that what made journalism so powerful those days was the way it appropriated many of the conventions of fiction (plot, point of view, interior mono-

Radical History Review

Issue 111 (Fall 2011)   DOI 10.1215/01636545-1268794

© 2011 by MARHO: The Radical Historians' Organization, Inc.

logue, etc.). The *9/11 Commission Report*, the official report on the events leading up to the September 11 attacks, also drew on fictional resources.[4] Ben Yagoda found the book exemplary because of its literary style and its allegiance to the truth. He liked some of its literary techniques, such as its starting in medias res, and its use of foreshadowing in some sentences. It tells two parallel stories: that of Islamic fundamentalists and that of the U.S. government's attempt to deal with the threat. For Yagoda it is like a "cinematic structure cutting back and forth between the two narratives."[5] Other reviewers also praised the book for the way it reads like a novel and for being "an improbable literary triumph."[6] A graphic adaptation of the report in 2006 made use of the agile and colourful style of superhero comics: it provides sound effects like "R-RUMBLE" when the South Tower collapses and "BLAMM!" when one of the hijacked planes crashes into the Pentagon.[7] The graphic adaptation received much praise for being unexpectedly moving and for its capacity to build suspense.[8] Also, "the captions pack a lot of punch."[9] The use of techniques coming from fiction thus elicited praise rather than rejection.

Ironically enough, when literature tried to draw from real images of 9/11 and from the language of journalism, many reviewers considered the move disrespectful and inappropriate. Maybe because reality had resembled fiction too much, and because some films, TV series, video games, and books had imagined the attacks before they took place,[10] the events of 9/11 did not seem to lend themselves to fictional adaptation at first. In fact, the representation of traumatic events in literature has proven a bone of contention for decades. Theodor Adorno's famous words come to mind: "To write poetry after Auschwitz is barbaric."[11] In the aftermath of the events, several writers and journalists claimed that fiction had nothing to offer that journalism and the news could not provide. Four days after the tragedy, the writer Ian McEwan admitted that all he could do was "watch the television, read the papers, turn on the radio again," recognizing that "the derided profession of journalism can rise quite nobly, and with immense resource, to public tragedy."[12] Lynne Sharon Schwartz wrote two months after the catastrophe that it was too soon to go back to fictional stories: "We will do what is needed; we will write the next sentence. Only not yet, not here on the bleak brink of November."[13] Jay McInerney met his fellow writer Bret Easton Ellis on September 11, 2001, and both agreed that they could not go back to the novels they were writing (set in New York) and were glad they did not have a book coming out that month, since nobody now showed any interest in fiction.[14]

Despite these initial misgivings, all these authors ended up writing their own 9/11 novels: McEwan wrote *Saturday* (2005), Schwartz *The Writing on the Wall* (2005), and McInerney *The Good Life* (2006). Ten years after the attacks, 9/11 fiction has become a genre in itself. Novels like Frédéric Beigbeder's *Windows on the World* (2004), Jonathan Safran Foer's *Extremely Loud and Incredibly Close* (2005), and Don DeLillo's *Falling Man* (2007) exemplify how literature has chosen to com bine real and fictional elements with a series of intermedial references in the depiction of 9/11. I here understand intermediality as the interplay between different media forms: photography, film, and the written word combine in novels that draw both from reality and from fiction.[15] Beigbeder, Foer, and DeLillo do not ignore the mediated nature of 9/11 but display it through the incorporation of other media in their fiction, which renders the representation of the trauma more effectively.

Frédéric Beigbeder's *Windows on the World* (2004)

In this book we find many examples of intermediality and the blurring of reality and fiction. A quick look at the acknowledgments section reveals how the author has drawn from different media: songs, photos, newspaper articles, eyewitness accounts, nonfiction, literature, film, and poetry. The book consists of short chapters that represent one minute each from 8:30 to 10:29 a.m., the time of the North Tower's collapse on September, 11. Two narratives interlock: one about Carthew Yorston, the other about Frédéric Beigbeder. Yorston is a Texan real estate agent who is having breakfast with his two young sons at the Windows on the World restaurant atop the North Tower. Carthew mostly narrates these chapters, but his sons, nine-year-old Jerry and seven-year-old David, also contribute as they struggle to survive and escape the tower. Yet the novel is not just a fictional account of what might have happened to the people trapped in the Windows on the World restaurant. It is also narrated by a French author called Beigbeder who is writing from the Ciel de Paris restaurant atop the Montparnasse tower in Paris and who inserts his own experiences and reflections into the novel. These chapters combine autobiographical elements, facts about September 11, and comments on what is happening to the fictional Texan family in the North Tower. They undermine the fictional chapters: as the narrator Beigbeder puts it in the opening sentence, "You know how it ends: everybody dies."[16]

This twofold narrative is also visually reflected in a media combination — the blend of two medial forms of articulation that are present in their own materiality — that we find in the final chapter of the novel.[17] There are two columns made up of words that reproduce both the shape of the twin towers and of newspaper columns. Thus, the role of journalism on 9/11 is visually underlined. Besides, Beigbeder reconstructs the towers through words: through his fictional account of the events and through his attempt to speak the unspeakable. This chapter also mixes image (the shape of the towers), media (the journal columns), and literature (the author's written thoughts and personal reflections on the events). With his narration Beigbeder symbolically reconstructs the towers and integrates them in our mind.

Another instance of media combination is the insertion of real photographs into the narrative. Two of them were taken at Montparnasse cemetery in Paris. In one of them we see an effigy of Charles Baudelaire in a thoughtful position. In the other we see the photo of what he seems to be looking at: the Tour Montparnasse and a big cross that, given the angle, looks like the doomed twin towers. These photos represent Beigbeder's way of approaching the subject: from his position as a writer in the Montparnasse tower in Paris he reflects on the effects of the collapse of the twin towers in New York. The other photograph is equally symbolic and works as an ironic comment on the use of good and evil as absolute terms. Beigbeder took it in the United Nations sculpture garden and it shows a statue of St. George slaying a dragon, which, in the distance, looks like the fuselage of an airplane. It is a monument against war entitled "Good defeats Evil" and was made with the remnants of a U.S. and a Soviet missile. The photograph works as an ironic comment on the use of good and evil as absolute terms, since at the time in the United Nations the members of the Security Council were voting on a resolution about the war in Iraq. These media combinations depend on the image but also on their written context to make full sense.

Apart from these media combinations, the work also includes many intermedial references, that is, references to other media by imitating their techniques.[18] As happened on 9/11, characters use references to disaster movies to make sense of the attacks. Carthew tries to convince his sons that they are merely seeing a new attraction like the ones in theme parks, with special effects, holograms, and actors. Beigbeder, the narrator, comments on the similarities with Hollywood films; he even says that the victims' suffering lasted 102 minutes, the same as the average Hollywood film and the same as the number of chapters in the book. According to the narrator Beigbeder, the dust cloud produced after the collapse of the towers seemed taken from disaster movies like *The Blob, Godzilla, Independence Day, Armageddon, Die Hard 2,* or *Deep Impact.*[19]

A *New York Times* article and a collection of eyewitness accounts serve as the basis for Beigbeder's reconstruction of the events.[20] In fact, the narrator Beigbeder quotes real survivors and rescue workers and mentions the names and stories of actual people. However, it is through fiction that readers begin to understand what happened those final hours. Well into the novel the narrator Beigbeder claims that art is a window on the world and that it constitutes the most appropriate means to face traumatic events:[21] "Nowadays, books must go where television does not. Show the invisible, speak the unspeakable."[22] Beigbeder goes where the media could not go by combining images from that very media with the power of fiction and the imagination.

Jonathan Safran Foer's *Extremely Loud and Incredibly Close* (2005)

Foer's novel tells the story of Oskar Schell, a nine-year-old boy traumatized by his father's death in the World Trade Center. When he finds an unknown key in his father's closet, he starts a quest to find the lock it opens, hoping to find out more about his father and about how he died. His story intermingles with that of his grandparents who survived the Allied firebombing of Dresden in 1945. Just as *Win-*

dows on the World has two narrative pillars (Carthew's and Beigbeder's stories) *Extremely Loud and Incredibly Close* combines two traumas: 9/11 and World War II. In literature, trauma narratives tend to depart from linear sequence and make use of experimental devices to reflect the unsettling experience. Stylistically there are visual images, textual gaps, repetitions, and shifting viewpoints as readers are made to feel the disorienting positions of characters.[23] Images prove especially important in the trauma process since to be traumatized is to be possessed by an image or an event not assimilated or understood at the time.[24] Precisely because the experience cannot be assimilated and put into words when it takes place, it is arranged on an iconic level and returns in the form of hallucinations, nightmares, and images that haunt the traumatized person.[25] Thus a traumatic experience is reenacted belatedly through a series of images that cannot be assimilated, preventing the linguistic retrieval.

Since *Extremely Loud and Incredibly Close* constitutes a narrative of trauma, images play a very important role: there are photographs inserted into the narrative, changes in typography, and blank pages. Some reviewers did not receive well the graphic aspect of the novel, considering these images senseless gimmicks or,[26] worse, an exploitation of trauma.[27] Even though the graphic adaptation of *The 9/11 Commission Report* did not to stir up controversy, when fiction drew from images, the act was curiously considered exploitative and unnecessary. In *Extremely Loud and Incredibly Close* images are necessary as insights into Oskar's traumatized mind. Different photos of locks and doorknobs that show Oskar's need to "unlock" his own trauma represent his quest.

In the aftermath of 9/11, images played a double role. They were used to "act out" the collective trauma, which according to the historian Dominick LaCapra is the tendency to relive or reenact the past through flashbacks, nightmares, and compulsively repeated words and images. Over time, these images also became a way to "work through" the trauma, a means to gain critical distance from the events.[28] Therefore, images can both act out trauma through repetition and also work through it by visually mediating the trauma. Oskar acts out his trauma through his scrapbook, which he calls "Stuff That Happened to Me" and which is made of random images that have impressed him and that he remembers. Among the fourteen images, we find a collection of keys, two turtles mating, and a man falling from the Word Trade Center. This last image, with slight variations, returns throughout the book. It represents the "unspeakable" for Oskar, since, even though he does not comment on it, it keeps returning belatedly through the flashbacks in his mind. This image is counterbalanced with other more hopeful ones like a flock of birds flying or a cat jumping.

The novel ends with a flip book made of images of that same man falling, but in reverse sequence; he seems to be falling upward. These images are directly linked to the last paragraphs in the novel in which Oskar finally confronts the photo of the falling man, working through his trauma and wondering if that man might have been his father. In the same way as we can flip those final pages in the novel and make the falling man return to the window, Oskar imagines time going backward:

> When I flipped through them, it looked like the man was floating up through the sky. And if I'd had more pictures, he would've flown through a window, back into the building, and the smoke would've poured into a hole that the plane was about to come out of. Dad would've left his message backward, until the machine was empty, and the plane would've flown backward away from him, all the way to Boston. . . . We would have been safe.[29]

Just as Beigbeder reconstructs the twin towers visually through the two newspaper-like columns in his "10:28" chapter, Foer returns to a safer time with the help of the flip book. By combining fiction and real images Foer creates an illusion that can help us work through trauma.

Don DeLillo's *Falling Man* (2007)

Falling Man tells the story of Keith Neudecker, a lawyer who barely escapes from the twin towers on 9/11 and who returns in shock to the apartment he used to share with his son Justin and estranged wife Lianne. Although they are all traumatized, they try to resume their life together. Unlike *Windows on the World* and *Extremely Loud and Incredibly Close*, this novel has no images actually inserted into it, but images do play an important role as an expressive means. After seeing many photographs and videos of the events of September 11, 2001, DeLillo constructed the initial pages from well-known images of 9/11:

> It was not a street anymore but a world, a time and space of falling ash and near night. He was walking north through rubble and mud and there were people running past holding towels to their faces or jackets over their heads. They had handkerchiefs pressed to their mouths. They had shoes in their hands, a woman with a shoe in each hand, running past him. They ran and fell, some of them, confused and ungainly, with debris coming down around them, and there were people taking shelter under cars.[30]

Smoke and ash, office paper flashing past, shoes discarded in the street, paper cups: the focus is on the visual, not on verbal narrative, much in the way of how traumatic memory works.

Keith's own description seems taken from an Associated Press photograph of a man covered in ash: "He wore a suit and carried a briefcase. There was glass in his hair and face, marbled bolls of blood and light."[31] Even Hammad, one of the terrorists, watches TV in a bar near the flight school that he attends and likes "to imagine himself appearing on the screen, a videotaped figure walking through the gatelike detector on his way to the plane."[32] This is another image we are all familiar with.

GOVERNMENT
EXHIBIT
FO07023
01-455-A (ID)

Abdulaziz Alomari and Mohamed Atta passing through security in the Portland, Maine, airport before
6 a.m. on September 11, 2001. Source: United States District Court Eastern District of Virginia

The falling man of the title seems to reference to another well-known Associated Press photograph of a man falling from one of the towers upside down, one knee bent.[33] Since the novel reenacts the workings of a traumatized mind, that image cannot be processed and cannot be integrated with other experiences. Thus the falling man in the fictional world of the novel actually refers to the safer, substitute image of a performance artist who, with the help of a harness, suspends himself upside down. This seems inspired by the staged jumps that the artist Kerry Skarbakka made from the roof of Chicago's Museum of Contemporary Art on June 14, 2005. In the same way as people rejected Skarbakka's performance because it caused the return, belatedly, of the image of people jumping to their death on 9/11, in the fictional world of the novel Lianne feels it causes the return of her father's suicide.

Keith is also haunted by an image of a shirt coming down from the towers that he remembers seeing during his escape on 9/11. He cannot put into words what happened to him, but the image of the shirt keeps reappearing in his mind. As the photographs of cats and birds in Foer's book stood in for those of falling people, the white shirt in DeLillo's novel serves a similar function. Trauma is coped with through disassociation. At the end of the novel we finally learn what Keith witnessed that day, and we realize what the white shirt stands for: "He could not stop seeing it, twenty feet away, an instant of something sideways, going past the window, white shirt, hand up, falling before he saw it."[34] Thus the integration of the image of the falling man is a necessary step for Keith to overcome 9/11, as it is for Lianne to deal with her father's suicide.

Some reviewers claimed that DeLillo offered nothing that we had not already seen in the media. For example, in the *Washington Post*, Jonathan Yardley complained that the only emotions in the novel derived from pictures on television.[35] Yet it is the use of images we recognize that makes the narration especially powerful. At the beginning they are only loose images that return to haunt Keith; at the end they are integrated into the narrative of events, of what happened not just outside but inside the towers, where the cameras could not be.

Conclusion

In these three novels we can see the ways in which literature has drawn from different media to deal with one of the most mediated events in history. The use of newspaper columns, photographs, radio transcripts, phone messages, e-mails, and interviews with eyewitnesses in *Windows on the World*, the use of moving images—a flip book—and other images inserted into *Extremely Loud and Incredibly Close*, and the references to well-known photographs of 9/11 in *Falling Man* all exemplify the importance of intermediality as an expressive means to approach a traumatic subject, to face the unspeakable and show it. Even though in the aftermath of 9/11 fiction was rejected as a suitable means for understanding the traumatic events, some authors rose to the challenge by drawing from other media and even using taboo images that had been hidden from the public. For example, the image of the falling man soon disappeared from the U.S. media because some critics felt its publication disrespectful to the dead (see Jaclyn Kirouac-Fram's article in this issue). According to Kalí Tal, once traumatic events are codified, they turn into a weapon in the struggle for political power. Thus the status quo may silence some voices or hide some images to enforce its ideological message.[36] Since the image of the falling man represented the destiny of many victims, the media favored other more hopeful images, such as a photograph taken by Thomas E. Franklin showing three firefighters raising the U.S. flag at ground zero: it came to represent loyalty and resilience. Traumatic events can be rewritten until they become codified in a set of safe symbols. They may undergo a process of mythologization as a strategy to cope with trauma, and Franklin's image turned something uncontrollable and frightening into a standardized narrative of patriotism. Literature recovered those images that had been hidden, those narratives that could only be imagined (like what happened inside the Windows on the World restaurant), and used them to emphasize the need to overcome our fears rather than hide them. Literature has the capacity to make us face the unspeakable, to act out cultural traumas to work through them, mediating between our urge to know and our need to deny.

Notes

The research for this essay has been financed by the Spanish Ministry of Science and Technology (MCYT) and the European Regional Development Fund (FEDER), in collaboration with the Aragonese Government (no. HUM2007–61035/FILO).

1. Jean Baudrillard, *The Spirit of Terrorism and Requiem for the Twin Towers*, trans. Chris Turner (New York: Verso, 2002), 29; Slavoj Žižek, *Welcome to the Desert of the Real: Five Essays on September 11 and Related Dates* (New York: Verso, 2002), 16.
2. Paul Virilio, *Ground Zero*, trans. Chris Turner (New York: Verso, 2002), 68.
3. Andrew O'Hagan, "Racing against Reality," *New York Review of Books,* June 28, 2007, www.nybooks.com/articles/archives/2007/jun/28/racing-against-reality/.
4. *The 9/11 Commission Report: Final Report of the National Commission on Terrorist Attacks upon the United States* (New York: Norton, 2004).
5. Ben Yagoda, "*The 9/11 Commission Report*: How a Government Committee Made a Piece of Literature," *Slate*, November 8, 2004, www.slate.com/id/2109277.
6. Richard A. Posner, "*The 9/11 Report*: A Dissent," *New York Times*, August 29, 2004.
7. Sid Jacobson and Ernie Colón, *The 9/11 Report: A Graphic Adaptation* (New York: Hill and Wang, 2006).
8. Julia Keller, "Call It What You Will: New Sept. 11 Book Is Riveting," *Chicago Tribune*, September 20, 2006.
9. "The 9/11 Report: A Graphic Adaptation," *Kirkus Reviews*, July 15, 2006, www.kirkus reviews.com/book-reviews/non-fiction/sid-jacobson/the-911-report/.
10. Some relevant examples would be Tom Clancy's novels *Debt of Honor* (1994) and *Executive Orders* (1996); the pilot episode of the TV series *The Lone Gunmen*; the free downloadable game called "Trade Center Defender"; Microsoft's Flight Simulator software; and films like *Turbulence* (dir Robert Butler, 1997), *Executive Decision* (dir Stuart Baird, 1996), and *The Siege* (dir Edward Zwick, 1998).
11. Adorno does not mean here that art cannot reflect a traumatic experience but that it has to do so through a new language that reflects the experience without minimizing it. Theodor Adorno, *Prisms* (1967; reprint, Cambridge, MA: MIT Press, 1981), 34.
12. Ian McEwan, "Only Love and Then Oblivion: Love Was All They Had to Set against Their Murderers," *Guardian,* September 15, 2001.
13. Lynne Sharon Schwartz, "Near November," in *110 Stories: New York Writers after September 11*, ed. Ulrich Baer (New York: New York University Press, 2002), 262.
14. Jay McInerney, "Brightness Falls," *Guardian*, September 15, 2001.
15. For the origins of the term see Marshall McLuhan, *Understanding Media: The Extensions of Man* (1964; New York: McGraw Hill, 1987); and Raymond Williams, *Television Technology and Cultural Form* (London: Fontana, 1974). For more recent research on the connections between different media, see Jay David Bolter and Richard Grusin, *Remediation: Understanding New Media* (Cambridge, MA: MIT Press, 2000); and Maddalena Pennacchia Punzi, *Literary Intermediality: The Transit of Literature through the Media Circuit* (Bern, Switzerland: Peter Lang, 2007).
16. Frédéric Beigbeder, *Windows on the World*, trans. Frank Wynne (London: Harper Perennial, 2004), 1.

17. See Irina O. Rajewsky, "Intermediality, Intertextuality, and Remediation: A Literary Perspective on Intermediality," *Intermédialités*, no. 6 (2005): 51–52.

18. Ibid., 52.

19. Beigbeder, *Windows on the World*, 1. References are to *The Blob* (dir Irvin S. Yeaworth Jr., 1958), *Godzilla* (any of several versions), *Independence Day* (dir. Roland Emmerich, 1996), *Armageddon* (dir. Michael Bay, 1998), *Die Hard 2* (dir. Renny Harlin, 1990), and *Deep Impact* (dir. Mimi Leder, 1998).

20. Jim Dwyer et al., "102 Minutes: Last Words at the Trade Center; Fighting to Live as the Towers Die," *New York Times*, May 24, 2002; Dean Murphy, *September 11: An Oral History* (New York: Doubleday, 2002).

21. Beigbeder, *Windows on the World*, 240.

22. Ibid., 301.

23. See Anne Whitehead, *Trauma Fiction* (Edinburgh: Edinburgh University Press, 2004), 6–7; Laurie Vickroy, *Trauma and Survival in Contemporary Fiction* (Charlottesville: University of Virginia Press, 2002), 28.

24. See Cathy Caruth, introduction to *Trauma: Explorations in Memory*, ed. Caruth (Baltimore: Johns Hopkins University Press, 1995), 4–5.

25. See Bessel A. Van der Kolk and Onno Van der Hart, "The Intrusive Past: The Flexibility of Memory and the Engraving of Trauma," in Caruth, *Trauma*, 172.

26. See Jennifer Reese, "Extremely Loud and Incredibly Close," *Entertainment Weekly*, March 23, 2005, www.ew.com/ew/article/0,,1039032,00.html; and Tim Adams, "A Nine-Year-Old and 9/11," *Observer* (London), May 29, 2005.

27. See Vivian Gornick, "About a Boy," *Nation*, April 25, 2005, 32.

28. Dominick LaCapra, *Writing History, Writing Trauma* (Baltimore: Johns Hopkins University Press, 2001).

29. Jonathan Safran Foer, *Extremely Loud and Incredibly Close* (Boston: Mariner Books, 2005), 325–26.

30. Don DeLillo, *Falling Man* (London: Picador, 2007), 3.

31. Ibid., 3. An Associated Press photograph of a man covered in ash and the story surrounding it are available on the *USA Today* Web site, www.usatoday.com/news/nation/2006-09-07-sept11-then-now_x.htm. The image also appeared on the famous cover of *Fortune*, on October 1, 2001, online at foliolit.com/wp3/wp-content/uploads/2010/10/Fortune_OCT8_01.jpg (both Web pages accessed February 2, 2011).

32. DeLillo, *Falling Man*, 173.

33. The photo of the falling man is reproduced in this issue in the article by Jaclyn Kirouac-Fram.

34. DeLillo, *Falling Man*, 242.

35. Jonathan Yardley, "Survivors of 9/11 Struggle to Live in a Changed World," *Washington Post*, May 13, 2007.

36. Kalí Tal, *Worlds of Hurt: Reading the Literatures of Trauma* (Cambridge: Cambridge University Press, 1995), 6–7.

The Dan Brown Phenomenon

Conspiracism in Post-9/11 Popular Fiction

Matthew Schneider-Mayerson

After the attacks of September 11, 2001, calls for artistic responses were met with works such as the film *United 93* and Don DeLillo's novel *Falling Man*, which garnered praise but failed to penetrate into mainstream popular culture.[1] In the search for cultural echoes of 9/11, few critics have mentioned the Dan Brown phenomenon, a peak of cultural production in the 2000s — not just *The Da Vinci Code*, which with 80 million copies sold is currently one of the twenty most popular texts ever published (in any language),[2] but the best-selling *Angels and Demons* and *The Lost Symbol*,[3] the popular filmic adaptations of these works, and the scores of copycat novels Brown inspired. To date, Brown's work has inspired few scholarly articles, and none of them links his popularity to the events of September 11, 2001.[4]

This article begins by asking why *The Da Vinci Code* gained such success at this historical moment, which leads me to connect Brown's thrillers, whose primary subjects are well-worn conspiracy theories about the history of Christianity, with the political atmosphere in the United States in the 2000s. I suggest that the attacks of 9/11 and the resulting war on terror generated an environment that encouraged conspiracism and thereby created a market for the conspiracy-suffused writings of this previously obscure novelist. Although Brown's novels entertain his readers with a dramatic exposition of ancient mysteries, their message feeds on the readiness of much of the American public to see conspiracies, of one sort or another, in the contemporary world.

Radical History Review

Issue 111 (Fall 2011)   DOI 10.1215/01636545-1268803

Before *The Da Vinci Code*

During the past few decades, a number of thrillers (such as Tom Clancy's *The Hunt for Red October*) have sold millions of paperbacks and inspired high-grossing Hollywood films.[5] But *The Da Vinci Code*, published in 2003, created a cultural wave that crossed several media boundaries: it inspired scores of copycat writers to produce books that were remarkably similar in content and style, with titles such as *The Rule of Four*, *The Templar Legacy*, and *The Alexander Cipher*; it led Brown fans to follow commercial "Grail trails" around the physical locations portrayed in his books; it was able, along with its prequel, *Angels and Demons*, to translate its literary success to the silver screen, grossing nearly $1.3 billion combined in worldwide ticket sales (excluding DVDs); and it even inspired diets, such as *The Diet Code: Revolutionary Weight Loss Secrets from Da Vinci and The Golden Ratio*.[6] A long line of detractors followed the Catholic Church in denouncing the novel, pushing it from book reviews to the news section of newspapers and Web sites.

The Da Vinci Code proved a surprise blockbuster, as Brown's career as a writer had been in jeopardy before its publication. His first three novels remained relatively unsuccessful, even though most of the content and style exhibited in *The Da Vinci Code* are present in *Digital Fortress* (1998), *Angels and Demons* (2000), and *Deception Point* (2001). All of Brown's novels take place in a single day, during which a male-female team solves an obscure puzzle that illuminates either a sinister hoax or a shocking truth. Unlike in most detective fiction, the clues here are so arcane and inscrutable that the reader cannot possibly solve the puzzles but is left marveling at the protagonists' impressive knowledge and quick intellect. Brown's prose often oozes with clichés, his characters are paper thin, and his dialogue stumbles clumsily, but his literary strength lies in his ability to limit every chapter to two or three pages yet conclude each with a cliffhanger. Critics and readers agree that despite their flaws, Brown's novels are hard to put down.

Nonetheless, all three of Brown's pre–*Da Vinci* novels failed to move the merchandise. *Digital Fortress* sought to capitalize on fears of Internet and information security as a cryptographer unveils a conspiracy between the National Security Agency and a U.S. senator. *Angels and Demons* merits more attention because of its similarities with *The Da Vinci Code* and its resuscitation as a best seller in 2005 *and* 2009, an almost unprecedented occurrence in publishing. In *Angels and Demons* the Harvard symbologist Robert Langdon attempts to thwart the plot of an ancient secret society, the Illuminati, to destroy the Catholic Church. The novel contains many sensationalized religious elements that might have ignited a moral conflagration — rampant deceit by a power-hungry church, for example, and the murder of the pope by a cardinal who is actually the pontiff's son — but the book was largely ignored. So was *Deception Point*, which exposes a bureaucrat's devious attempt to mislead the world into believing that NASA has discovered a meteorite containing interstellar fossils so as to save NASA from a presidential candidate who would privatize the agency.[7]

All of Brown's works are conspiracy novels with an epic historical scope that eclipses that of similar popular authors, such as Robert Ludlum. Each claims that the general public remains ignorant of the forces that move history; voters, members of Congress, and presidents are impotent compared to powerful individuals and secret organizations that manipulate the public and control the world. *The Da Vinci Code*'s plot is no different: Langdon follows a coded trail mapped out centuries earlier to uncover the greatest hoax in history. Jesus Christ, it turns out, did not die on the cross but escaped as the husband of Mary Magdalene and sired a royal bloodline that continues to the present day. The Catholic Church has denied Jesus' mortality and along with it the egalitarian concept of the "sacred feminine," and it attempts to prevent the exposition of the damning truth. Langdon's quest involves uncovering a conspiracy of monumental proportions, one that has lasted nearly two thousand years.[8]

Each of Brown's earlier books displays notable similarities with *The Da Vinci Code*, yet few Americans read any of the three at the time of their publication. What had changed, in Brown's novels and among his potential audience, by the mid-2000s? Surprisingly few scholars have engaged this question, and the answers suggested by journalists and reviewers are usually simplistic one-liners.[9] The introduction to the recent collection *The Da Vinci Code in the Academy* begins with the query, "One book has functioned to trigger a cultural explosion, but what were the ingredients, waiting to react?"[10] While it contains interesting chapters on the novel's relation to alchemy, goddess worship, and postmodernism, none of its contributors attempt to answer its editor's initial question and explain the novel's very popularity. A handful of scholars have done so, and their work is worth noting. The psychologist Mariam Cohen speculates that *The Da Vinci Code* resonates with deep, unconscious emotions formed in children in the presence of seemingly omnipotent adults.[11] The religious historian Bernard Hamilton offers two simple explanations for the novel's success: first, people love puzzles; second, the novel taps into a popular literary theme, the quest for the Holy Grail.[12] Kent Drummond claims that the book's attraction, primarily for educated readers, is its apparent intellectual sophistication.[13] The most practical explanation in the academy for Brown's success is provided by the marketing professor Stephen Brown (no relation), who writes that Dan Brown "razzle-dazzles 'em" by crafting an "unputdownable" thriller; he taps "the appeal of puzzles, mysteries, enigmas, secrets, quizzes, codes, ciphers and all the rest" that "is deeply engrained in the human psyche."[14] Many of Brown's popular critics echo this insight. Stephen Brown adds that the novelist Brown deliberately courted the crusades against *The Da Vinci Code* to publicize the work.

The explanations provided by Cohen, Hamilton, Drummond, and Brown are all persuasive but problematically ahistorical. As George Lipsitz has noted, "popular culture comes to us as a commodity" often lacking a clear connection to its production and consumption. However, Brown's novels and films and their reception are inextricably rooted in a particular historical moment.[15] An overlooked factor in the aforementioned explanations of Brown's success after 9/11 is the political soil in which the Dan Brown phenomenon took root: the post–9/11 war on terror.

Brown as a Conspiracy Theorist

In *The Da Vinci Code*, written between 2001 and 2003, Brown acknowledges the power and attraction of conspiracy theories through his protagonist: *"Everyone loves a conspiracy,"* Langdon says ironically, and adds, in a comment that might as well refer to the post-9/11 period, "and the conspiracies kept coming."[16] Intended as an offhand remark, this assertion reflects the rise of post-9/11 American conspiracism and points to an unappreciated factor in the success of Brown's novel.

Conspiracy theories abounded after 9/11. The actual attack was itself the result of a remarkably complex international conspiracy, but just as psychologically significant and lasting was the threat of more to come. With the post–Cold War confidence in American impregnability now punctured, cells of bearded al-Qaeda agents determined to destroy the nation were suddenly waiting in the wings. In October of 2001, 86 percent of those polled believed that further terrorist attacks "in the next several weeks" were "very likely" or "somewhat likely," a number that remained over 50 percent for almost two years.[17] Levels of fear waxed and waned according to the announced "threat level" (or color) and unrelenting media coverage. The issue achieved a ubiquity unparalleled in the United States since the height of Cold War hysteria in the 1950s.[18]

At the same time, a growing number of people were open to fears of *internal* conspiracies. The Bush administration's buildup to the 2003 invasion of Iraq created a reservoir of mistrust that spilled over once the war began and the occupation continued. The failure to find the alleged weapons of mass destruction, and the subsequent inability of the occupation to bring the promised peaceful democracy and stability to Iraq, led to a growing suspicion that the war had been concocted and sold to the public by a cabal of ideologues in pursuit of goals that long predated 9/11. A growing minority of the public soon went further. A 2006 poll found that 36 percent of Americans considered it "very likely" or "somewhat likely" that government officials either allowed the attacks or carried them out themselves.[19] A *Time* article in 2006 announced the surprising endurance of such beliefs in its very title: "Why the 9/11 Conspiracy Theories Won't Go Away." The "9/11 Truth" movement seemed to hit its peak after the U.S. invasion of Iraq, with regular conventions, Web sites, and even films, *Time* reported, but its popularity had actually increased over time.[20] The movement was perhaps both a partial cause and a partial consequence of an increasingly widespread tendency to look for ulterior motives in governmental actions. General "trust in government" statistics, which had hovered in the mid-50s from roughly 1985 to 2002, had dropped to 17 percent by 2008.[21] At the same time that Americans witnessed an increase in violence and death in Iraq, learned of torture at Abu Ghraib and elsewhere, and watched the justification for the war evaporate, *The Da Vinci Code* maintained its place at the top of best-seller lists. Although initial sales proved impressive, the novel's true success lay in its staying power: it was the best-selling work of fiction in 2003 and 2004, as mistrust of the Bush administration grew, and second in 2005. Brown was previously a relative unknown, but his new novel tapped into the widespread affirmation of conspiracism to create a cultural phenomenon.

Perhaps even more striking was the latter-day success of Brown's previously ignored *Angels and Demons*. In mid-January of 2004, it rode Brown's name, his trademark conspiracy theories, and a new national atmosphere to a spot on the *New York Times* best-seller list, where it remained for almost a year, eventually selling over 40 million copies. Brown's publishers seized the moment and rereleased the novel in May of 2006 to coincide with the blockbuster film version of *The Da Vinci Code*, starring Tom Hanks.[22]

Democracy and Conspiracy Theories

In the six years between the publications of *The Da Vinci Code* and *The Lost Symbol*, released in 2009, a great deal had changed in U.S. politics, but the conspiracism that marked Brown's two previous best sellers had become, if anything, more popular throughout the United States. This is reflected in the eagerly awaited *The Lost Symbol*, which portrays the sinister reach of Freemasonry in Washington, D.C. Once again, Robert Langdon exposes the penetration of a conspiracy into the elite of powerful decision makers, in this case the U.S. government, thereby affirming post-9/11 fears of internal conspiracies.

Although all of Brown's novels portray a protagonist desperately searching for a hidden truth, a historical smoking gun, their ultimate manipulation in the final pages suggests that truth and history are malleable. In *The Lost Symbol*, the reader learns that Freemasonry's secrets are deeply entwined with the founding of the United States, but only the highest-ranking members of government are privy to this information. In fact, the greatest danger derives not from the novel's villain's serial butchery or his potential ascension to godhood but from his threat to release on the Internet videos of "innocent" presidents and senators engaging in Masonic rituals. Langdon laments that "no one would understand," and that "the truth will be twisted."[23]

This element of secrecy that ties Brown's heroes to most of his villains provides a key to situating the Dan Brown phenomenon. The conclusions to Brown's popular novels are rarely remarked on, but from a political perspective they prove telling. In each novel, a great truth is discovered, and the reader learns of it alongside Langdon; the general public, however, is allowed to — must! — remain ignorant. In *The Da Vinci Code*, a descendant of Jesus Christ tells Langdon that when he eventually finds the location of Christ's remains, "I trust that you, of all people, can keep a secret."[24] *The Lost Symbol*, in which Langdon discovers the *true* history of the United States, only to decide that its citizens cannot be trusted to interpret it—"the Ancient Mysteries cannot be shouted from the rooftops"—constitutes not a departure but a logical progression in the Langdon series.[25]

This antidemocratic impulse is the unacknowledged backbone of the politics of Brown's novels. *The Lost Symbol* goes further than the others by tacitly endorsing the Bush administration's most repressive tactics in the war on terror. As the background for the novel moves to Washington, D.C., "interrogational torture," the USA PATRIOT Act, and waterboarding are mentioned without any comment from Langdon or Brown.[26] Even the novel's concept of "noetic science"—the cutting-edge scientific theory that "particles themselves came in and out of existence based solely on [a scientist's] *intention* to observe them"—has political overtones. The portrayal of noetic science, developed in a lab beneath the Smithsonian Institution, evokes the infamous claim made by a Bush aide (most likely Karl Rove) that the United States is "an empire now, and when we act, we create our own reality."[27]

Conclusion

The political issues that lie beneath the surface of Brown's popular novels and films are some of the dominant themes of the post-9/11 period, and their exposition here uncovers a new site for further study. While many artists of the past decade explicitly tackled the controversial political issues of the era, most did not. Popular authors, filmmakers, musicians, advertisers, and other cultural producers of this period subtly or unconsciously reflected, represented, or protested political issues and actions, and their work presents important sources for cultural-political analysis. *The Da Vinci Code* and the Dan Brown phenomenon in general were and are considered, by almost all observers, to be apolitical page-turners, but it was the attacks of 9/11 and the resulting domestic political and social atmosphere that turned Brown into one of the most popular authors of all time.

Notes

1. Don DeLillo, *Falling Man* (New York: Scribner's, 2007); *United 93* was directed by Paul Greengrass and came out in 2006.
2. Dan Brown, *The Da Vinci Code* (New York: Doubleday, 2003). See also "Doubleday Books—Authors—Dan Brown," www.randomhouse.com/doubleday/catalog/author.pperl?authorid=3446 (accessed December 13, 2010). With the release of *The Lost Symbol* (New York: Doubleday, 2009), this number has surely risen.
3. Dan Brown, *Angels and Demons* (New York: Doubleday, 2000); *The Lost Symbol*.
4. Stephen Brown, "The Marketing Code: Unlocking the Secrets of Dan Brown's Success," *European Business Review* 18 (2006): 322–32.
5. Tom Clancy, *The Hunt for Red October* (Annapolis, MD: Naval Institute Press, 1984).
6. Ian Caldwell and Dustin Thompson, *The Rule of Four* (New York: Dial Press, 2004); Steve Berry, *The Templar Legacy* (New York: Ballantine, 2006); Will Adams, *The Alexander Cipher* (New York: Harper, 2007); "The Numbers: Box Office Data, Movie Stars, Idle Speculation," www.the-numbers.com (accessed February 24, 2010); Stephen Lanzalotta,

The Diet Code: Revolutionary Weight Loss Secrets from Da Vinci and the Golden Ratio (New York: Grand Central Publishing, 2006).

7. Dan Brown, *Digital Fortress* (New York: St. Martin's Press, 1998); Dan Brown, *Deception Point* (New York: Simon and Schuster, 2001).

8. As many critics noted, *The Da Vinci Code* is only the latest manifestation of a long history of anti-Catholicism in the United States, and this was a dominant interpretation of the book: it inspired dozens of polemical books and hundreds of Web sites with refutations by Catholics and criticism from the Vatican.

9. There are, however, dozens of academic or semiacademic works, generally published by defensive and zealous Christians or offended historians, debunking the novel's claims to truth. See, for example, Amy Wellborn, *De-coding Da Vinci: The Facts behind the Fiction of "The Da Vinci Code"* (Huntington, IN: Our Sunday Visitor Publishing Division, 2004); Sharan Newman, *The Real History behind "The Da Vinci Code"* (New York: Berkley Publishing Group, 2005); and Carl E. Olson and Sandra Miesel, *The Da Vinci Hoax: Exposing the Errors in "The Da Vinci Code"* (San Francisco: Ignatius Press, 2004).

10. Bradley Bowers, ed., *The Da Vinci Code in the Academy* (Newcastle, UK: Cambridge Scholars Publishing, 2007), vi.

11. Mariam Cohen, "The Da Vinci Code Dynamically De-coded," *Journal of the American Academy of Psychoanalysis and Dynamic Psychiatry* 33 (2005): 729–40.

12. Bernard Hamilton, "Puzzling Success: Specious History, Religious Bigotry, and the Power of Symbols in *The Da Vinci Code*," *Times Literary Supplement*, June 10, 2005, 20–21.

13. Kent Drummond, "Culture Club: Marketing and Consuming *The Da Vinci Code*," in *Consuming Books: The Marketing and Consumption of Literature*, ed. Stephen Brown (New York: Routledge, 2006), 60–72. Readers might fall under the impression that they have learned a great deal about ancient history, Renaissance painting, and the life of Jesus Christ, for example. I, for instance, recently found myself informing a friend that the original plan for the symbol of the modern Olympics was a pentagram, which at one point in time symbolized peace and balance—before recalling that this particular piece of information was gleaned from a Brown novel, a work of fiction.

14. Brown, "Marketing Code," 326.

15. George Lipsitz, *Time Passages: Collective Memory and American Popular Culture* (Minneapolis: University of Minnesota Press, 1990), 14.

16. Brown, *Da Vinci Code*, 181.

17. CNN/USA Today poll, October 19, 2001 to October 21, 2001, qn17.

18. See, for example, W. Lance Bennett, Regina G. Lawrence, and Steven Livingston, *When the Press Fails: Political Power and the News Media from Iraq to Katrina* (Chicago: University of Chicago Press, 2007); and Amy Gershkoff and Shana Kushner, "Shaping Public Opinion: The 9/11–Iraq Connection in the Bush Administration's Rhetoric," *Perspectives on Politics* 3 (2005): 525–37. See also Michael Ryan, "Framing the War against Terrorism: US Newspaper Editorials and Military Action in Afghanistan," *International Journal for Communication Studies* 66 (2004): 363–82.

19. Thomas Hargrove, "Third of Americans Suspect 9–11 Government Conspiracy," Scripps Howard News Service, August 1, 2006.

20. Lev Grossman, "Why the 9/11 Conspiracy Theories Won't Go Away," *Time*, September 3, 2006, 135; Phil Molé, "9/11 Conspiracy Theories: The 9/11 Truth Movement in Perspective," *Skeptic Magazine*, June 9, 2011, www.skeptic.com/eskeptic/06-09-11/.

21. Pew Research Center for the People and the Press, "Public Trust in Government, 1958–2010," people-press.org/trust (accessed July 28, 2010).

22. Michael Fleming, "Columbia Moves on 'Symbol,'" *Variety Online*, April 20, 2009, www .variety.com/article/VR1118002603?refCatId=13.

23. Brown, *Lost Symbol*, 437.

24. Brown, *Da Vinci Code*, 482.

25. Brown, *Lost Symbol*, 491.

26. Ibid., 78, 298, 500.

27. Ron Suskind, "Faith, Certainty, and the Presidency of George W. Bush," *New York Times Magazine*, October 17, 2004, 44-45, 64, 102, 106.

Traffic advisory sign outside London after the July 7, 2005, terrorist bombings. Credit: Demi

9/11 and the United Kingdom

Jeffrey R. Kerr-Ritchie

That fateful Tuesday morning, I was working at home. I taught in the history department at the State University of New York at Binghamton but commuted to New York City almost every weekend to spend time in our apartment. A former student of mine who lives in New York City called me to tell me to switch on the television because the World Trade Center (WTC) and the Pentagon were burning. After tuning in, I watched for fifteen minutes, and then went back to my desk. With the benefit of hindsight, I can only surmise that my long-standing contempt for the corporate media's newspeak blinded me to the importance of the events unfolding. I could not return to New York City until Saturday morning because all the bridges onto the island borough of Manhattan had been sealed off. As I approached the city, what immediately struck me was an acrid burning smell. I am narrating the 9/11 attacks this way partly because its facts are too familiar for me to add anything significant, but also because this was the personal experience of a British citizen who had been living and working in the United States since 1985.

What about the reaction to the 9/11 attacks in the United Kingdom? This must be divided into popular reactions and the government's official response. Many British people expressed their sympathy for those Americans who had lost their lives. "We are all Americans now," went a common refrain. It was certainly the reaction I encountered when communicating with family and friends in subsequent weeks. There is little doubt that millions of people around the world shared this feeling. On the other hand, there were those in Britain and elsewhere who thought that the U.S. government's policies in the Middle East, especially sanctions resulting in the

Radical History Review

Issue 111 (Fall 2011)   DOI 10.1215/01636545-1268812

© 2011 by MARHO: The Radical Historians' Organization, Inc.

deaths of innocent Iraqi children and Washington's consistently dishonest brokerage of the Palestine-Israel dispute, meant that the chickens had come home to roost.

At the time, most British people remained unaware that some of their fellow citizens had lost their lives in the bombings. On the one-year anniversary of the 9/11 attacks, it was revealed that sixty-seven British citizens, alongside sixteen foreign nationals with close British ties, had died. Reading about their brief lives proves a sobering experience. Many had their lives ahead of them; some had American spouses; and a few parented young children. Quite a few worked for businesses with transatlantic connections. The London-based publishing firm Risk Waters was holding a conference in a restaurant at the WTC that morning. Numerous British personnel worked for the financial brokerage firm Cantor Fitzgerald or for other businesses like Eurobrokers, Eurobank, and AON Corporation. Some office workers in London's financial district, the City, recalled losing friends and fellow workers.[1] Other foreign nationals who worked in various capacities at the WTC also died and went unnoticed at the time. The important point is that the WTC constituted a hub of global financial capital.[2] The international dimensions of the 9/11 attacks should not be sacrificed on the nationalist altar of U.S. patriotism.[3]

If it is difficult to get at ordinary British people's precise responses to the 9/11 attacks, this does not hold true for the official reaction from the British government. Prime Minister Tony Blair made immediate contact with President George W. Bush, offering the British people's sympathy as well as governmental support to its American ally. The latter came very quickly in the form of military intelligence, boots on the ground, and moral support for the U.S.-led invasion of Afghanistan starting October 7, 2001. The latter's objective was to remove the Taliban regime accused of aiding and abetting the organizers and perpetrators of the 9/11 attacks. Although some raised their voices in opposition to the war on Afghanistan in London (and in Washington), these critiques remained cries in the wilderness.[4] Blair recognized an opportune moment to strike when nerves were raw, truth was abstract, and any serious attempt at understanding could be dismissed as irrational dissent and a lack of patriotism. In a matter of weeks, the medieval Taliban regime was removed at a minimal cost of casualties to U.S. and coalition forces. This was not only a successful war; it was also a good war because, as the American and British corporate media never failed to remind their citizens ad nauseam, the bad guys had been defeated.

And the Anglo-American alliance had not terminated. From a broader policy of a war on terror the Americans and the British spearheaded an illegal invasion of the sovereign nation of Iraq in March 2003. Much like the war in Afghanistan, the invasion was quickly over. The coalition casualties were low, the world was rid of a ruthless dictator, and men and women in uniform constituted the glory of two nations. One problem, however, was that Iraq had nothing to do with the 9/11 attacks. Islamic fundamentalists who allegedly perpetrated the 9/11 attacks did so from Afghanistan, not from Iraq. Moreover, Iraq was a secular state run by a socialist nationalist Ba'athist regime whose toleration of religious organizations depended on the latter's readiness not to meddle in the affairs of state.[5] Moreover, the massive antiwar protests globally in late February 2003 involving up to 10 million ordinary women, men, and children reflected a deep sense of popular unease about the ways in which the resources of the state were being used to make a disingenuous case for going to war. If there was ever a recent historical moment at which people saw through the lies and deceit of professional politicians—at which the emperor was stark-bollocks naked—it was in those final weeks leading up to the invasion of Iraq. The political blowback came with the resignation of Blair in 2007. He explained that it was time to leave after a decade of public service; a more honest account would have admitted that the prime minister had squandered his trust with the British people.[6] Bush left office because he had already served a maximum two terms; but his dismal approval ratings can be partly attributed to his getting it so terribly wrong with the invasion of Iraq.

There has been much debate about why Blair invaded Iraq. The two factors of oil and the establishment of U.S. geopolitical influence in the region are probably most important in explaining why Bush went to war (and why the U.S. military remains in large numbers after the official withdrawal during the summer of 2010). The claim that Iraq's president Saddam Hussein held weapons of mass destruction has subsequently been proven a campaign of misinformation designed to rationalize a war already decided on by Bush.[7] Blair's own explanation—that he knew the Americans were going to invade and that it was better that they did not go alone—seems partially true. The more complete explanation is that the special relationship between Washington and London made it implausible that a U.S. government could launch such an operation without the complicity of the British government.[8] This constitutes a vital historical dimension of post–World War II U.S. and British foreign relations that international leftists should not underestimate in the future.[9]

On the morning of July 7, 2005, four bombs exploded on London's public transport system. At 8:51 a.m., three Tube trains emanating from King's Cross St. Pancras station were blasted off the tracks. At 9:47 a.m., a double-decker bus crossing Tavistock Square blew up. Fifty-two people were killed and more than seven hundred sustained injuries. Subsequent investigations revealed that the attacks were the work of four suicide bombers, all young British male citizens of the Islamic faith. Fourteen days later, on July 21, there were four more attempted bombings. These devices failed to explode except for the detonators. The six accused were all Muslim men residing in London. The next day, armed police officers shot to death the Brazilian electrician Jean Charles de Menezes at Stockwell Tube station in the mistaken belief that he was a suicide bomber. These fourteen days shook London and the nation.[10]

Stunned but resilient, the British populace partook of a two-minute silence to honor the slain victims of the most deadly bombings in London since World War II. Part of this resilience no doubt stemmed from a certain familiarity with attacks on the capital city. An older generation could recall Germany's wartime blitz campaign designed to break the hearts and minds of Londoners during the early 1940s. A younger generation including myself recalls the Irish Republican Army's mainland bombing campaign beginning in the 1970s, whose primary objective was to force the British government to the negotiating table on behalf of the beleaguered Catholic minority in Northern Ireland. This resilience of Londoners contrasted with the response of many New York City residents, whose lack of familiarity with bombing campaigns (alongside a rather paradoxical parochialism for a cosmopolitan city) explains why the 9/11 attacks came as such a shock and appeared so deeply personal. This was certainly my impression on the streets of Lower Manhattan, especially around Union Square, in the weeks following the attacks. Moreover, many New Yorkers were simply not expecting these attacks that literally came like lightning bolts out of a clear blue sky. In contrast, many Londoners anticipated some sort of retribution — not if, but when — given the 9/11 attacks, the deadly invasions of Afghanistan and Iraq, and the nadir of Western relations with the Islamic world. What they did not expect were British bombers.

Much like Bush post-9/11, Blair and his spin doctors explained that the people who carried out the 7/7 bombings were beyond the civilized pale. They would stop at nothing. Their actions put them outside acceptable norms of protest, military contest, and rational debate. Democratic values were anathema to them. They supported violence and anarchy rather than law and order. In the words of one newspaper letter writer, they committed "mindless atrocities."[11]

Such explanations appealed to the British government for three reasons. First, they were the logical outgrowth of a belief that the 9/11 attacks constituted simply ruthless and mindless acts. Second, the 7/7 bombings and the appalling loss of life they meant provided subsequent justification for the decision to invade Afghanistan and Iraq. Even though the bombers used military plastic and homemade chemical explosives, just imagine what death and destruction they might have wrought if they had had access to weapons of mass destruction. Third, these people and their supporters can expect little sympathy and no quarter from the state in its war on terror. Such acts of barbarism — and their prevention in the future — demand the implementation of radical new emergency powers. The Anti-Terrorism, Crime, and Security Act was rushed through the British Parliament three months after the 9/11 attacks. Ten months after the 7/7 bombings, Blair's government passed the 2006 Terrorism Act, which included the new offense of the "glorification" of terrorism

Police cordon at Russell Square, London, after the 7/7 bombings of the Tube.
Credit: Francis Tyers

and extended the detention of terrorist suspects held without charge from fourteen to twenty-eight days.[12]

During the past decade, the British state has been taking liberties. These include, but are not restricted to, illegal detention, wrongful arrests, incursions into civilian liberties, and secret reconnaissance units. The police arrested two men under the Terrorism Act of 2006 when they discovered two large containers marked "hydrogen peroxide" in an apartment in the city of Bristol—only to discover the contents were vegetable oil.[13] On September 18, 2007, Mohammed Atif Siddique, a twenty-one-year-old student from Scotland, was found guilty of two charges under the 2000 Terrorism Act and the 2006 Terrorism Act. One source claims this arrest illustrates "how far democratic rights have been eroded and legal norms abandoned."[14] According to the former Scotland Yard antiterrorist head who dealt with the Irish Republican Army and its bombing campaign, Britain was turning into a police state.[15] Even William Rees Mogg, the conservative editor of the British establishment newspaper the *Times* from 1967 to 1981, believes that the 2006 Terrorism Act "is a fundamental attack on traditional liberties," "liberties which go back to Magna Carta."[16] What these latter indictments fail to mention, however, is that this more recent attack on civil liberties by the state has taken the form of racial profiling and antiterror stop-and-search tactics, a long-term policy that disproportionately targets immigrant communities and people of color.[17]

Where are we now, a decade after the 9/11 attacks and six years after the 7/7 bombings? Limitations of space allow for only two points concerning the challenges ahead. First, we must immediately halt military and political interventions by the Anglo-American alliance in the Islamic world.[18] Boots on the ground and martial foreign policy should be replaced by support for a political solution to end a thirty-year civil war in Afghanistan as well as honest brokerage by Washington and London in resolving the Palestinian-Israeli conflict. Second, we must rescue the democratic tradition from political elites who dare to evoke it in our name during moments of crises. Both Bush and Blair asserted that terrorists rejected our democratic values, and yet both suppressed these values with the force of state power. Ordinary people must make their governments more, not less, accountable during moments of new emergencies. That is when we must speak out, march more, protest louder, and organize further than during quieter moments, because it is then that we truly affirm our liberties. In 1930, the British political scientist Harold J. Laski wrote, "We acquiesce in the loss of freedom every time we are silent in the face of injustice."[19] In 1989, the U.S. rap group Public Enemy told us to "fight the power." This means that we must be prepared to court unpopularity every time we seek to explain, contextualize, and historicize 9/11, 7/7, and beyond.

Notes

My thanks to Jim O'Brien and Andor Skotnes for editorial improvements.

1. "British Victims of September 11," *Guardian*, September 10, 2002.
2. For a useful historical account of financial capital's transatlantic links between Wall Street and the City of London, see Ron Chernow, *The House of Morgan: An American Banking Dynasty and the Rise of Modern Finance* (New York: Grove, 1990).
3. On September 9, 2010, students with the Young Republicans Club planted American flags in the ground outside Langley High School in McLean, Virginia, commemorating each victim of the 9/11 attacks. The students and the reporter were oblivious of non-American victims of the attacks. See "They are not forgotten," *Washington Post*, September 10, 2010.
4. Barbara Lee, the federal representative for California's ninth congressional district, was the only member of the House to vote against President Bush's blank check to wage war in the aftermath of the 9/11 attacks. For a pictorial narrative opposing Britain's military presence in Afghanistan, see the 2007 YouTube video "Why Are We in Afghanistan Again?" narrated by the British socialist politician Tony Benn (www.youtube.com/watch?v=-bSzAuisI4I; accessed March 4, 2011).
5. Charles Tripp, *A History of Iraq* (Cambridge: Cambridge University Press, 2000).
6. I have not read Blair's recently published memoir and do not plan to. But according to media reports, he does not regret the decision to invade Iraq along with the Americans.
7. Derrick Z. Jackson, "A Madness for War," *Boston Globe*, March 29, 2006.
8. What I am saying is that U.S.-U.K. policies toward the Middle East have remained similar, despite different administrations in Washington (Bush I, Clinton, Bush II, Obama) and London (Major, Blair, Brown, Cameron).
9. Jeffrey Kerr-Ritchie, "Our American Cousin: Critical Comments on the Special Relationship between the United States and the United Kingdom" (manuscript in progress).
10. Nafeez Mosaddeq Ahmed, *The London Bombings: An Independent Inquiry* (London: Duckworth, 2006); "Six on Trial over Failed London Bombings," *Guardian*, January 15, 2007. I have narrated the events of July 2005 because these are less familiar to readers.

11. "Letters to Editor," *Guardian*, July 9, 2005. As a scholar of slavery and abolition in the nineteenth-century Americas, I am struck by the similarities between the language of slaveholders in response to slave revolts and conspiracies and this more recent terminology employed by political leaders.

12. "Terrorism Act Comes into Force," *Guardian*, April 13, 2006.

13. "Bristol Terror Suspects Released," *Times*, July 20, 2007.

14. Niall Green, "Britain: Youth Convicted under Antidemocratic Terrorism Acts," World Socialist Web Site, September 25, 2007, www.wsws.org/articles/2007/sep2007/terr-s25.shtml.

15. "Britain 'Sliding into Police State,'" *Guardian*, January 28, 2005.

16. "Taking Liberties with History," *Times*, March 7, 2005.

17. Arun Kundnani, "Racial Profiling and Anti-terror Stop and Search," Institute for Race Relations, January 31, 2006, www.irr.org.uk/2006/january/ha000025.html.

18. Hundreds of thousands of civilians have been killed in Afghanistan and Iraq since 2001. See, e.g., Gilbert Burnham et al., "Mortality after the 2003 Invasion of Iraq: A Cross-sectional Cluster Sample Survey," *Lancet*, October 11, 2006, www.brussellstribunal.org/pdf/lancet111006.pdf. My thanks to Jim O'Brien for this citation. This human loss should be no less sobering than that from the 9/11 attacks and the 7/7 bombings.

19. Harold J. Laski, *Liberty in the Modern State* (New York: Viking, 1949), 21.

9/11 and the Increase in Racism and Islamophobia

A Personal Reflection

Amir Saeed

I am a British citizen of Pakistani origin. If asked, I would describe myself as Scottish Pakistani. From a personal perspective, I used to say that I was part British, my argument being that I was literate in English and had citizenship rights and responsibilities. In short, I had adapted, to a degree at least, to the ambiguous notion of "British" culture. Religion was an element of my personal identity but not an essential part of my life; it was not *the* overriding ideology. Unlike that of many other Muslims, my faith was not of overwhelming importance. What was important was to have the right to practice my faith (if I chose) without fear, intimidation, and ridicule.

This willingness to put secular rights over religion mirrored the political maturity awakened in me in the 1980s, a time when, in Scotland at least, skin color seemed more important than religion. In many respects my political identity was modeled on inclusive definitions of "black." I understood the term *black* as meaning people of Third World origin—whether Latin American, African, or Asian—who were victims of European imperialism. To me they constituted part of the colonized globe and thus deserved my support.

Yet the events of 9/11 and the subsequent levels of hostility have made me question my own notions of identity and belonging. Increasingly I experience and see Muslims having to emphasize our Britishness. It seems that we are given a stark

Radical History Review
Issue 111 (Fall 2011)   DOI 10.1215/01636545-1268821
© 2011 by MARHO: The Radical Historians' Organization, Inc.

choice: to be British or to be Muslim. In short, assimilate not just integrate. In reaction, I have come to take my Muslim faith more seriously, at the same time that the radicalism of my political understanding has deepened.

Islamophobia

The moral panic surrounding the events of 9/11 and 7/7 (the date of the London Underground and bus bombings in 2005) has led to a debate led by the political right under the guise of community cohesion that has suggested a return to "core national values" and/or "core national culture," alongside stricter immigration and policing controls. We rarely hear precise meanings for the

The anti-Muslim English Defense League protests in Newcastle, May 29, 2010. Credit: Gavin Lynn

terms *national* and *culture*. Recently, a neo-right-wing discourse (some of it from previously center-left commentators) has questioned the whole concept of multiculturalism, which is said to have "failed." Furthermore, much of the blame for this "failure" has been attached to Muslims' alleged incompatibility with the "democratic" principles of the West.

These attacks on Muslims have amounted to Islamophobia. This contemporary form of racism manifests itself in a number of different hybrid forms, but all are premised on generalizing human beings' existence and experiences into simple homogenous groupings. Islamophobia can sometimes resemble the biological arguments employed to justify slavery and imperialism: "All Muslims, like all dogs, share certain characteristics. A dog is not the same animal as a cat just because both species are comprised of different breeds. An extreme Christian believes that the Garden of Eden really existed; an extreme Muslim flies planes into buildings—there's a big difference."[1]

All across the Western world, Muslim communities face increasing physical and verbal intimidation. In the United Kingdom, far-right political groups such as the British National Party have adopted an ever more anti-Muslim agenda. Likewise, the country has seen the emergence of groups such as the English Defence League, which have adopted "street tactics" to intimidate Muslim communities. The Institute of Race Relations has noted that although Muslims account for 3 percent of the population in the United Kingdom, they represent 44 percent of all victims of racial violence in the country.[2]

An anti-Muslim English Defence League demonstrator wearing a "No Surrender to al-Qaeda" sweatshirt and an English police officer in Newcastle, May 29, 2010. Credit: Gavin Lynn

Writers from various parts of the political spectrum have debated the reasons and consequences of 9/11 and subsequent events. However, the views of Muslim minorities in the West have been oversimplified or ignored in favor of quoting fundamentalist or extremist opinions, which could be seen as supporting the claim that Islam is inherently confrontational. Drawing on Samuel Huntington's theory of a "clash of civilizations" was the idea that Islam posed a threat to the enlightened Western way of life, its culture, and its values. In the days, weeks, months, and years after 9/11 this anti-Islamic discourse has acquired new efficacy particularly among politicians, journalists, and commentators in the United States and the United Kingdom.

Part of my academic research has involved talking to a large number of Muslims from various ethnic, gender, and class backgrounds. While they apparently had different commitments to Islam, they all agreed on one facet: that Islam had become the new enemy and that Muslims living in the United Kingdom were included in that category. This constituted a new development. During the early 1990s media representations of Islamic fundamentalism focused on the Middle East, Asia, and Africa. While some events like the condemnation of Salman Rushdie's *Satanic Verses* and the first Gulf War produced anti-Muslim hysteria from some quarters, an onslaught on British Muslims or Western Muslims was not sustained. Yet the events of 9/11, the war against terrorism, and the public attacks on asylum seekers have resurrected latent stereotypes. This has been accompanied by debates concerning the compatibility of Muslims with Western societies. Are Muslims the enemy within? Are Muslims integrating enough? Is Islamic culture democratic? What role do women have in Islam? Suddenly Islam came under scrutiny, and any defense of Islam seemed accompanied by further accusations of Islamic militancy.

However much they seek to identify themselves as British, young Muslims regularly find that others assume them to be first and foremost Muslim. In Britain today, especially after the events of 9/11 and the beginning of the so-called war on terror, Muslims have been identified as a group of potentially "false nationals" and systematically constructed as the other. A discourse has been produced that directly links British Muslims with support for terrorism, fundamentalism, "illegal immigration," and an "Oriental" stereotype of the East. British Muslims are repeatedly implored by voices in the media and by politicians of all sides to make more strenuous efforts to "integrate" into British society, and to reassert their loyalty to the British state in a manner that no non-Muslim antiwar group would ever be instructed to do. In short, demands for assimilation seem to translate to "be quiet and behave."

In the United Kingdom, the then prime minister, Tony Blair, implored British Muslims to take collective responsibility and accept British values: "When it comes to our essential values — belief in democracy, the rule of law, tolerance, equal treatment for all, respect for this country and its shared heritage — then that is where we come together, it is what we hold in common. It is what gives us the right to call ourselves British."[3]

My Jihad

The events surrounding 9/11 and especially the war on terror have made me pay ever closer attention to my religious roots. My secular outlook has been replaced by a more religious and (I say so hesitantly) more Islamic perspective. While popular culture and public opinion seemed to decry the inhumane nature of Islam following 9/11, the following passage from the Koran seemed highly relevant: "Whoever slays a soul . . . it is as though he slew all mankind, and whoever keeps it alive it as though he kept alive all mankind. Al Quran 5:35."[4] In Islam it is clear that life must be respected and the right to life accorded to all beings. Unfortunately, those who appear as the strongest critics of Islam seem to have the weakest knowledge of it.

Rather than seeing Islam just as a religion, a closer examination of the Koran for me showed that it was a political ideology that could provide a framework for me to understand contemporary capitalist society. Indeed, Islamic scholars may argue that social justice and challenging oppression constitute the cornerstones of Islam: "What is wrong with you that you not fight in the cause of Allah and for those who are weak, ill treated and oppressed among men, women and children and whose cry is: Our Lord! Rescue us from this town whose people are oppressors and raise for us from You one who will protect us and raise for us from You one who will help. Al Quran 4:74/5."[5] For me, capitalism quite simply (using the classic socialist phrase) puts "profit before people." For me it is apparent the war on terror marks an attempt by proponents of free market capitalism, and by the United States in particular, to control resources in what they consider to be a less civilized part of the world. Yet having been stigmatized by popular culture as one of the "enemy within," I have experienced a change in my social and political conscience in the past few years. More and more I see myself as belonging to the *ummah*, the global Islamic community that supersedes nationality. Explained briefly, there are two tiers to Muslim identity; one is related to faith and one related to country, but faith overrides any other component of identity.

It is with this personal background that I have to approach any further research on race and ethnic studies. Given that academia is supposed to be rational, objective, and scientific, my conclusions may be open to criticism. Yet the work of As'ad Abukhalil (describing his recent book *Bin Laden, Terrorism, and Islam*) may provide some thought to critics of a subjective approach, "The style and tone of this book are emotional, and may strike the academic reader as odd. But hiding behind the cloak of objectivity is often used more to conceal than to reveal."[6]

Anti-Muslim demonstrations have occurred regularly in the United States and in Britain: a protester in Washington, D.C., September 15, 2007. Credit: City of Anthrax

More and more Muslims, it appears, are now facing the same challenges by drawing strength from an Islamic identity that can provide solidarity with other Muslims, as well as an avenue of escape from constant identification in negative terms. This constitutes a political process, and it implies a positive (re)conceptualization of Islamic identity transcending local, negative attributions.

This Islamic challenge or struggle has been popularized in the media as intrinsically violent. For example, the use of the term *jihad* conjures up images of violent irrational terrorism. Yet jihad does not necessarily mean a call to arms and a prelude to bloodshed. A jihad can be personal and may include debate, reasoning, marching, and indeed voicing concern in a written format.

A progressive Islam centered on the inclusion of all disparaged groups (regardless of religion, ethnicity, and even sexuality) is my jihad. At the genesis of Islam the main converts were slaves and women, the two most oppressed groups at the time. That they saw something liberating and empowering within the Hadiths (sayings/teachings) of the Prophet Muhammad (peace be upon him) illustrates for me that Islam has a liberal and radical foundation inherent in its teachings. Unfortunately, the fundamentalist interpretation of Islam that is conservative and exclusive is mirrored by an equally conservative mainstream media, thus implying inevitable and natural cultural conflict.

Hopefully this new Muslim *ummah* can (as it indeed has done) draw links with antiwar and anticapitalist movements to challenge the barbaric nature of globalization and the U.S.-led war on terrorism. Public opinion can be mobilized to challenge the powers. Furthermore, this challenge can be led by Muslims: for example, the antiwar movement in Birmingham (UK) is directed with great energy by a young Muslim woman. So while on the one hand we have the negativity and hostility of the mainstream press and the body politic, an alternative voice can be found that, based on the principles of social justice and challenging oppression, can help build and sustain a challenge to the capitalists.

Notes

1. Will Cummins, "Muslims Are a Threat to Our Way of Life," *Daily Telegraph*, July 25, 2004.
2. Harmit Athwal, Jenny Bourne, and Rebecca Wood, "Racial Violence: The Buried Issue," Institute of Race Relations, London, Briefing Paper No. 6 (2010), www.irr.org.uk/pdf2/IRR_Briefing_No.6.pdf (accessed February 20, 2011).
3. Will Woodward, "Radical Muslims Must Integrate, Says Blair," *Guardian*, December 9, 2006.
4. *The Qu'ran: Text, Translation, and Commentary (English and Arabic Version)*, trans. Abdullah Yusuf Ali (New York: Tahrike Tarsile, 1987), 114.
5. Ibid., 87.
6. As'ad Abukahlil, *Bin Laden, Islam, and America's New "War on Terrorism"* (New York: Open Media Books, 2002), 10–11.

David Rees's second *Get Your War On*, October 9, 2001. Courtesy of David Rees

"Get Your War On"

Teaching the Post-9/11

Jeffrey Melnick

Over the past five years I have been teaching a course called "9/11 Culture" at a small business college in the Northeast. This is an advanced American Studies seminar and it is important to me that students confront a wide variety of texts (including literary novels, popular songs, rumors, CD covers and inserts, telethons, stand-up comedy routines, political rhetoric, Hollywood and independent film, poetry, photographs, the "Portraits of Grief" series in the *New York Times*, and comic strips, to name a few) and develop skills for historicizing and interpreting them all. As the course evolved from a two-week experimental winter-session offering to a regularly scheduled spring-semester class (always oversubscribed, at that), I became increasingly interested in developing metrics — admittedly and purposefully subjective ones — that might help me track what my students' reactions to certain incendiary texts could teach *me* about the evolving culture of 9/11, at least in our little corner of the world. One of the most surprising pieces of evidence has come with my students' evolving response to David Rees's Internet clip art–based comic strip *Get Your War On*,[1] which, until recently, I taught as a major part of the first third of the class on immediate cultural responses to 9/11 — along with rumors, photographs, a telethon, and a few songs. In what follows I want to track the surprising ways that *Get Your War On* has acted as a guide to the cultural and political expectations that my students enter the class with. The short version is that my students have never really connected with Rees's work: my work has been to figure out why.

Radical History Review

Issue 111 (Fall 2011)   DOI 10.1215/01636545-1268830

© 2011 by MARHO: The Radical Historians' Organization, Inc.

This 9/11 class has never explicitly concerned itself with capital *p* Politics: the real burden of the course has more to do with the construction of a grammar and rhetoric of what I call "9/11 culture" in American popular arts than with the motivations, strategies, or outcomes associated with the U.S. invasion of Afghanistan in 2001 and of Iraq in 2003. Yet the wars shadow every moment of the class. I always begin the class by showing *America: A Tribute to Heroes*, the celebrity telethon that was broadcast on September 21, mostly to help students begin to understand the rapid deployment of *hero* as a keyword in our post-9/11 discourse. The obsessive overuse of the word has come to represent an outright mocking of real struggle.[2]

A screening of the telethon quickly establishes this devaluation of *hero* for my students. The telethon was directed by Joel Gallen, whose major credits before this night mostly had to do with industry celebrations of itself: the MTV Movie Awards, the Academy Award Preshow, a Rock and Roll Hall of Fame Induction Ceremony. (The 9/11 show would become a kind of template for Gallen over the next few years, and he would get jobs directing the Hurricane Katrina telethon and a special called *CNN Heroes*, "honoring ordinary people who do extraordinary things," as well.) The choice of Gallen represented an apt harmonizing of director and material: in many ways *Tribute* felt like a tribute to entertainment-industry largesse, a display of how well our celebrities were taking up the task of instructing the rest of us how to act in this newly ordered universe.

The entire narrative arc of the telethon can be captured by taking a quick look at the first speaker and the last. Two musical performances bookend the telethon: a repurposing by Bruce Springsteen of his lament "My City of Ruins" to apply to New York rather than his adopted hometown of Asbury Park, New Jersey, and an unintentionally hilarious group singing of Katharine Lee Bates's "America the Beautiful" led by an unflappable and, more than likely, stoned Willie Nelson. Inside this frame, however, comes the real story. First up is Tom Hanks, playing the humble but dedicated son, who acknowledges that he is there simply as an entertainer, hoping to raise "spirits" and a "great deal of money." "Most of us here," Hanks admits, "are not heroes"—just entertainers.

But this diffidence is a feint. By the end of the show the telethon's writers (including Ronald Reagan's speechwriter Peggy Noonan and Bill Clinton's aide Ann Lewis) and the director have worked hard to ensure the audience understands that it is now time to get our war on. While a few of the entertainers on the show manage to go thrillingly off script—I am thinking here of Neil Young's tentatively peacenik version of "Imagine," Wyclef Jean's complex mix of sight and sound (wearing a flag, singing the anti-imperialist and anti-slavery "Redemption Song"), and Julia Roberts's possibly improvised "let's love one another" remarks at the end of her Peggy Noonan–penned spot—the real burden of the show is to posit World War II as the context for understanding 9/11 and thus to prepare Americans for a new "just" war. This work gets accomplished by the mien and rhetoric of the final two presenters.

First comes Robert De Niro, wearing his familiar "I'm in pain, I see the cosmic unfairness that defines the universe, and yet I'm resolute" face. Until De Niro's appearance, *Tribute* was defined by a direct appeal to the tastes and wallets of baby boomers. But the actor, born *during* World War II and here invoking the so-called Greatest Generation through his quotation of Franklin Delano Roosevelt's "Four Freedoms" speech of 1941, accesses a deeper history than the show had heretofore admitted. In doing so he appeals to a nostalgic sense of unity that (allegedly) characterized the United States during the era of World War II. Clint Eastwood emerges as the final presenter, putatively appearing to introduce the celebrity chorus led by Nelson. Eastwood looks uncomfortable, badly mangles his call-to-war remarks, and is most memorable for wearing a hitched-up blazer suggesting that he was, perhaps, packing heat. Even so, Eastwood did the work of organizing the American public to understand 9/11 as the "twenty-first century's day of infamy." "Oh they left us wounded," Eastwood says, "but renewed in strength." With broad strokes, the script for Eastwood has him very carefully framing the 9/11 attacks as an act of war. "In the conflict that's come upon us," Eastwood argues, today's Americans will be as resolute as their parents and grandparents were in earlier wars. Finally, his insistence that instead of "300 million victims" the terrorist attack would instead create "300 million heroes" constitutes a crucial act of redefinition: in essence Eastwood is drawing attention away from the rescue workers most commonly named as the heroes of the day and instructing his audience to consider what sacrifices they will make for the cause, vague as that might have been on September 21. No one appearing on *Tribute to Heroes* says "Islamofascists"—that ugly coinage was not yet circulating as widely as it would in the coming years—but attentive viewers certainly understood the connections they were asked to draw between World War II–era fascism and the current crisis.

In every section of my 9/11 culture class, the students have understood the prime directive of *Tribute to Heroes*. While some of them always want to laugh at Eastwood's get-the-hell-off-my-property crazy grandpa routine, many more sit in stunned silence, chastened by what they see as this too-immediate saber rattling. During the five years that I have taught this class, it has been easy to track changes in my students' first responses to the course subject and materials. The four-year college where I have been teaching this course is populated almost exclusively by "traditional" students between the ages of seventeen and twenty-two—a large percentage hailing from the Northeast corridor. The first sections I taught were full of students who were high school seniors when the towers fell, intent on sharing personal memories and reflections of 9/11. More recently the seats have been filled by young people who were twelve or thirteen at the time; they tend to carry much less baggage into the classroom than the earlier cohort. But consistent across all sections, winter, spring, and fall, has been a general revulsion toward the call to war that punctuates the celebrity telethon. If the United States was going to find it necessary to launch a military response to 9/11, my students suggest, this response should have been framed by regret and drenched in grief.

The second week of the class usually deals with a collection of other "first responses" (defined by me as works that appeared during the rest of 2001) to the attacks, from amateur photographs of the day to the more formal "Portraits of Grief" in the *New York Times*. Another required text here is Rees's *Get Your War On*. If you have not seen the strip, or have not looked at it recently, do me (and yourself) a favor and go look at a few weeks of it. It starts with these words: "Oh yeah! *Operation: Enduring Freedom* is in the house!"

My students' resistance to Rees has always puzzled me. Student evaluations are notoriously untrustworthy tools, and I try to read them as critically as the next pedagogically conscious and personally defensive instructor. But it has been a real challenge to make much out of the unified chorus of voices singing, over the span of a half decade, "this book sucks" when it comes to thinking and writing about *Get Your War On*. There are formal challenges, of course: in fact, if I were to be totally honest, I would have to admit that, outside of a few notable exceptions, I have never had much success teaching comic strips, graphic novels, or other nonfilm combinations of text and image. (Miné Okubo's memoir of her internment during World War II, *Citizen 13660*, is a notable exception.[3])

Get Your War On relies perhaps above all on the incendiary and innovative language that fills its panels, while its launching and definitive visual element—what film scholars call the "establishing shot"—is the appearance of Clip Art figures. These miserable and seemingly interchangeable office workers are *Dilbert*'s pissed-off and alcoholic cousins; they are the heirs to an important subgenre of contemporary American film that focuses on the alienating challenges and indignities of white- and pink-collar office life. The visual repetition is put to sharp political use, as Rees's characters blandly (and at times bizarrely) comment on the increasingly surrealistic nature of U.S. political discourse after 9/11. In the strips Rees uses not only his standard Clip Art repetitions but also adds in some key hip-hop phrases to remind us of repetition's functionality: at an actual hip-hop performance these phrases would be instructional, directive, a call to collective action.

Rees, in *Get Your War On*, delivers angry and confrontational work: he is responding to what the novelist Lynne Sharon Schwartz would soon refer to as the "butchery" of language that followed the tragedy of the attacks. Conventionalized grief—expressed in meaningless catchphrases—is a major target for Rees. Students in my 9/11 class regularly felt uncomfortable with Rees's desire to challenge *any* seemingly "authentic" articulation of post-9/11 American grief.

It is more than possible that my inability to "sell" *Get Your War On* has to do with my own shortcomings in framing and contextualizing its artistic accomplishments. But I think the anti-Rees consensus that my students have expressed in all the years I have offered the course grew from more than a simple resistance to Rees's aesthetic strategies. It is worth noting that Americans very quickly made some (tentative) cultural agreements in the days and weeks after the attacks about which sorts of responses to the attacks would be endorsed and which would be condemned. Numerous talking heads instructed us nightly that we were now done with tall buildings blowing up, done with "irony" (this might be traced to Roger Rosenblatt speaking on the *News Hour* on PBS), done with anything really fun in popular culture whatsoever. Tracking my students' reactions to *Get Your War On* over the years has made it quite simple to see how fully this ideology of "proper" artistic response reached this population. In fact, my students quite regularly articulated (at first) that it was "too soon" for confrontational arts such as Rees's comic art. More interesting to track is how temporary this idea of a fragile American populace, in need of protection from the likes of Rees, turned out to be.

"Too soon" was a key phrase deployed in these days—and really up through the release of the film *United 93* (dir. Paul Greengrass, 2006); "too soon" was used widely to draw that always crucial boundary between purity and danger. A primary text here is the appearance of the stand-up comic Gilbert Gottfried at a Friars Club roast hosted by Hugh Hefner in late September 2001, archived later in the film *The Aristocrats* (dir. Paul Provenza, 2005). Explaining that he had to leave the show early to catch a flight to Los Angeles, the comedian complained that he could not get a direct flight and would have to change planes at the Empire State Building. Rim shot followed by hilarious laughter? As if. Instead, Gottfried faced boos and calls of "too soon." It was not too soon to hold a roast at the notoriously risqué Friars Club event. But it was too soon to tell a joke about planes and tall buildings.

None of my students, as far I can recall, ever actually uttered the words "too soon" in the first few iterations of the 9/11 culture class, but that certainly captures the tenor of their responses to Rees—and most of all, it tells us something about the stony silence that defined our class session on the Web comic. The students in my first few sections of "9/11 Culture"—not yet conditioned by Facebook tagging or YouTube commenting—did not seem ready (or able) to "talk back" to Rees. They were simply shocked into silence.

If the first generation of students in my 9/11 class found Rees's strip to be too much too soon, by the middle years of my experience teaching the class (around 2004–7) the strip—which I doggedly kept teaching—reached these students as too obvious. Here I had neglected to evaluate its value in the syllabus up against the larger cultural context my students operated in. To put it simply, even these (by and large) politically conservative business students were already well prepared to resist dominant cultural narratives having to do with post-9/11 unity, with unquestioning fealty to the U.S. war efforts in Afghanistan and Iraq, and even to the idea that 9/11 constituted the defining event of their young lives. The common sense of the culture (especially of American youth culture) had been altered by Michael Moore's *Fahrenheit 9/11* (2004) and perhaps even more so by the way that mainstream and underground rap artists had begun to say "no," in numerous ways, to the central militaristic dictates of their time. In my own, admittedly haphazard, polling of these students, it seems clear that it was Jay-Z's partnership with the British artist Panjabi MC on "Beware" in 2006 ("We rebellious, we back home screaming 'Leave Iraq alone'") that caught their ears most dramatically.

By the time I taught the class in the spring of 2006 it was becoming clear to me that a new key moment for our study of 9/11 art and the post-9/11 in general had come with the moment of the next American tragedy, Hurricane Katrina's devastation of New Orleans and other sites on the Gulf Coast and the abandonment of the region and its people by the U.S. federal government. While questions of race, privilege, and power have been largely submerged in artistic conversations surrounding 9/11, Katrina forced artists in the United States to confront the country's central dilemma. A few musicians worked hard to link the very different realities of 9/11 and Katrina. Jay-Z, for instance, offered up a Katrina song in the fall of 2006 that he called "Minority Report." Using this title was, no doubt, the rapper's way of foregrounding how black disenfranchisement was the headline story in the U.S. government's neglect of Katrina's most vulnerable victims and of musing on his own relative privilege. But it was also a way for Jay-Z to invoke Steven Spielberg's 9/11–themed movie of that name, with its obsessive circling around the question of prior knowledge.

Nothing reached my students as powerfully as Kanye West's off-script moment ("George Bush doesn't care about black people") during a telethon held just after the flood in September of 2005. Having been prepared in the 9/11 culture class to understand the kinds of consensus-building work that celebrity telethons usually accomplish, the students were completely ready to see how West's speech act tore the fabric of togetherness supposedly binding "us" all together at such moments. West's moment was replayed, it seems, 24/7 on YouTube and elsewhere, and my students cited it again and again as a major contributor to their developing sense that they had work to do analyzing the cultural myths that had seemed commonsensical to them for so long. In his fascinating book *American Ground: Unbuilding the World Trade Center* (2003), William Langewiesche writes of the "prodigious energy" originally required to raise the twin towers as high as they went, and how their destruction literally "released that energy back into the city."[4] West's relatively simple act of rebellion helped my students see how much energy Katrina had released into the culture, and helped them develop a critical map of 9/11 culture that left Rees's once revelatory critique seeming a little obvious. Now when I asked my students to reflect on why they seemed relatively unmoved by *Get Your War On* they tended to say, "We know all this already."

In the past few years (2008–10) I finally faced pedagogical reality and stopped teaching *Get Your War On*: in terms of student reception the strip—like a number of other expressions of early post-9/11 outrage—had leapfrogged from "too soon," to "too obvious" and finally to "too tame."

It seems that Rees's *Get Your War On* served as the "foxhole" movies of World War II must have served their audiences—creating a vocabulary for talking about the horror in front of us *right now* as we search for fuller and more complex ways to process our feelings of confusion and repulsion, our second and third thoughts. This next generation of art—"September 12th art" is what the British journalist Mark Lawson named it, writing optimistically less than a year after the attacks[5]—has carried a much heavier burden than September 11th art. September 11th art— Oliver Stone's *World Trade Center* (2006), Toby Keith's "Courtesy of the Red, White and Blue," even Bruce Springsteen's "The Rising"—has little to offer my students. But September 12th art has regularly challenged and engaged them. From Steven Spielberg's trilogy—*Minority Report* (2002), *War of the Worlds* (2005), and, above all, *Munich* (2005)—and James McTeigue's *V for Vendetta* (2006), to novels like Schwartz's *The Writing on the Wall* and Moshin Hamid's *The Reluctant Fundamentalist*,[6] to the use of Middle Eastern sounds in rhythm and blues and hip-hop music by Truth Hurts, Erick Sermon, Jay-Z, and others, these students have consistently and productively wrestled with the culture of the aftermath and developed usable and ambitious criteria for determining what matters.

One objective I always had in mind in teaching the Rees strip (along with digital photography, rumor culture, and so on) was as an introduction to the larger question of how the growth of Web 2.0 existed in a mutually constitutive relationship with post-9/11 culture. The tapestry of new hardware, new platforms, and new user behaviors we have come to call Web 2.0 has, to reduce the matter considerably, changed the Internet from predominantly a one-way street to a much more complicated weave of highways, side streets, and dead ends.

I have always billed this class to students—without necessarily bothering them about Michel Foucault—as a history of the present. But insisting on the primacy of the current moment also means that it will prove particularly difficult for students to develop a sense of the relevance of their own positionality as they evaluate the materials under investigation. In other words, short of billing the class as an exercise in thinking and writing about our own experience of 9/11, it remained very difficult in the early semesters to get students to *both* attend to the larger contours of history *and* be willing to investigate their own deep complicity in that history. Let me be clear: the robust narcissism of young people made it relatively easy to get these classes to see that 9/11 was about them. (Later, I would have John Cameron Mitchell's 2006 movie *Shortbus* to enlist in class, with the drag queen Justin Bond's great line about young people swarming to New York after 9/11 because 9/11 was the "only real thing" that had ever happened to them). What is more difficult, of course, is to get the students to see that 9/11 is not *only* about *them*.

For those of us teaching in and around topics in cultural studies drawn from contemporary history, it seems necessary to confront the group psychology, the evidence of denial and complex personal investment that shape our classroom dynamics. Reading student silence is notoriously tricky: Is it active resistance? Engaged intellectual struggle? Lack of preparation? This classroom work remains a tentative and open-ended venture. In taking on the challenge of teaching these histories of the present we, at the very least, encourage students to examine ideologies in the making, while they also chart the relevance of their own social location.

Notes

1. David Rees, *Get Your War On*, www.mnftiu.cc/category/gywo/war1 (accessed March 3, 2011). The archive of strips can be found on this site.
2. The telethon was broadcast on all three of the major broadcast networks. Much of it can usually be viewed on YouTube. Warner Bros/WEA released a DVD version late in 2001.
3. Miné Okubo, *Citizen 13660* (New York: Columbia University Press, 1946).
4. William Langewiesche, *American Ground: Unbuilding the World Trade Center* (New York: Northpoint, 2002), 4.
5. Mark Lawson, "After the Fall," *Guardian*, August 16, 2002, www.guardian.co.uk/film/2002/aug/16/artsfeatures.september11.
6. Lynne Sharon Schwartz, *The Writing on the Wall* (New York: Counterpoint, 2005); Moshin Hamid, *The Reluctant Fundamentalist* (Orlando, FL: Harcourt, 2007).

Teaching 9/11

Lessons from Classrooms in the United States and Pakistan

Magid Shihade

During the years 2005–9, I taught a course on September 11, 2001, as an adjunct in different departments and colleges including the University of California at Berkeley and Davis, the University of Pittsburgh, and Lahore University of Management Sciences (LUMS) in Pakistan.

Initially, I was ambivalent about teaching the course. Yet considering how seminal the event has proven in global politics, I felt it important to engage college students with a critical assessment of the event and with how it was explained and then used by the U.S. and other governments, by the media, and by the public at large. The course is especially important for this generation, which grew up in the post-9/11 world and whose cultural and political identities have been shaped in part by the so-called global war on terror. Many in this generation of students saw 9/11 as a defining moment of their youth. It is the largest world-historical event in their lives, and it factors significantly in their memory. As most of them were between twelve and fifteen years old when the event took place, coming of age for them meant coming into the post-9/11 world.

My principal aim in the course was to challenge deeply held (especially by American students) beliefs about the U.S.-led global politics of post-9/11. I wanted to introduce students to literature and films that critically assess the dominant American narrative surrounding the event and its aftermath. I sought to propose an alter-

Radical History Review

Issue 111 (Fall 2011)   DOI 10.1215/01636545-1268839

© 2011 by MARHO: The Radical Historians' Organization, Inc.

native way to understand such events, not only in explaining what happened and why but also, and more important, what obstacles in our modern societies hinder a critical understanding of such events. I attempted to make students less trusting of the official and dominant narratives, especially when it comes to issues of conflict and war. Not to do so, I felt, would only contribute to reenacting histories of war and suffering.

Structure of the Class

The class was structured around reading materials, movies (including documentaries), class presentations, and discussions. I used visual media because many students are affected more by the visual than by the verbal, and I could thus communicate ideas that proved hard to tackle through readings and discussions alone.[1] Students were asked to discuss the main issues presented in the films to see what links they could see to 9/11 and its aftermath, especially how these points might challenge, or at least place in context, the official or dominant narratives. Later on, I required students to submit a written response as a means of providing space for those who hesitated to speak in the classroom to comment on the film.

Students themselves introduced the literature in class through presentations to avoid the lecture format that might put students on guard against the material presented.[2] Students in teams presented the reading to the class and led the discussions; I served an only complementary role in keeping the class focused on the material presented in the reading.

Other faculty and administrators typically received the course topic with initial enthusiasm and curiosity. Many affirmed the importance of the subject and the need to engage students with it, since the war on terror had been having a huge impact on their lives and on the larger society. I made the point that students should understand the world we live in at this moment of war on terror, including the impact of these policies on people at home and abroad. It seems that there is a global interest in the subject, and not without reason. The impact of the U.S.-led war on terror is felt everywhere.

I divided the material and topics of the course into three parts organized so as to gradually engage the students with critical material on the event and its aftermath. These three stages were designed to tackle difficult issues related to the topic and were organized according to their level of acceptance in the public discussion (i.e., from the most accepted to the least). In the three sections that follow, I will discuss the dynamics of the course as it played out in the U.S. institutions where I taught. Later, I will describe how the course in Pakistan played out somewhat differently.

Part One: Shaking the Belief in Post-9/11 Policies

This stage proved the easiest in the class, since many students already had doubts and critiques of the policies pursued by the United States since 9/11 and the policies of its allies in the region, especially after the failures of the wars in Iraq and Afghanistan. Although the media discussion of these policies tended to focus on Americans killed and American money spent, rather than on the ethical and legal grounds of waging these wars, the coverage did allow me an opportunity to question the war on terror itself, if only on issues of "efficiency, practicality, and feasibility."

Students were at least ready for this first part of the class. Even the students who supported these policies were already accustomed to critiques that they had heard in mainstream U.S. media. The material (films and literature) introduced helped change the opinion of most of those supportive of the official polices, or at least make them question the wisdom, objectives, and/or results of such policies. This constituted an important step in that it prepared all students for the possibility of questioning more of their beliefs as we moved to the subsequent material. Only a few students continued to use the same official or dominant arguments, while a few dropped the class, unwilling or unable to deal with what was to come in it. Some complained to the department that the course made them feel uncomfortable. The course, they argued further, contained "anti-American and anti-Israeli propaganda."

Part Two: Unsettling the Official Propaganda Regarding the Wars in the Arab and Muslim Worlds

The second part of the course proved more complicated, because even the critics of the official policies were not ready to read, see, and hear from Arabs and Muslims about how U.S. policies have influenced their lives. The literature and films made most students feel uneasy about the devastation that U.S. policies brought on people in Afghanistan and Iraq. Even those students who had a liberal outlook on politics, and who were critical of U.S. policies, were not fully aware of the extent of the misery created by the wars. While many students criticized U.S. policies as harmful for Americans in the long term, only a small minority in the class opposed the policies because of their impact on peoples in the Arab and Muslim worlds.

In this part of the class, we focused on literature and films that shed light on the impact of U.S. policies on the receiving end in Afghanistan and Iraq. The course also made a link between Israel's policies in Palestine (which intensified after 9/11) and U.S. policies in the Arab and Muslim worlds. We discussed who capitalized on the conditions of the post-9/11 world, in which the slogan of a war on terror was used to implement different objectives according to the needs and abilities of different parties, resulting in much suffering that Americans in general did not recognize.

By the end of this part most students were ready for the class to end. Many already were convinced of the problems of the U.S. war on terror, while the rest were not ready for more than that possibility. Yet we still had another third of the semester to complete. This final part proved the most difficult both for students and for me.

Part Three: Questioning Officialdom

In this stage, students had to confront material that discussed the very core of the official story concerning what happened on 9/11 and, more important, why the killing of Americans in 9/11 was deemed more important than the killing of Iraqis, Afghanis, and Palestinians, or any other group of people.

In this part, I introduced different versions of inside-job theories, along with criticisms of them to give students material to make independent judgments. We also discussed how different entities, from New York to Tel Aviv, had exploited the event to their advantage. Students were introduced to literature discussing pre-9/11 plans that matched U.S. foreign policies after the event. In addition, and regardless of who was behind the attacks of 9/11, students were also introduced to narratives of American and Israeli officials commenting on the event as an "opportunity" to be used to shape policies and achieve objectives already on the books long before 9/11.

This third stage of the course drew most protests. Almost on a daily basis, administrators received complaints from students of "anti-American" and "anti-Israeli" propaganda in the class. At one school, the complaints warranted a "special meeting" with me, in which I was presented with material I had written outside the classroom, as well as with specific words and arguments I made in class.

I was questioned about my writing (elsewhere) that education should be about critical thinking rather than about conformity with the official or dominant narratives, that education ought to benefit all people rather than a specific segment of society. Educational institutions should not constitute factories for degree granting, I had argued, but rather should be sites of liberation from already held beliefs and of real democracy, where alternative narratives were welcomed rather than censored. One administrator reprimanded me for an activist pedagogy. I responded that while my writings outside the classroom should not form part of the "special meeting," the pedagogy of the status quo was also an activist pedagogy, one that benefits a minority in the United States and elsewhere and that comes at the cost of many lives, in addition to being intellectually quite poor. I added that students should not have to pay as much as they do in these colleges.

Back in the classroom, while some students started to miss our meetings, others — both at this school and at the others — continued to attend and even proposed to show documentaries that they felt all students should see. The class then became a battle between students who did not want to have their beliefs in the government, the state, and authority at large completely shaken and the minority of students who had little faith in authority and felt that the problem lay with a blind faith in the official narrative. Such discussions were not pleasant or easy to deal with. Yet this is what we, in part, ought to be doing in the classroom.

In reflecting on the course in the last meeting, some students (whether orally or through written course evaluations) stressed the importance of gaining information and knowledge; others were convinced that whatever information people get, governments will continue to do what they want, and people at large will be paying the price, especially those targeted by certain policies. The goal, they agreed, is thus to get educated so that people do not follow the government's policies of war so easily. No major difference manifested about this general conclusion in terms of age or gender.

The Pakistani Students and Final Thoughts

Although I did not have many complaints in Pakistan, students' reactions to the material in many ways resembled those in the United States. By the time I came to Pakistan, the Pakistani government was engaged in its own version of the war on terror. In Pakistan, as in the United States, students who attend colleges form part of the larger society. Some are connected to the power structure in each country, while others benefit from the status quo and others still are made to believe that the status quo benefits them and that a radical change will negatively affect their life and privileges. This holds especially true in the case of an elite institution like the one I taught at in Pakistan.

One major difference between students in the United States and those in Pakistan lies in the way they dealt with the material we read and watched. Some of the American students reacted as innocent victims personally impacted by the event and its aftermath. Even movies about the war on Iraq (such as *Redacted*) created a backlash among some American students who felt that these movies represented the U.S. soldiers too harshly. For them, the real victims were not Iraqi civilians, such as the raped Iraqi girl in *Redacted* (dir. Brian DePalma, 2008), but the soldiers forced to go to Iraq. These students did not concern themselves with the killing and raping of Iraqis. They were concerned, like the general American public, including much of the antiwar movement, with "supporting the troops" and with what benefits Americans in the end. Pakistani students were much more likely to identify with the civilian victims. They see direct U.S. involvement in their country through the drone attacks and special operations on the ground that are not much talked about in the United States. While people in Pakistan talk about Blackwater (the security company that keeps changing its name but not its actions), there is hardly any discussion about it in the United States.

Pakistani students were also generally more inclined to suspect official narratives and not to put much trust in the government. This healthy attitude toward authority is less present among American students. U.S. education emphasizes the importance of political participation, on the one hand, but it also pushes (directly or indirectly) for trust in the government and its institutions. American students tend to see bad policies as resulting only from misinformation, lack of information, or the actions of one or more ill-intentioned individuals. In other words, to them it is not a matter of structural flaws at the core of the U.S. system and state.

Pakistani students, for their part, are likely to believe that their own government has done the bidding of the United States. While they believe this to have been the case for a long time — especially since the 1980s, when the Pakistani government helped the United States finance, arm, and train militants to fight in Afghanistan — now, they feel, their government is killing its own people just to please the Americans and to avoid more direct U.S. involvement in the country. The backlash of militants against the public, they feel, is one of the results of the war on terror that their government has unleashed at the behest of the Americans. While one might dispute these arguments, Americans will find themselves in a better position for change if they trust their governments less than they do.

By the end of the semester, some students came to question the core of the 9/11 narrative, while others questioned the policies that followed the event and criticized the damage these policies had caused for people abroad and at home. Thus, despite the protests of some students and administrators and the challenges they brought, teaching the course — giving students an opportunity to critically assess the event of 9/11 and its aftermath — remained worthwhile.

Notes

1. The films I most frequently used were *Canadian Bacon* (dir. Michael Moore, 1995), *Five Fingers* (dir. Laurence Malkin, 2006), *Goya's Ghosts* (dir. Milos Forman, 2006), and *Sorry, Haters* (dir. Jeff Stanzler, 2005).

2. The books that I most frequently used in the class were M. Shahid Alam, *Israeli Exceptionalism: The Destabilizing Logic of Zionism* (New York: Palgrave Macmillan, 2009); Talal Asad, *On Suicide Bombing* (New York: Columbia University Press, 2007); Jonathan Cook, *Israel and the Clash of Civilisations: Iraq, Iran, and the Plan to Remake the Middle East* (London: Pluto Press, 2008); Derek Gregory, *The Colonial Present: Afghanistan, Palestine, and Iraq* (Malden, MA: Blackwell, 2004); Mahmood Mamdani, *Good Muslim, Bad Muslim: America, the Cold War, and the Roots of Terror* (New York: Pantheon, 2004); Steven Salaita, *Anti-Arab Racism in the USA: Where It Comes from and What It Means for Politics Today* (London: Pluto Press, 2006); and Slavoj Žižek, *Welcome to the Desert of the Real: Five Essays on September 11 and Related Dates* (London: Verso, 2002).

LIFE DURING WARTIME

ᴡᴡTHURSDAY, MARCH 20, 2003ᴡᴡ

The New York T[imes]

BUSH ORDERS S[...]
MISSILES APPA[...]

— DEFIANT RESPONSE —

Iraq Leader Exhorts His
People to Draw Arms
[aga]inst Invaders

Once again, a feeling of helplessness
in the face of obsession...

The First Eight Years of
Life during Wartime, 2003–2011

Joshua Brown

Introduction by Andor Skotnes

Many of us remember when, on March 20, 2003, the United States invaded Iraq. In the preceding weeks and months, many people — many of us — around the world had worked in unprecedented international solidarity to stop this invasion, culminating in worldwide demonstrations on February 15 and 16 that involved millions of people in more than sixty countries. In New York City alone, hundreds of thousands marched, or attempted to march, on a cold day with a suffocating police presence. In part because of this global mobilization, the Bush administration's heavy-handed diplomatic efforts failed to line up United Nations or significant international support for its essentially unilateral attack. Bush invaded anyway, setting off a cycle of astounding violence that has yet to end.

Thus many of us experienced frustration, outrage, or despondency on that day in March 2003. As Joshua Brown put it in the inaugural cartoon of his *Life during Wartime* series, "Once again a feeling of helplessness in the face of obsession . . . ." Of course, Brown was not really helpless, for, with this image, he initiated a stream of cartoons that continue to this day, dedicated to exposing the hypocrisies and lies of the so-called war against terror in all of its international and domestic manifestations. If the imperial establishment has justified this war by a peculiar and often changing historical interpretation of 9/11, Brown's four hundred–plus cartoons during the past decade, posted all over the Web and found in many hard-copy forms,

Radical History Review
Issue 111 (Fall 2011) DOI 10.1215/01636545-1268848

have sought to challenge and subvert this phony historicizing. We thus invited Brown to assemble a retrospective of *Life during Wartime* for the current issue of *Radical History Review*.

Brown has a long-standing involvement with this journal. He first joined the editorial collective in the late 1970s, continuing as a member for more than two decades. He contributed the artwork for the first of his many *RHR* covers in 1979. He is also an accomplished historian—elsewhere in this issue, for example, we publish his article, coauthored with another longtime *RHR* colleague, Steve Brier, on the remarkable work of the September 11 Digital Archive. A look at his Web site (www.joshbrownnyc.com) will provide a sense of his historical and artistic work. It is safe to say that Brown stands as one of the most prolific, inventive, and effective historical-political artists working in the United States today.[1]

So we at *RHR* are proud to present this retrospective of Brown's *Life during Wartime*, and we salute the artist for his continued participation in the struggle to get history right and to promote real social change.

—Andor Skotnes

Note

1. For his account of the first six years of *Life during Wartime*, see Joshua Brown, "The Historian as Cartoonist: Drawing George W. Bush," History News Network, January 19, 2009, hnn.us/articles/59952.html.

With the start of the Iraq war, the color-coded terrorist threat level was raised, and a military presence became visible at major transportation hubs such as New York's Pennsylvania Station.

Trying to locate information on triumph-all-the-time TV.

ᴧᴧᴧ MONDAY, JUNE 21, 2004 ᴧᴧᴧ

Profile in Confabulation

In the original color version of this cartoon, Rice's hand is red.

All-purpose weapon

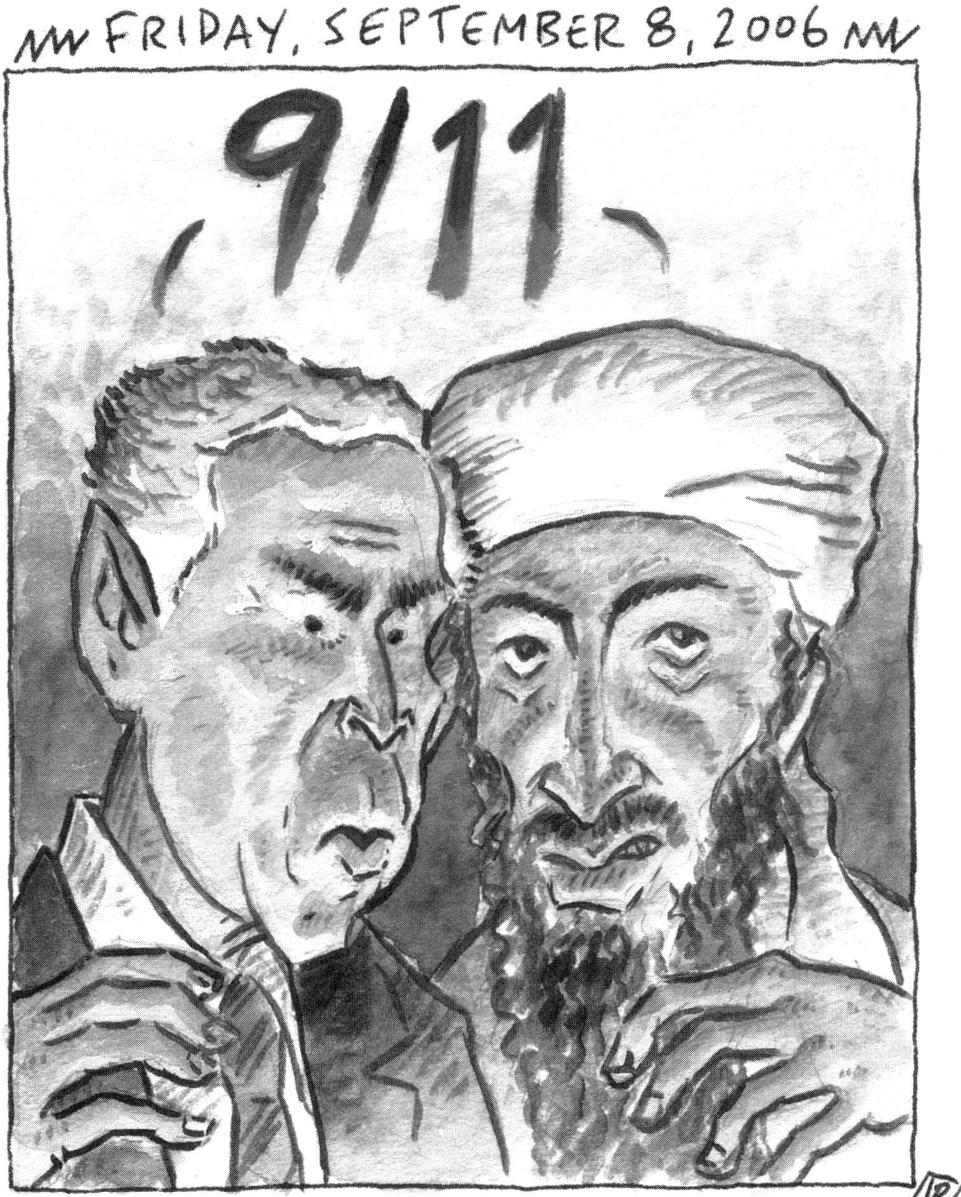

Before the House Judiciary Committee, Michael Mukasey, George W. Bush's third attorney general, rejected opening a criminal investigation into the use of waterboarding by the CIA.

TRANSITION PORTRAIT 4

YOU HEARD IT HERE FIRST—

WHAT OBAMA ISN'T TELLING US ABOUT GUANTANAMO

WHY ARE REPUBLICANS + DEMOCRATS UNITED IN ONE CRY:

We will never allow terrorists to be released into the U.S.!

WHY WHEN THE UNABOMBER, OMAR ABDEL-RAHMAN (WTC 1), ZACARIAS MOUSSAOUI, AND OTHERS ARE ALREADY IN PRISONS IN THE U.S.?

SO WHY ARE DEMOCRATS + REPUBLICANS SO ADAMANT ABOUT NOT CLOSING GUANTANAMO?

BECAUSE THERE IS ONE TERRORIST WE CANNOT AFFORD TO HAVE ON U.S. SOIL—

WE REFER, OF COURSE, TO **GODZILLA!**

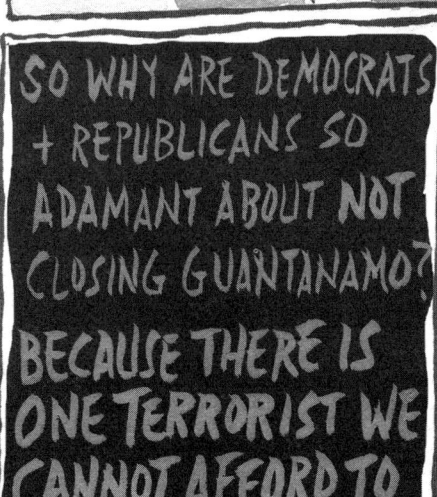

I may be Japanese but I call Osama a friend!

STANDS TO REASON—RIGHT?

SATURDAY, MAY 8, 2010

Senators Scott Brown (R-Mass) and Joseph Lieberman (I-Conn) introduced the Terrorist Expatriation Bill, which would strip of his or her citizenship any American, naturalized or native born, found to have supported or joined a terrorist group—with no hearing and with no basis except the say-so of the State Department.

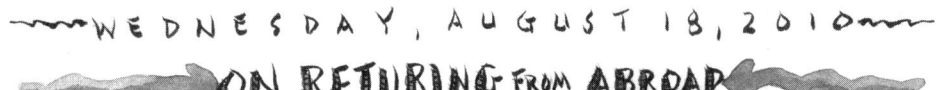

WEDNESDAY, AUGUST 18, 2010

ON RETURING FROM ABROAD

America is experiencing an Islamist cultural-political offensive designed to undermine + destroy our civilization.

NEWT GINGRICH

I'm going to keep doing what I'm doing. It doesn't matter to me.

SHERIFF JOE ARPAIO

The president didn't send me over here to seek a graceful exit.

GENERAL DAVID PETRAEUS

BEN BERNANKE

WAIT! WAIT! I DIDN'T MEAN TO GET OFF!

SATURDAY, OCTOBER 23, 2010

Juan Williams was fired as a National Public Radio commentator after he professed on "The O'Reilly Factor" that, "when I get on the plane, I got to tell you, if I see people who are in Muslim garb and I think, you know, they are identifying themselves first and foremost as Muslims, I get worried. I get nervous." Proclaiming himself a victim of political correctness, Williams accepted a lucrative contract offered him by Fox News.

SUNDAY, JANUARY 2, 2011

Representative Peter King (R-NY), the new chair of the Homeland Security Committee, announced he would hold hearings on the "radicalization of the American Muslim community."

Paul L. Atwood served in the U.S. Marine Corps during the Vietnam War and as a result committed himself to work for peace and to study U.S. foreign policy in depth. He is a senior lecturer in American studies and research associate in the William Joiner Center for the Study of War and Social Consequences, both at the University of Massachusetts Boston. He is author most recently of *War and Empire: The American Way of Life* (2010).

Sonia Baelo-Allué is an associate professor in the Department of English and German Philology at the University of Zaragoza (Spain), where she primarily teaches U.S. literature. Her current research centers on trauma studies and 9/11 fiction. She has published widely on the genre of blank fiction, the concept of intermediality, and the representation of violence in literature. Her recent publications include *Bret Easton Ellis's Controversial Fiction: Writing between High and Low Culture* (2011).

Bob Batchelor is an assistant professor in the School of Journalism and Mass Communication at Kent State University and the director of the online master's degree program in public relations. He is the author or editor of ten books, including *The 2000s* (2009) and the four-volume *American Pop: Popular Culture Decade by Decade* (2009). He serves on the editorial board of the *Journal of Popular Culture* and is currently writing a critical analysis of John Updike.

Stephen Brier, who joined the editorial collective of *RHR* in 1976, was the founding director of CUNY's American Social History Project. Brier currently teaches urban education at the CUNY Graduate Center and is a faculty member at CUNY's Joseph S. Murphy Institute for Worker Education and Labor Studies, where he teaches labor history to trade unionists.

Joshua Brown is the executive director of the American Social History Project and a professor of history at the CUNY Graduate Center. A 2010 Guggenheim Fellow, his current projects include a history of Civil War visual culture and a graphic novel on Reconstruction entitled *Ithaca* (serialized on the *Common-place* Web site).

Mary Marshall Clark is the director of the Columbia University Oral History Research Office, the world's oldest university-based oral history archive. She is also the director and cofounder, with the sociologist Peter Bearman, of the nation's first master's program in oral history, launched at Columbia University in 2008. Clark and Bearman undertook a longitudinal oral history project on the multiple impacts of September 11, 2001, on New York City. Currently Clark is directing an oral history project on the legal, moral, and social consequences of establishing Guantánamo Bay as a site of imprisonment and torture.

Ann Cvetkovich is Ellen C. Garwood Centennial professor of English and professor of women's and gender studies at the University of Texas at Austin. She is the author of *Mixed Feelings: Feminism, Mass Culture, and Victorian Sensationalism* (1992), *An Archive of Feelings: Trauma, Sexuality, and Lesbian Public Cultures* (2003), and *Depression: A Public Feelings Project* (forthcoming). She is coeditor (with Janet Staiger and Ann Reynolds) of *Political Emotions* (2010) and, with Annamarie Jagose, of *GLQ: A Journal of Lesbian and Gay Studies*.

Chitra Ganesh and **Mariam Ghani** have collaborated since 2004 on Index of the Disappeared, which is both a physical archive of post-9/11 disappearances and a mobile platform for public dialogue. Recent Index presentations include installations of the full archive, parasitic installations in existing libraries, and site-specific selections of particular documents. Ganesh's drawing-based practice excavates buried narratives typically excluded from official canons of history, literature, and art. Her work has been exhibited internationally, including at the MoMA PS1, the Museum of Contemporary Art in Shanghai, the Saatchi Museum, and the Gwangju Contemporary Arts Centre. She is the recipient of numerous awards, including grants from the Art Matters Foundation and the Joan Mitchell Foundation. She holds a bachelor of arts from Brown University in comparative literature and art semiotics and a master of fine arts from Columbia University. Ghani's work explores how histories, places, identities, and communities are constructed and reconstructed, as well as the shifting private and public narratives that comprise and contest those constructions. Her videos and installations have been exhibited internationally, including at the Sharjah Biennial, the Beijing 798 Biennial, the Tate Modern, and the Museum of Modern Art. She has a bachelor of arts in comparative literature from New York University, a master of fine arts from the School of Visual Arts, and she teaches in the Art and Public Policy program at NYU.

Ivan Greenberg earned a doctorate at the CUNY Graduate Center and is the author of *The Dangers of Dissent: The FBI and Civil Liberties since 1965* (2010). He is completing a second book dealing with U.S. surveillance practices.

Jeffrey R. Kerr-Ritchie, born and raised in London, has lived and worked in the United States since 1985. He teaches and writes on slavery and emancipation at Howard University. This article draws from a forthcoming book, "Our American Cousin: Critical Comments on the Special Relationship between the United States and the United Kingdom."

Jaclyn Kirouac-Fram is a doctoral candidate in the Department of American Studies at Saint Louis University. Through an approach that blends visual culture studies, urban studies, and critical race theory, her research examines how representations of the metropolis and its residents affect contemporary urban culture.

Linda Levitt is an assistant professor of communication studies at Stephen F. Austin State University. Her research interests include media studies and cultural memory, and she is particularly focused on their intersection, interrogating the role of media in shaping public memory.

Micki McElya is an assistant professor of history at the University of Connecticut, where she teaches courses on the twentieth- and twenty-first-century United States and on the histories of women and gender, and on sexuality. She is the author of *Clinging to Mammy: The Faithful Slave in Twentieth-Century America* (2007) and is at work on "Grave Affairs: Arlington National Cemetery and the Politics of Death and Honor."

Jeffrey Melnick now teaches in the American Studies Department at the University of Massachusetts Boston, after twelve years at Babson College. His most recent book is *9/11 Culture: America under Construction* (2009). He has just begun work on a new project, provisionally titled "Creepy Crawling with the Manson Family."

Jim O'Brien is a freelance editor and indexer who formerly taught history and writing at the

University of Massachusetts Boston and still teaches on a volunteer basis in the campus's learning-in-retirement program. He has been a member of the *Radical History Review* editorial collective since 1999, and since 2007 he has cochaired Historians Against the War.

Thomas Riegler studied history and politics at Vienna and Edinburgh Universities, with a PhD from Vienna University. He now works as a journalist and independent historian. He has published on a wide range of topics, including terrorism, film studies, and contemporary history. He is the author of *Terrorismus: Akteure, Strukturen, Entwicklungslinien* (*Terrorism: Actors, Structures, Trends*, 2009) and *Im Fadenkreuz: Osterreich und der Nahostterrorismus 1973–1985* (*In The Crosshairs: Austria and Middle Eastern Terrorism 1973–1985*).

Amir Saeed is a senior lecturer in media and cultural Studies at the University of Sunderland. His research interests are in "race," racism, and media influence. His recent publications concern topics such as Islamophobia, racism after 9/11, Muslim hip hop, Malcolm X, and social media in relation to the Palestinian occupation.

Matthew Schneider-Mayerson is completing his dissertation at the University of Minnesota on the "peak oil" movement, online communities, and conservatism in contemporary U.S. political culture. He has published "'Too Black': Race in the 'Dark Ages' of the National Basketball Association," "What Almost Was: The Politics of the Contemporary Alternate History Novel," and "Popular Fiction Studies: The Advantages of a New Field." His teaching and research interests include professional sports, genre fiction, and the nexus between twentieth-century U.S. popular culture and politics.

Magid Shihade is a faculty member at the Ibrahim Abu-Lughod Institute of International Studies at Birzeit University. His research interests include modernity, violence, identity, and the anthropology and politics of knowledge. He serves on the editorial boards of the *Journal of Alternative Perspectives in the Social Sciences*, *Resistance Studies Magazine*, and *Interface: A Journal about and for Social Movements*, and he is the author of *Not Just a Soccer Game: Colonialism and Conflict among Palestinians in Israel* (2011).

Andor Skotnes is a professor of history at The Sage Colleges in Troy, New York; he teaches courses in the history of the Americas and in oral history. He is the author of *Race and Class Struggles on the Middle Ground*, to be published later this year. He has been a member of the *Radical History Review* editorial collective for twenty years.

James Stone is an assistant professor in the Department of Cinematic Arts at the University of New Mexico. He teaches several courses in film history, among them "International Horror Film," "The Cinema of Alfred Hitchcock," and "Silent Film." His writing has explored British cinema's relationship with American culture and, most recently, the subject of cinema and terrorism.

Kent Worcester is the author or coeditor of six books, including *C. L. R. James: A Political Biography* (1996), *Arguing Comics: Literary Masters on a Popular Medium* (2004), and *A Comics Studies Reader* (2009). He has been interviewing New York–area cartoonists for the *Comics Journal* for the past fifteen years.